Contracting for Publi Services

Contracts and contractual relationships have become the predominant mode of organization for public service delivery in recent years, and the successful management of contracts has become a core task for public service managers. In the wake of New Public Management reforms, and as public–private partnerships have proliferated, it has become more important than ever before for public service managers to understand the contracting process and its institutional context. This insightful and comprehensive text offers a thorough introduction to the key phases of the contracting process and the skills required by managers in its implementation, including:

- policy for contracting
- strategic purchasing
- understanding markets
- communicating the contracting decision
- designing and drafting the contract
- the role of the consumer
- the regulation of service provision

Illustrated throughout with practitioner case studies from a range of OECD countries, the book presents an important new theoretical 'contract management model' and a 'mature contract model', and explores the mechanisms, formal rules and informal norms that influence the way governments contract for public services. This book is essential reading for all students of public management and all public service managers.

Carsten Greve is Professor of Public Management and Public–Private Cooperation at the International Center for Business and Politics, Copenhagen Business School. He is the author of numerous scholarly articles and several books, including *The Challenge of Public–Private Partnerships: Learning from International Experience* (co-edited with Graeme Hodge). He is also the vice-study leader for the MPA programme at the Copenhagen Business School.

ROUTLEDGE MASTERS IN PUBLIC MANAGEMENT

Edited by Stephen P Osborne, Owen Hughes, Walter Kickert

Routledge Masters in Public Management series is an integrated set of texts. It is intended to form the backbone for the holistic study of the theory and practice of public management as part of:

- a taught Masters, MBA or MPA course at a university or college;
- a work-based, in-service, programme of education and training; or
- a programme of self-guided study.

Each volume stands alone in its treatment of its topic, whether it be strategic management, marketing or procurement and is co-authored by leading specialists in their field. However, all volumes in the series share both a common pedagogy and a common approach to the structure of the text. Key features of all volumes in the series include:

- a critical approach to combining theory with practice which educates its reader, rather than solely teaching him/her a set of skills;
- clear learning objectives for each chapter;
- the use of figures, tables and boxes to highlight key ideas, concepts and skills;
- an annotated bibliography, guiding students in their further reading; and
- a dedicated case study in the topic of each volume, to serve as a focus for discussion and learning.

Managing Change and Innovation in Public Service Organizations
Stephen P. Osborne and Kerry Brown

Risk and Crisis Management in the Public Sector
Lynn T. Drennan and Allan McConnell

Contracting for Public Services
Carsten Greve

Contracting for Public Services

Carsten Greve

Routledge
Taylor & Francis Group

LONDON AND NEW YORK

to BP, FGP and SGP

First published 2008 by Routledge
2 Park Square, Milton Park, Abingdon, Oxon OX14 4RN

Simultaneously published in the USA and Canada
by Routledge
270 Madison Ave, New York, NY 10016

Routledge is an imprint of the Taylor & Francis Group, an informa business

© 2008 Carsten Greve

Typeset in Perpetua by
Keystroke, 28 High Street, Tettenhall, Wolverhampton
Printed and bound in Great Britain by
TJ International Ltd, Padstow, Cornwall

British Library Cataloguing in Publication Data
A catalogue record for this book is available from the British Library

Library of Congress Cataloging in Publication Data
Greve, Carsten.
    Contracting for public services / Carsten Greve. – 1st ed.
        p. cm.
    Includes bibliographical references and index.
    1. Public contracts. 2. Public administration. 3. Public works.
    4. Government purchasing. 5. Contracting out. 6. Public–private
    sector cooperation. I. Title.
    HD3860.G738 2007
    352.5'38–dc22   2007003126

ISBN10: 0–415–35654–7 (hbk)
ISBN10: 0–415–35655–5 (pbk)

ISBN13: 978–0–415–35654–1 (hbk)
ISBN13: 978–0–415–35655–8 (pbk)

Contents

CONTENTS

APPENDICES

Figures, tables and boxes

FIGURES

TABLES

BOXES

Foreword

The **Routledge Masters in Public Management** is a series of original texts authored by some of the most established authors in the field of public management and public services management. This series is aimed at offering students and practitioners accessible, coordinated and comprehensive books in this field.

The series has a coordinated format, including the use of learning points, text boxes, annotated reading and student questions. Each volume will stand in its own right as a major textbook in public management. Taken together, however, the series offers an integrated and up-to-date collection of core textbooks that can form the backbone of any student's study of public management – whether based upon an MBA or MPA programme, a 'stand-alone' course or through a period of individual study. Taking an expert look at an increasingly important and complex discipline, this is a groundbreaking new series that answers a real need for serious textbooks on public management.

Each volume focuses upon a core area within public management – such as marketing, human resource management, the management of innovation and change, and the outsourcing of public services. They provide:

- an overview of the key state of knowledge on this area;
- a critical approach to the practice of this task in public services; and
- exercises and resources to support reader learning in each area.

As such, these volumes go far beyond the 'toolkit' or 'recipe' format that has dogged so many individual textbooks in this field in the past. They encourage the development by the reader both of core managerial skills and of critical thinking about public management. This is, the editors believe, an important and unique contribution to the literature on public management. This Routledge series, **Routledge Masters in Public Management**, is thus intended to serve the growing market of public service professionals who are seeking a deeper and broader understanding of the role and importance of the management of public services across the world.

This current volume, by *Carsten Greve*, addresses the essential task of the outsourcing of public services. It examines the context of public services contracting, the core skills involved and offers a critical appreciation of the state of our knowledge about this important field. It will support the work of those public service managers, whether they are based in governmental, third sector or other organizations that are involved in the outsourcing of public services, as either a client or contractor. It is, we believe, essential reading for the informed and effective public manager.

Stephen P. Osborne, Owen Hughes and Walter Kickert
February 2007

Acknowledgements

This book has been underway for some time. I would like to thank a small number of people for their inspiration and help while the book was being written.

Associate Professor Niels Ejersbo, University of Southern Denmark, and Professor Graeme Hodge, Monash University, Australia, have both provided much inspiration in the projects we have done together over the years. This book could not have been written without conversations with them on contracts, privatization and public–private partnerships (although they have not read this particular manuscript, I hasten to add). I have also learned much from other colleagues in universities and business schools – thank you to you all.

At Routledge I would like to thank Francesca Heslop and Emma Joyce for their support. The word 'patience' has gained a new meaning after the process which took much longer than anticipated. I would also like to thank the series editors, especially Professor Stephen Osborne, for giving me the opportunity to write this book and for urging me to finish the project.

The continuing support of the International Center for Business and Politics at Copenhagen Business School is greatly acknowledged. I also greatly benefited from informed discussions and case studies from my students at the Master of Public Administration springtime course on Marketization and Partnerships in 2005 and 2006 at the Copenhagen Business School.

Finally, a big thank you to my family, who has suffered more than reasonably while this book was being written. I sincerely appreciate all your love and support.

All errors in the text are my responsibility.

Carsten Greve
Copenhagen 2006

Abbreviations

BOO	Build own operate
BOOT	Build-own-operate transfer
CCT	Competitive compulsory tendering
CEO	Chief Executive Officer
DEG	Digital-era governance
DFBO	Design finance build operate
IRA	Independent regulatory authority
NAO	National audit office
NPG	New public governance
NPM	New Public Management
O&M	Operations and Management contract
PDA	Personal digital assistant
PFI	Private Finance Initiative
PPP	Public–Private Partnership
PSO	Public service organization
VFM	Value for money

Part I

Introduction

Chapter 1

Introduction

The contractual age in public service delivery

LEARNING OBJECTIVES

By the end of this chapter you should:

- be clear about the basic definition of what a contract is;
- be able to figure out the main arguments for and against contracting out;
- be able to place contracting in the broader public management reform context;
- be familiar with various interpretations of 'the contract state'; and
- be clear about the approach of the text and its structure.

KEY POINTS OF THIS CHAPTER

- Contracting is an essential part of the New Public Management (NPM) agenda that focuses on competition (or marketization) and adopting management techniques from the private sector which enables a results-based management system, but is also a part of the wider New Public Governance (NPG) agenda that specifies relationships between government and society.
- The main reasons to contract are to save money, get value for money, be innovative, and help a country's industry in getting orders. The main hindrances for contracting are the risk of fear of quality degradation, changed accountability structures and lack of transparency.

- ■ Empirical research has focused on economic efficiency and effectiveness, and while evidence for some savings has been found, they are generally less than the contracting proponents have often suggested.
- ■ There are variations of the contract state: the hollow state, the enabling state and the strategic contracting state.

KEY TERMS

- ■ **Contract** – a formal agreement between a purchaser and a provider which states the term of delivery of a service or a product.
- ■ **Contracting** – the design and implementation of contractual relationships between purchasers and suppliers.
- ■ **The contract state** – a public sector that relies on contracting and collaboration with private sector providers as one of its main institutions for the delivery of public services.

Contracting has become a central feature of modern government, and one of the key institutions to deliver public service to the citizens and build new infrastructure. Contracting has been a feature in the ongoing public management reforms, often associated with the phenomenon of the New Public Management (NPM) (Fortin 2000; Kettl 2000; Pollitt and Bouckaert 2004; Savas 2000). There is now a considerable literature on what contract management means and implies for the public sector that we will draw on in this book (Brown *et al.* 2006; Cooper 2003; Kelman 2002).

This chapter will introduce the concept of 'contract' and 'contracting', and then go on to examine the main arguments that have occurred for why governments should contract for public service delivery and why they should sometimes abstain from contracting. The chapter will also look at the various labels and concepts that have been attached to 'the contract state'. This meaning has changed over time as contracts are now seen as more integrated in the relationship between the public sector and the private sector today than it was 20 years ago or more.

CONTRACTING

In order to engage private providers in delivering public services, the purchaser must enter a contract between one or more providers. The contract is the key document around which communication between purchasers and providers revolves. The contract is a formal agreement between a purchaser and a provider.

A contract is an agreement between a purchaser and a provider (buyer and seller) which states the terms of delivery of a service or product (Domberger 1998: 12). Contracting is 'the design and implementation of contractual relationships between purchasers and suppliers' (ibid.).

OECD describes contracting out (which it calls outsourcing) as: 'the practice whereby governments contract with private sector providers for the provision of services to government ministries and agencies, or directly to citizens on behalf of the government' (OECD 2005: 131).

Cooper (2003: 12–13) observes that 'contracts in the business world . . . operate on a horizontal model, based not on authority but on a foundation of negotiations. The rules of the relationship are established by mutual consent and can be enforced by either of the parties to the agreement.' He contrasts this approach with a vertical approach where:

> the political process that produces the decision to contract, the appropriations to be used for that purpose, and the techniques of accountability to be employed to maintain oversight of contract operations come from a vertical, authority-based processes starting from the Constitution and flowing down through legislative processes and administrative agencies to the point where contracts are made and managed.
>
> (Cooper 2003: 12)

The challenge for public managers, according to Cooper (2003), is that they operate at the intersection between the horizontal and the vertical approach to contracts.

A contract, in the words of the new institutional economics professor Oliver Williamson, is 'an agreement between a buyer and a supplier in which the terms of ex-ante change are defined by a triple: price, asset specificity, and safeguards, and which assumes that quantity, quality and duration are all specified' (Williamson 1996: 377). Asset specificity is 'a specialized investment that cannot be redeployed to alternative uses or by alternative users except at a loss of productive value' (ibid.), and where a safeguard is 'the added security features, if any, that are introduced in a contract in order to reduce hazards (due to mainly asset specificity) and to create confidence' (ibid.).

A contract is much more than just a formal agreement. Contracts may be seen in an institutional perspective. Following North (1990) and Knight (1992), institutions are formal and informal rules that enable and restrain human action. Contracts have a legal, 'black letter law' side to them. But contracts are also embedded in norms about what signing a contract means. Perhaps sociologist Durkheim put it most poignantly when he said that 'not everything in a contract is contractual'. There are norms and expectations about behaviour that cannot be put into writing. And there are other rule systems on which the individual contract is dependent. How the legal system works in a particular country is of importance to how contracts are implemented and understood. The argument may be summed up as follows:

5

> It is true that there is a body of contract law and that a contract is a legal instrument. Even so, great latitude is left to the contracting parties to shape the agreement and decide how it will be operated. In that sense, contract law in its traditional private law form is facilitative, supporting the ability of parties to an agreement to have the tools to fashion and implement it. Negotiations resulting in meeting of minds is the dominant dynamic in most contracting.
>
> (Cooper 2003: 13)

Each country's tradition and rules for settling disputes is important when contractual agreements are made and carried out. Contracts have a broader context. Understanding a sector or a country's 'contract culture' is important when designing or working in a contractual environment (Greve and Ejersbo 2005). The contract culture is embedded in both the formal legal framework, the political and business culture, and in the informal ways that purchasers, providers, employees and the users of services ('the customers') view and practise contracting.

Writing a contract is not always easy, as is evident from both the literature and practical experience in many governments. There are several reasons why it is not easy to write a contract. First, there are principal–agent problems: there is a problem for the purchaser in knowing the exact details of what may be produced. The service provider may withhold knowledge about the production methods in order to get an easier deal. The service provider may hold back evidence, and then later use that slack to not work as hard as the purchaser may have wished. This is known as hidden information. Another problem is if the action of the provider cannot be controlled thoroughly. The service provider may then have an incentive to not work quite as hard as possible. This is known as 'hidden action'. In the literature, this is called the principal–agent problem. The principal (the purchaser) wants a certain job done, but the agent (the provider) may hold back information and/or avoid control.

Second, there are costs associated with controlling the contract output. There are also costs involved in writing and monitoring a contract, known as transaction costs. Transaction costs have been defined as:

> The ex ante costs of drafting, negotiating, and safeguarding an agreement, and more especially, the ex-post costs of maladaption and adjustment that arise when contract execution is misaligned as a result of gaps, errors, omissions, and unanticipated disturbances; the costs of running the economic system.
>
> (Williamson 1996: 379)

WHY CONTRACT FOR PUBLIC SERVICES?

Contracting has been used to achieve the best quality for the lowest cost. Donald F. Kettl (1993) argued that a government has to be a 'smart buyer'. Governments must know what they want to buy, who to buy it from and later assess what they have bought. Undoubtedly, this continues to be a key focus for many governments around the world. Recently, however, it has been argued that there is more to contracting than just obtaining a good deal (Cooper 2003). The American scholar responsible for procurement policy in the Clinton administration in the USA, Steven Kelman (2002), has come up with the term 'Strategic contracting'. He sees a trend towards contracting being used to further an organization's mission. Contracting is a strategic management tool, not just a technique to achieve better and cheaper products or services in the short term. Strategic contracting sets contracting right at the centre of any government's public management strategy. This means that top executives in the public sector must be aware of contracting as a phenomenon and cannot always delegate that responsibility to lower line managers. Strategic contracting fits well with the main principles of the NPM movement.

The decision to contract out can be argued for in many ways, Often the arguments serve as legitimization for choosing the contract option instead of an in-house production. This chapter looks more closely at the various arguments that have been given for contracting. A key point is that reasons for contracting change over time. 'Innovation' has taken over from 'saving money'. Romzek and Johnston (2002: 425) commented that 'research suggests that ideology, cost savings, and load shedding are the primary factors behind most decisions to contract out government services'. OECD (2005: 132) suggests the following key reasons for contracting out government services:

- to reduce costs;
- to access expertise not available in-house to meet one-off needs;
- to access expertise on a long-term basis in order to be able to vary its quantity and mix over time; and
- to replace current government operations in extreme cases where their provision is unsatisfactory. This is rare and limited to cases where there is a long history of poor performance.

Saving money

A classic argument for contracting for public service delivery is that it will save the government money. Savas (2000: 119) places 'reduce the cost of government' at the top of his list of reasons why governments should want to use the private sector for public service delivery. In his summary of a large number of studies, Savas (2000: 149) concludes that 'there is by now a lengthy list of quantitative studies demonstrating quite conclusively that, in general, contracted services cost less and are at least as good in quality as corresponding services produced in-house by government agencies'. Savas believes that the savings do not come from firing people, but rather that they work harder and better under a private management than under a public management regime: 'The productivity gains through contracting result, in general, from more work performed per employee per unit time, not from lower wages' (Savas 2000: 157). People believe that the market is more efficient than hierarchy. Therefore, providing services on the market will mean more competition which again means that prices will be set at a competitive level. A widely reported study was made by Simon Domberger and colleagues in the 1980s, and they found that savings of around 20 per cent were the average in contracting out (Domberger *et al.* 1986; Domberger and Hall 1996; Domberger and Jensen 1997). As we will see below, the figure was later disputed, but there is no dispute about the widely spread 'common knowledge' that contracting out is expected to lead to savings.

> The objectives of privatization as contracting out or outsourcing appear to have become a moving target. The extent to which this has occurred as a result of organizations now viewing contracting out in a more sophisticated way, or as a result of a changed organizational learning from unmet early expectations of sizeable cost reductions, is uncertain. Nontheless, the primacy of cost reductions as an early commercial driver is clear.
>
> (Hodge 2000: 25)

Cooper (2003: 5) simply observes that 'It is still true that the primary argument most often given support to contracting out by government for goods and services is that it will save money'.

That is fine in theory. In practice it does not always work like that. First, it depends on what service is in focus. It is easier to plan savings for cleaning a building than it is for the Navy to buy a new helicopter. Second, the amount of savings is also dependent on how well run the service already is. An efficient public service production may mean that there is little a private provider can do to save money. Estimations exist of how much money can be saved. A 'rule of thumb' in the early literature and in practice used to be that around 20 per cent of costs could be saved. The 20 per cent figure comes from an early analysis of refuse collection in the UK carried out by Simon Domberger and colleagues in the 1980s (Hodge 2000: 101–103; see Box 1.1).

BOX 1.1 THE 20 PER CENT RULE

The '20 per cent' savings figure often appears in the literature on contracting out, but where did it come from? Early studies, conducted by E.S. Savas in the 1980s, had shown some results in refuse collection from the US. Professor Graeme Hodge explains the background:

In the UK another team of economists (Domberger, Meadowcroft, and Thompson 1986) studied the possible influence of competitive tendering on the production of cost of local government refuse collection service. Their analysis of 610 authorities through 1983–84 revealed cost differentials of 22 per cent when contracting was being undertaken with the private sector, and 17 per cent when the service was tendered but retained in-house. Controls for a wide range of variables were present. . . . Finding that the cost difference between the 'contracted out' and 'contracted in' arrangement was not statistically significant, Domberger, Meadowcroft, and Thompson concluded that both resulted in cost reductions 'of around 20 percent.' This is the origin of the now much quoted '20 percent cost reduction rule' used as a basis for contracting out.

(Hodge 2000: 101–103)

Many authors have also stated that savings of this magnitude are possible; for example, the American scholar and pro-contracting-out advocate E.S. Savas (2000). Empirical research shows more cautious results. Australian professor Graeme Hodge (2000) has done a meta-analysis of all empirical studies of contracting out. Based on all available English-language studies in the 1980s and 1990s showing statistical results, Hodge (2000: 155) concludes that:

A massive distribution of findings is available from the literature. Literally, we can find what we wish to find and quote from dozens of studies justifying our own predetermined beliefs about contracting. Focusing in on those research studies that had reported the statistical measurements themselves, it was observed that they were mostly from local government, U.S. in origin and mostly from refuse collection, cleaning and maintenance services. A significant association between cost savings and contracting was found corresponding to around 6 to 12 percent, depending on how the average was taken, and assuming a few percent for the cost of the contracting process. Overall, therefore, it was found that contracting resulted in cost savings, although the precise figures were subject to some important qualifications.

BOX 1.2 META-ANALYSIS OF CONTRACTING OUT STUDIES

There is often much controversy surrounding the evidence of how efficient private service production is compared to public service production. In normal policy discourses, numbers and figures on how much can be saved if governments contract out services to private providers are numerous. Governments themselves try to project the planned savings. The Australian researcher Graeme Hodge (2000) set out to find out what the empirical studies on contracting out were saying about efficiency effects and other effects. He conducted a meta-analysis of all the available studies on contracting out that were published in English, and that had statistically based results. He found out that most studies were in refuse collection or cleaning; services where performance targets could be set without too much trouble, and where regulation and accountability were relatively straightforward. He also noted that most studies reported findings from US and UK local governments. Hodge showed that there were savings connected to contracting out, but not as many as proponents sometimes claim. He found the savings to be between 6 and 12 per cent depending on how the average was taken and allowing for a few percentages to cover transaction costs. He also noted that the knowledge on whether contracting out affects quality remains an open question because there is simply not sufficient empirical data to demonstrate any effects.

Value for money

The argument about saving money is often coupled with a belief that quality can be maintained even though money is saved. The chief argument for this is that private companies have more efficient ways of organizing work and that they create value for money (VFM). Therefore, they can both save the government money and make themselves a profit. Trade unions often argue against this: they claim that money cannot always be saved without sacrificing the level of quality. Some people also think that making a profit in public services such as care for the elderly is not acceptable. Arguments tend to become heated in this debate. The value-for-money argument is probably the most widely used argument for contracting out. The argument is easy to communicate from politicians to citizens. It remains the most powerful reason governments have when they want to contract out services. From the empirical evidence that exists, the relationship to in particular the quality component is difficult to detect: Hodge (2000: 156) concludes that 'as best we know at present, contracting does not reduce or increase quality, as a general rule'.

A level playing field

Establishing a level playing field is sometimes used as an argument in its own right (Martin 1999). Public and private organizations must enjoy the same conditions when they compete for bids; however, this has not always been the case. Public organizations complain that they are not getting sufficient independence to organize their bids. Sometimes they are not even allowed to bid by law. In Britain there was a rule against government bids. In Denmark own bids are used, but are not often successful in winning contracts. From the private companies' perspectives, governments are often favoured because the cost calculations they use are different and government organizations often have privileged knowledge of the service that is going to be provided because they may have provided it for generations. Creating a level playing field is a task in itself, and there exist tools that can check the state of a playing field (Martin 1999).

Industrial policy

Contracting may be used to boost activity in the private sector. For industrial policy reasons, governments may wish to encourage growth in a certain kind of sector or among certain groups of companies. Using contracting to allow private companies to win more contracts is a well-known technique for governments. Some companies or industries become almost dependent on the willingness of governments to contract for services and products. The American defence industry is a well-known example of this. Many of the big weapons and aircraft companies receive much of their income from the US Defence Department. Likewise with NASA which depended on many organizations that work chiefly for them. In Europe and the Asia-Pacific area there is less dependence between governments and whole industries although there are examples of long-term contracts in both areas.

Contracting may be used strategically to further certain sectors in a country. For many years the Danish public sector has toyed with the idea of exporting welfare systems. The idea is that if Denmark is a leading nation in welfare states systems, then other countries could benefit. Contracting out is going to help Danish firms in establishing reputations and gaining knowledge as world-class providers, and this asset may be marketed in other countries. The Falck company which runs most of the country's ambulances and extinquishes fires is a case in point. Falck laid the foundations for their later international strategy by being a key provider to Danish local government.

Innovation

One of the more recent arguments is that contracting enhances innovation. Innovation has been a highly popular concept in the public sector during recent years. Innovation may be thought of as 'the introduction of new elements into a public service – in the form of new knowledge, a new organization, and/or new management or processual skills. It represents discontinuity with the past' (Osborne and Brown 2005: 4). Public organizations are learning to be more innovative alongside their counterparts in the public sector. There are at least four core values connected to the innovative organization according to Paul C. Light (1998), a leading US expert on the field: trust, honesty, rigor and faith. Innovation need not only take place within a public organization. By collaborating, public and private organizations can learn from each other. Often public and

11

private organizations will collaborate in various forms of public–private networks (Klijn and Teisman 2004). Public organizations obtain better services from it. Private organizations may learn from the public sector's need for specific services. Instead of focusing only on savings, contracting becomes a way to renew the services, to improve the quality, and to explore new ways of providing services that neither of the parties may have thought of before.

Contracting can play a part in the innovation process. A contract is a key institutional device that can connect public and private organizations, and through the contract, the different strengths and weaknesses of each organization can be specified. Innovation through contracting means that private sector providers can get an opportunity to show their different innovative suggestions from improved public service delivery. For the public sector employees to engage in innovative dialogues, they have to have contract management capacity and individual competencies (we will return to those elements in Chapters 3 and 5). The private providers have found that the better conditions of innovation in collaboration with public purchasers are best found in public–private partnerships (we return to partnerships in Chapter 7).

Reasons change over time

In the official argument, a change is observable in many countries. Arguments about contracting were once about saving money. While that argument is still heard, it is not so common any more. In this era of globalization of the economy, governments also use contracting to secure or boost a local industry. When companies can compete 'at home', they may be able to export their services to other countries. The industrial policy argument has gained more influence even though some countries have always relied on industrial policy aspects (e.g. the US defence industry). Recently, arguments for contracting have tended to revolve around innovation. Synergy between public purchasers and providers is the attraction from both the public sector and the private sector. More pragmatic governments can use this argument. It is not really about public or private providers, the argument runs, but more about creating a new environment where innovation can flourish and ideas flow more freely.

Cooper (2003: 5) observes that:

> the best deal is not measured by any one criterion. Although price is a factor, other critical issues include efficiency, effectiveness, equity, responsiveness, and responsibility. Furthermore, because these different criteria are frequently in conflict, a determination as to what constitutes a good deal requires a process of working through a set of trade-offs among these factors.

WHEN IS CONTRACTING NOT APPROPRIATE?

Experience tells us that there may be several reasons not to choose contracting. A short list is given below.

Fear of quality degradation

Critics argue that quality is likely to fall if services are contracted out. This is due to companies' interest in making money rather than developing services. If contracts are short term, companies are likely to cut corners to make the largest possible profit, the argument goes. They may never return to the purchaser again. In the language of principal–agent theory (Pratt and Zeckhauser 1992), the providers (as agents) will try to hide information and their actions. While the fear of quality degradation seems wide-spread, there is actually little empirical knowledge on how the level of quality is affected by contracting out, as Hodge (2000: 156) observed. This has to do with the fact that 'quality' is a contested concept and not always easy to measure in the public sector (Beckford 1998).

Control and accountability changes

Critics point to the fact that control becomes difficult when a contract is placed between the purchasing organization and the providing organization. Control can no longer be direct, but has to take notice of what is written down in the contract (this subject is discussed at length in Chapter 9).

Lack of transparency

An often heard comment is that control becomes difficult due to lack of transparency in contract arrangements. Often legislation on openness in government applies to government organizations, but not to contractors. Contractors often do not have the same obligation to be open to the public about their actions. Note, however, that this may vary between countries. In some countries, a relatively strict policy concerning openness is in place. Other countries allow more broad access to information about government actions, including actions of contractors.

THE SERVICE CONTEXT: WHAT PUBLIC SERVICE DELIVERY IS BEING CONTRACTED FOR?

In advanced, industrialized countries (e.g. Denmark), a number of services may be contracted out to private providers:

- The secrets of the intelligence service stored in computer systems are maintained by a private computer firm – a private contractor.
- If you are picked up by an ambulance or have a fire extinguished, you call a private sector company – a private contractor.
- If you want to travel in a bus in central Copenhagen, you ride with a private bus company – a private contractor.
- If the government wants legal advice, it uses its own chief legal adviser in the form of a private law firm – a private contractor.
- If you want to enjoy a meal in a government agency, you eat in a canteen run by private cooks – a private contractor.

It seems as if contracting supplies several of a state's essential needs: the need to guard the secrecy of military intelligence, matters of life and death, and the need to get sound legal advice when travelling in a bus to and from work, and eating a healthy lunch while at work. In other countries, contracting is used for guarding prisoners, and even maintaining supplementary services to military forces (as is the case with private contractors helping US armed forces and allies in the war in Iraq). Of course, there are also many areas of public service delivery where contractors are not used, and where public organizations remain dedicated to producing goods and services in-house. OECD (2005: 131) has published a review of the recent decades experience with contracting out:

> The range of services outsourced in OECD countries is very wide. They include blue collar support services (building cleaning, catering), professional services that are considered ancillary to the core mission of the ministry or agency (information technology), and core government functions (prisons).

A delicate problem is the borderline between the public sector and the private sector:

> Perhaps more fundamentally, the competitive tendering process and the documents that have established it seemingly lack any definite sense of which activities are clearly public functions and therefore not potentially subject to contracting out.
>
> (Peters 1996: 39)

E.S. Savas (2000), in his book on privatization and public–private partnerships, lists a range of services that may be or have been contracted out. A general rule is that the more complex the goals of a service are, the more challenging it is to contract that service out. Walsh (1995) and others have noted how the service specification is of critical importance to a successful contracting-out process. Observers have noted how the types of services that are contracted out have shifted over the years:

> Contracting for public services may have begun with 'brush-and-flush' activities – blue-collar services such as refuse collection, and street and building cleaning. But

in recent years, the policy reach has been extended to a variety of high-tech white-collar services. Prominent examples include the contracting of the National Physical Laboratory . . ., the vehicle driving testing service, and the UK's ballistic missile early warning system.

(Domberger 1998: 160)

CONTRACTING AS PART OF THE GLOBAL PUBLIC MANAGEMENT REVOLUTION

The world of public service delivery has changed dramatically in recent times. It used to be as follows. Public organizations would deliver public services to citizens. Public organizations would enjoy a *de facto* and *de jure* monopoly of service delivery. The governance model followed a stable hierarchical chain of command. Public organizations would not be inclined to combine their forces with other organizations. Independent regulation was not needed so much, as ministers and governments would make the decisions and be held accountable if anything went wrong. If not it would be a matter for the courts, either the administrative courts or the ordinary courts. This is no longer the case. Competition for public service delivery is now widespread. What Donald F. Kettl (1993) called 'the competition prescription' has taken a hold of public sectors everywhere on the globe. Public services are now increasingly put out to tender, contracted out and delivered by private sector providers. These providers can be for-profit companies, or they can be non-profit organizations. Providers can also be alliances or joint partnerships where private firms and non-profit organizations have joined forces to deliver services in a particular area.

A means for providing services through other organizations is contracting. Contracting is 'the design and implementation of contractual relationships between purchasers and suppliers' (Domberger 1998: 12). A contract is an agreement between a purchaser and a provider (buyer and seller) which states the terms of delivery of a service or a product.

Throughout the world, the public sector has been transformed dramatically during the past couple of decades. The New Public Management (NPM) movement focused on marketization of public services and on adopting management techniques from the private sector (Hood 1991; McLaughlin *et al.* 2002). On a short formula, NPM has been described as 'incentivization, marketization and disaggregation' (Dunleavy *et al.* 2006). Politicians either wanted to 'make managers manage' or 'let managers manage' (Kettl 1997). Making managers manage is based on the principal–agent framework that derives from new institutional economics. Letting managers manage puts faith in managers' own abilities to meet new challenges once they are freed from 'red tape'. There has always been a tension in NPM reforms between these two different forces. Kettl (2000) described the movement as 'a global public management revolution' that was shedding the old habits of bureaucracy and focus on inputs, to a new kind of public sector focused on management, governance and results, and he emphasized that this was going on

15

globally; from Mongolia and Sweden to New Zealand and the United States. It has been convincingly documented how many OECD countries moved to public management reform inspired by the NPM agenda (Pollitt and Bouckaert 2004; OECD 2005). Each country has implemented NPM reforms in accordance with its own historical public management traditions and institutions. Christensen and Lægreid (2001) call this the transformative perspective. Many envisaged the New Public Management state as an alternative to the traditional administrative state (Hughes 2003).

In this NPM world, contracting has played a significant part (Fortin and van Hassel 2000). Contracting means collaboration with private sector organizations for delivery of public services. Contracting made the split between 'purchasers' and 'providers' possible. Contracting therefore has to be understood properly in the context of the reforms associated with NPM. Seconding private actors that are for-profit organizations (such as firms and companies) and non-profit organizations (such as voluntary organizations) has been an important part of the NPM agenda. A leading public management scholar Jan-Erik Lane (2000) has even suggested that contracting *is* NPM. Lane sees a trend away from the old traditional modes of service delivery towards a contract-based service delivery, and he argues that contracts are what set new waves of reform apart from the old service delivery style. It has been argued that we have entered 'the contractual age' (Fortin 2000) (Table 1.1).

Table 1.1 Seminal studies in contracting for public service delivery (in chronological order)

Author(s)	Main contribution	Comments
E.S. Savas (1987) *Privatization: The Key to Better Government*	Savas' original analysis of the theme of privatization broadly understood. Research was already being published in the 1970s.	Savas still publishes on contracting out and privatization. Savas' knowledge of contracting out is deep, but his work is often biased in a pro-privatization direction.
Donald F. Kettl (1993) *Sharing Power*	First study that took contract management seriously and identified 'the smart buyer problem'.	Kettl's work has since inspired work on contract management capacity and strategic contracting management.
H. B. Milward (1996) *Symposium on the hollow state*	Identification of 'the hollowing out of the state' as one of the consequences of contracting. Later confirmed in empirical studies in Arizona, USA.	The hollow state has long been a metaphor for what was going to happen with the public sector if public service delivery was contracted out too much. Recent research has focused on governing in the hollow state. Critics assert that the state is not hollow, and the contracting only goes on in the margins of the public sector.

Simon Domberger (1998) *The Contracting Organization*	Domberger did the original empirical studies of contracting in the 1980s that established the later controversial 20 per cent rule. In this book, Domberger compares contracting in the public sector with outsourcing practices in the private sector.	Domberger's work was groundbreaking because of his commitment to assessing both the public sector and private sector practice, but the work has not been followed up in the literature (probably because of the huge task it implicates).
Graeme Hodge (2000) *Privatization*	Meta-analysis on the effectiveness of contracting out based on studies of all available statistically based results published in English.	Hodge's work managed to break new ground in providing empirical assessment for what was often an ideological discussion on the pros and cons of private sector involvement in public service delivery.
Jan-Erik Lane (2000) *New Public Management*	The first full treatment, if somewhat controversial, of NPM as a theory mostly of contracting. Lane gives full treatment to the challenges faced in public management by the contract agenda.	Lane's work has been criticized for being too informed by the principal–agent theory, but his work does contain criticisms of this theory as well and is not a complete endorsement of the theory.
Yvonne Fortin and Hugo van Hassel (2000) *Contracting in the New Public Management*	A work that firmly placed contracting in the framework of the NPM, and also considered the public law implications of the contract state.	Later work has tried to emphasize what effects contracting has on the overall function of the public sector and to what extent public and private law collide.
Stephen Osborne (2000) *Public– Private Partnerships*	First international assessment of the impact of the move from contracting to public–private partnerships. Recognition of PPPs as a theme in contracting.	The widespread attention to PPPs by governments has been noticed by researchers. Many researchers have followed on from this line of research, including Hodge and Greve (2005).
Barbara Romzek and Jocelyn M. Johnston (2002) Effective contract implementation and management	Romzek and Johnston has tried to make a preliminary model of effective contract management implement and accountability based on empirical studies in Kansas, USA. Empirical studies have gone on since the 1990s	Their model forms the basis for further revisions and tests, but the elements for a more robust theory of contracting are there.
T. Brown and M. Potoski (2003) Contract management capacity	The research from these authors tries to show that the contract management capacity is needed on a variety of variables. Aims towards an empirically based theory of government contracting.	Builds on earlier ideas by Kettl, and seeks to take contract management seriously as a subject of its own and not just as a subset of the (now criticized) NPM agenda.

17

The move towards a new public management and marketization model of public service delivery is neatly summed up by the following characterization:

> More recently, some countries have moved this agenda [the management model] one step further and introduced forms of public organization in which a 'quasi market' takes the place of traditional forms of coordination (market governance). This became the ideal type of the 1990s, when contracting out, competitive tenders, and principal–agent separation were employed to force officials to respond to financial signals and competitive pressures. Sometimes called 'contractualism' or 'entrepreneurial government', the market governance model sought to create greater flexibility, reduced planning and less regulation. Programs and the agencies running them were to be rewarded through an incentive-based system in which increased performance resulted in increased reward. In addition, choices made by consumers would help to determine whether programs would receive continued public support.
>
> (Considine and Lewis 2003: 133)

The term 'public service organizations' (PSOs), used by Osborne and Brown (2005), is a good signal of what contracting has done to public service delivery. They are not exclusively public *sector* organizations, but public service organizations because they deliver public services; however, they could be organized as private companies or voluntary organizations. There is much more openness as to who should deliver the service than there was in the traditional administrative state.

In recent years, the debate on public management has been expanded to embrace a discussion around the concept of governance. Broadly stated, governance is about the interactions between government and society (Kettl 2002). For some years, the catch-phrase was 'from government to governance', meaning a move from a traditional hierarchical, top-down form of government to a supposedly more network-based, interorganizational relationship between different public and private organizations (Pierre 2000). While this crude image has been revoked in the literature, there has been a growing interest to see management tools in the wider context of interorganizational relationships. Osborne (2006) has coined the term 'new public governance' (NPG) to characterize the new form of steering societies. According to Osborne (2006: 83), new public governance:

■ has its theoretical roots in organizational sociology and network theory;
■ sees the state as plural and pluralist;
■ focuses on interorganizational relationships;
■ views relationships to external organizational partners as interdependent agents within ongoing relationships;
■ sees the main governance mechanisms as trust or relational contracts;
■ has neo-corporatism as its value base.

18

It is obvious how the contract state fits into this general picture. Writers such as Milward and Provan (2000) have long been interested in contracting and interorganizational relationships, and some of the recent writers, such as Sanger (2002), view the providers as networks or alliances. The different variations of how a contract state can be conceived of are presented in the following section.

VARIATIONS OF THE CONTRACT STATE

What are the consequences of contracting for the way the state is structured? There have been various predictions and characterizations of what might happen to the state if contracting becomes a widespread phenomenon.

The hollowing out of the state

This model has been written about extensively in the literature. American researchers Milward and Provan (1993) described a state where many services are contracted out and only a 'hollow' core remains. The term was taken from an analysis of 'the hollow corporation' in the business literature (Milward 1996: 193). In Milward and Provan's view, contracting out and relying on third parties is what happened in many areas of social policy in the 1990s. The hollowing-out thesis has since attracted many sceptics. According to Milward (1996: 193):

> In the general sense the hollow state refers to any joint production situation where a governmental agency relies on others (firms, non-profits or other government agencies) to jointly deliver public services. Carried to extreme, it refers to a government that as a matter of policy has chosen to contract out all its production capability to third parties, perhaps retaining only a systems' integration responsible for negotiating, monitoring, and evaluating contracts.

There are those who do not believe that enough contracting out has taken place to earn the description 'hollow' in the first place. Other critics of the thesis argue that the state is not hollow, but that it is simply a smarter way of organizing than is the usual hierarchy. There was concern over lack of governance capacity in relation to private organizations. However, in later research Milward and Provan (2000) showed how government could influence private organizations through network steering and thus 'govern the hollow state'.

The enabling state

British scholars Deakin and Walsh (1995) characterized the state's role as 'enabling'. The state would 'enable' organizations to perform the tasks that the purchasers had specified in the contracts. The enabling state paints a more optimistic picture about the possibility for governance of private organizations. The concept of enabling is similar to the more well-known phrase of 'steering, not rowing' or the entrepreneurial state, popularized by Osborne and Gaebler (1993) (and originally coined by E.S. Savas in his 1987 book on *Privatization: The Key to Better Government*) in their famous book on *Reinventing Government* that paved the way for Al Gore and Bill Clinton's programme for the National Performance Review in the 1990s in the USA.

The strategic contract state

At various points in time, the term has simply been 'the contract state' or 'the contracting state' (Harden 1992). Adding knowledge from Kelman (2002), the term may be expanded to 'the strategic contracting state'. The state contracts for public services, but not only when a good bargain is in sight. The state uses contracting in order to fulfil its mission and its vision for what good governance is. Contracting is more than simply obtaining value for money for a specific service. Contracting is a way of organizing the public sector and to make employees deliver the best possible service. Contracting is deeply embedded in the principles of NPM and its focus on results.

Which contract state?

There has been a trend in discussing the contract state from seeing it as a way of loadshedding to seeing contracting as a strategic device for governments to improve the mechanisms of service delivery. One of the early predicaments focused on the dangers for public management in contracting out public service delivery. 'The hollowing out of the state' (Milward 1996) envisioned a society where governments would have little control over how public services were delivered. Governments would lose out to (mostly) private providers of services, and there would be little or nothing to do for the public managers 'left behind' in the remaining parts of the public sector. An even earlier characterization was that of the 'shadow state' (Guttman and Willner 1975) where contracting out was seen as political device for governments to shed responsibility for services and to foster a huge private provider industry. That is still the view of some in how the United States approach contracts for public services (Guttman 2003). There was another theme in the 1990s when people gradually focused on how governments could act in leading change. This came with the NPM wave in public management theory and practice. Deakin and Walsh's term 'the enabling state' focused on the possibilities governments had for directing service delivery without having to do the hard work of actually delivering services. This was in accordance with Patrick Dunleavy's (1991) much discussed 'bureau-shaping bureaucrat' that favoured all the important policy work close to the political circles, while being ignorant of the more mundane public service delivery at the street level. Governments would be 'enablers' that allowed for-profit and nonprofit providers to come forward and display their creativity in solving public policy problems and delivering public services. Contracting out was still seen at the margins of government although Kettl (1993) early on had urged governments to think more coherently and systematically about contract management while still advocating a 'smart buyer' approach. The more recent theme of 'strategic contracting' proposed by Kelman (2002), or the theme of contract management capacity (Brown and Potoski 2003), give evidence of a more confident approach to the role of contracting out in the modern state. Contracting out must be placed at the strategic apex of public organizations, and politicians and public managers must be responsible for building an adequate contract management capacity.

The challenges of the contract state remain, even though the role of government has shifted to a more pro-active status. As Cooper (2003) has reminded us, contracting for public services takes place at the intersection between horizontal governance and vertical governance. Governments may want to be more market-like and engage closely with private sector providers, but they still have to attend to the lines of authority which is where they receive their legitimacy from. In this respect, governments cannot turn into a business. What is new in recent years is the trend towards using contracts strategically: to contract only for some services and not for others. Contracts must also be wired into the long-term strategy of the organization if they are to have a solid future in public policy and management reality. There is no doubt that the institutional realities must be aligned with the concrete initiatives and steps towards contracting (Greve and Ejersbo 2005; Brown *et al.* 2006). Just as public management cannot be grasped without considering its institutional context (Lynn 2006), public sector contracting cannot be treated as a technical matter, but must take the institutional characteristics of each country and each public delivery system into account.

CONCLUSIONS

This chapter has examined the reasons for injecting competition into public service delivery. The primary reasons appear to be: saving money; getting value for money; efficiency; creating a level playing field; industrial policy, and innovation. The second part of the chapter looked at different models of the state when contracting is a prominent feature: the hollowing-out model, the enabling state model, and the strategic contract state model.

Structure of the book

The issue of competition and contracting for public service delivery is discussed in this book. The book is structured as follows. The first part is the introduction. Chapter 1 introduces the concepts of competition and contracting. Chapter 2 presents the contract management model. Chapter 3 looks at contract management capacity. Chapter 4 discusses the use of information technology in contracting. This is a new area, and little has been written before on the relationship between contracting and IT. Chapter 5 discusses the conditions of training for contract management. Chapter 6 concerns the provider perspective, and looks at the changing role of the market, and the globalization of public service production. Chapter 7 discusses public–private partnerships (PPPs), and debates whether they should be thought of as something new or if they are an extension of the contracting phenomenon. Chapter 8 is about regulation and accountability that accompanies contracting, and distinguishes between three types of regulation: hierarchical regulation, management-based regulation, and market-based regulation. Chapter 9 outlines the conclusions of the book. A mature contract management model is discussed, and the future of the contract state is laid out.

Two case studies are included at the end of the book. The first concerns the contracting out of railways services in Jutland, Denmark, and shows the challenges for both purchasers and providers in contract management and implementation. The second describes the case of a local government's effort to contract out most of its services, and shows how strategic contracting management works in practice.

DISCUSSION QUESTIONS

1 How is contract management wired into the fabric of the NPM in your country? Is contracting seen as a neutral arrangement that has always been there or part of a public management trend?
2 How fierce is the competition in your area? Has the government got a policy for competition for public service delivery? Are there any areas that are not suitable for competition?
3 What are the formal and the informal sides of contracting in your particular context? Should the informal norms be written down as formal rules? Is the legal system geared to contracting for public service delivery? Do purchasers and providers build up trust or have adversarial relationships?
4 Should contracting be used only as a pragmatic tool for getting more value for money, or does strategic contracting – where contracting is integrated in a strategic public management framework – have a future?

REFERENCES

Bartle, J.R. and R.L. Kosorec (2001) *Procurement and Contracting in State Government 2000.* Syracuse: Maxwell. Government Performance Project Learning Paper Series.

Beckford, J. (1998) *Quality – A Critical Introduction*. London: Routledge.

Brown, T. and M. Potoski (2003) Contract management capacity in municipal and county government, *Public Administration Review* 63(2): 141–164.

Brown, T., M. Potoski and D. Van Slyke (2006) Managing contracted public services, *Public Administration Review* 66(3): 323–331.

Christensen, T. and P. Lægreid (2001) *New Public Management – The Transformation of Ideas into Practice*. Aldershot: Ashgate.

Considine, M. and J. Lewis (2003) Bureaucracy, network, or enterprise? Comparing models of governance in Australia, Britain, the Netherlands, and New Zealand, *Public Administration Review* 63(2): 131–140.

Cooper, P. (2003) *Governing By Contract*. Washington, DC: GQ Press.

Deakin, N. and K. Walsh (1995) The enabling state, *Public Administration* 74 (spring): 33–48.

Domberger, S. (1998) *The Contracting Organization: A Strategic Guide to Outsourcing*. Oxford: Oxford University Press.

Domberger, S. and C. Hall (1996) Contracting for public services: a review of antipodean experiences, *Public Administration* 74(1): 129–147.

Domberger, S. and P.H. Jensen (1997) Contracting out by the public sector: theory, evidence, prospects, *Oxford Review of Economic Policy* 13(4): 67–78.

Domberger, S., S.A. Medowcroft and D.J. Thompson (1986) Competitive tendering and efficiency: the case of refuse collection, *Fiscal Studies* 7(4): 69–87.

Drewry, C., C. Greve and T. Tanquerel (eds) (2005) *Contracts, Performance Measurement and Accountability in the Public Sector*. Amsterdam: IOS Press.

Dunleavy, P. (1991) *Democracy, Bureaucracy and Public Choice*. Hemel Hempstead: Harvester Wheatsheaf.

Dunleavy, P. *et al.* (2006) New public management is dead – long live digital-era governance, *Journal of Public Administration Research and Theory* 16(3): 467–494.

Fortin, Y. (2000) 'Introduction', in Fortin, Y. and van Hassel, H. (eds) *Contracting in the New Public Management*. Amsterdam: IOS Press.

Fortin, Y. and H. van Hassel (eds) (2000) *Contracting in the New Public Management*. Amsterdam: IOS Press.

Greve, C. and N. Ejersbo (2005) *Contracts as Reinvented Institutions in the Public Sector. A Cross-cultural Comparison*, Westport, CT: Praeger.

Guttman, D. (2003) Contracting United States government work: organizational and constitutional models, *Public Organization Review: A Global Journal* 3(3): 281–299.

Guttman, D. and B. Willner (1975) *The Shadow Government*. Pantheon Books.

Harden, I. (1992) *The Contracting State*. Buckingham: Open University Press.

Hodge, G.A. (2000) *Privatization. An International Review of Performance*. Boulder, CO: Westview Press.

Hood, C. (1991) A public management of all seasons, *Public Administration* 69: 3–19.

Hood, C. (1998) *The Art of the State. Culture, Rhetoric, and Public Management*. Oxford: Clarendon Press.

Hughes, O. (2003) *Public Management and Administration*. London: Palgrave.

Kelman, S. (2002) Strategic contracting management, in J.D. Donahue and J.S. Nye (eds) *Market-based Governance*. Washington, DC: Brookings.

Kettl, D.F. (1993) *Sharing Power. Public Governance of Private Markets*. Washington, DC: Brookings.

Kettl, D.F. (1997) The global revolution in public management: driving themes, missing links, *Journal of Public Policy and Management* 16(3): 446–462.

Kettl, D.F. (2000) *The Global Public Management Revolution*. Washington, DC: Brookings.

Kettl, D.F. (2002) *The Transformation of Governance*. Baltimore, MD: Johns Hopkins University Press.

Klijn, E-H. and G. Teisman. (2004) *Managing Uncertainties in Networks: Public–Private Controversies*. London: Routledge.

Knight, J. (1992) *Institutions and Social Conflict*. Cambridge: Cambridge University Press.

Lane, J.E. (2000) *New Public Management*. London: Routledge.

Light, P. (1998) *Sustaining Innovation*. San Francisco, CA: Jossey Bass.

Lynn, L. Jr. (2006) *Public Management. Old and New*. London: Routledge.

Martin, L. (1999) *Determining a Level Playing Field for Public–Private Competition*. Arlington, VA: The PriceWaterhouseCoopers Endowment for the Business of Government.

McLaughlin, K., S. Osborne and E. Ferlie (eds) (2002) *The New Public Management*. London: Routledge.

Milward, H.B. (1996) Symposium on the hollow state: capacity, control and performance in interorganizational settings, *Journal of Public Administration Research and Theory* 6: 193–195.

Milward, H.B. and K. Provan (1993) What does the hollow state look like?, in B. Bozeman (ed.) *Public Management: The State of the Art*. San Francisco, CA: Jossey Bass.

Milward, H.B. and K. Provan (2000) Governing the hollow state, *Journal of Public Administration Research and Theory* 10(2): 359–379.

North, D.C. (1990) Institutions, *Journal of Economic Perspectives* 5(1): 97–112.

OECD (2005) *Modernising Government*. Paris: OECD.

Osborne, D. and T. Gaebler (1993) [1992] *Reinventing Government. How the Entrepreneurial Spirit is Transforming the Public Sector*. New York: Plume.

Osborne, S. (2000) *Public–Private Partnerships*. London: Routledge.

Osborne, S. (2006) The new public governance? *Public Management Review* 8(3): 377–387.

Osborne, S. and K. Brown (2005) *Managing Change and Innovation in Public Service Organizations*, London: Routledge.

Peters, B.G. (1996) *The Future of Governing. Four Emerging Models.* Lawrence: University of Kansas Press.

Pierre, J. (ed.) (2000) *Debating Governance.* Oxford: Oxford University Press.

Pollitt, C. (2003) *The Essential Public Manager.* Buckingham: Open University Press.

Pollitt, C. and G. Bouckaert (2004) *Public Management Reform. A Comparative Analysis* Oxford: Oxford University Press.

Pratt, J.W. and R.J. Zeckhauser (eds) (1992) *Principals and Agents. The Structure of Business.* Cambridge, MA: Harvard Business School Press.

Romzek, B. and J. Johnston (2002) Effective contract implementation and management: a preliminary model, *Journal of Public Administration Research and Theory* 12(3): 423–453.

Sanger, M.B. (2002) *The Welfare Marketplace, Privatization and Welfare Reform.* Washington, DC: Brookings.

Savas, E.S. (1987) *Privatization: The Key to Better Government.* New Jersey: Chatham House.

Savas, E.S. (2000) *Privatization and Public–Private Partnerships.* New Jersey: Chatham House.

Walsh, K. (1995) *Public Services and Market Mechanisms.* London: Macmillan.

Williamson, O.E. (1996) *The Mechanisms of Governance.* Oxford: Oxford University Press.

FURTHER READING

Readings on contracting as part of NPM

A good general overview of contracting as part of NPM is the collection of papers from Fortin and van Hassel (2000) – *Contracting in the New Public Management* (Amsterdam: IOS Press). The introductory chapter by Fortin is especially good. Walsh (1995) gives an account of the early days of contracting. Domberger's (1998) book on contracting – *The Contracting Organization* (Oxford: Oxford University Press) – offers one of the most balanced treatments of the subject (despite its subtitle *A Strategic Guide to Outsourcing*). If you are looking for insights into how the private sector contracts (or outsources), then Domberger is a good choice because it includes an extensive discussion of private sector practices. Lane's *New Public Management* (2000) (London: Routledge) has an in-depth treatment of NPM as contracting. A recent overview of how contracting relates to performance-based management and accountability may be found in Drewry *et al.* (eds) (2005) *Contracts, Performance Measurement and Accountability in the Public Sector* (Amsterdam: IOS Press).

Readings on competition of public services

There are several books which deal with competition in public services. For a good overview of the various forms of competition models, see Savas (2000) *Privatization and Public–Private Partnerships* (New Jersey: Chatham House), although the author has a clear pro-privatization bias. Peters' (1996) *The Future of Governing* (Lawrence: University of Kansas Press) provides a thorough review of the ingredients in 'the market model' for public service delivery. Hood (1998) *The Art of the State* (Oxford: Clarendon Press) is a thoughtful and well-crafted work on public management, including the individualized style of public management that deals with competition.

Readings on strategic contracting

The best work on strategic contracting is found in Kelman's (2002) 'Strategic contracting management' in Donahue and Nye (eds) *Market-based Governance* (Washington, DC: Brookings). There is also a good treatment of the strategic use of contracting in Domberger's (1998) *The Contracting Organization* which compares public sector practices with private sector practices.

Chapter 2

Managing contracts

A conceptual model

LEARNING OBJECTIVES

By the end of this chapter you should:

- have a clear understanding of the different elements in managing contracts;
- be able to link the different elements together in a conceptual model;
- have acquired an understanding of the challenges facing contract management.

KEY POINTS OF THIS CHAPTER

- Contract management consists of several elements, including formulating a policy, purchasing smartly and cleverly, and regulating responsively. This chapter develops a heuristic model of contracting for public service delivery.
- Governments must know what they want to buy from providers and specify their performance or output targets.
- Contracts have both a formal side and an informal side to them (when seen from an institutional perspective). Public managers must grasp both types of institutions in order to deal effectively with contractual relationships.
- Providers differ in form and size, but the most common distinction is between for-profit providers (companies), non-profit providers (voluntary organizations, for example), other public organizations and networks or

> consortia of providers. Providers operate at the local, the national and increasingly also at the global level.
> ■ Contract management is placed in an institutional context of both formal and informal rules that shape the strategies of contract managers and providers.

KEY TERMS

■ **Contracting out policy** – the official policy, found in documents and legislation and political statements, that governments follow to contract out public services to external providers.

■ **Strategic purchasing** – how governments know what and how they want to purchase goods and services from external providers.

■ **Provider of public service** – an organization (for-profit, non-profit or a public organization) delivering public services under contract and usually after a round of competitive tendering.

In this chapter, a conceptual model of contracting is presented. The model is derived from the different contributions to the literature on government contracting (see Brown and Potoski 2003; Kettl 1993; Romzek and Johnston 2002). Authors have written about the different steps in a contracting cycle (Cooper 2003; Savas 2000). Here, the different steps are organized into distinct elements. The model forms the basic structure of the book.

The model consists of the following elements:

■ contracting out policy;
■ strategic purchasing and communication;
■ the contract;
■ the providers;
■ consumption;
■ regulation; and
■ institutions/institutional framework.

CONTRACTING OUT POLICY

Contracting out rests on the assumption that competition is required for effective public service delivery. For many years, there has been a belief among policy-makers that competition is what public services delivery need. Donald F. Kettl (1993) calls this the competition prescription. Kettl (1993: 3) observes a trend that 'substitutes market for government control, that replaces command-and-control authority with competition'. The competition prescription is quite simple. Let public services be produced on the market instead of being produced by public organizations in a hierarchy. Let private providers compete for contracts. Award the contract to the bidder with the best combination of price and quality. The competition prescription has many advocates. Privatization expert and advocate Savas (1987, 2000) sees privatization as 'the key to better government'. The promise has always been that private providers are able to deliver more efficient services at a lower cost because they are forced to compete in the marketplace. International organizations such as the OECD (1997) advocated the injection of more competition into public services. Although the OECD's policy recommendations have been modified somewhat, competition still plays a major role in the OECD's approach to better public service delivery. A summary of OECD's policy may be found in the report *Modernising Government* that came out in 2005 which summed up the previous twenty-plus years of initiatives towards public management reform, including contracting, in the OECD countries (OECD 2005).

Public services are hard to measure and set clear objectives for. There is a reason why services were public in the first place. Public services are complex, and the more complex they are, the harder it is to specify a clear contract. Donald F. Kettl (1993) has called this the complexity problem. Another part of the answer is that public providers do not know exactly what they want from the market. Providers often complain that purchasers have not made up their minds about what kinds of services they want delivered. Sometimes, purchasers are not up to date with what the market can provide. Consequently, purchasers may ask for types of service delivery that have already been overtaken by new service developments.

Competition is now relevant in many policy areas, and is used for both simple and complex services. Competition is traditionally used when schools or other public buildings have to be cleaned (Hodge 2000). Social services are increasingly exposed to competition (Van Slyke 2003). Childcare is another service where there are private providers delivering the services. Prison services have been delivered by private companies in a number of countries recently (Sand 2004). Competition is also relevant when the military buys new equipment, or NASA buys components for its space programmes. Ambulance driving and fire-fighting are areas where some countries have experience with competition. Savas (2000: 72–73) offers an extensive list of areas where contracting out has been applied in real-life contexts: from addiction treatment, adopting, air polution abatement, airport operation over paratransit system operations, park management and maintenance, parking enforcement, parking lot and garage operation to waste water treatment, water meter reading and maintenance, zoning and subdivision control, and zoo management! Snow removal was one of the first areas where contracting out was used and that led Savas to introduce the term privatization or alternative service delivery during the 1970s (Milward 2006).

A general contracting out policy, or more specifically a 'competition strategy for public service delivery', is a strategy or policy that governments follow in order to ensure that public services are competitive. A competition strategy consists of cognitive,

29

normative and regulative institutions (Scott 1995). Cognitive institutions promote the notion that competition may be applied to public service delivery. Normative institutions argue that competition and involvement of private sector providers are a desirable policy for governments to pursue and citizens to gain from as customers. Regulative institutions build the competition prescription into rules and regulations that will guide companies' and citizens' behaviour. We can also think of competition as different forms of ideas with different types of interests behind it (Campbell 2004). Ideas can be programmes that governments put forward. Ideas can be paradigms that specify a particular selection of ideas. Ideas can be frames that put competition into a context. And ideas can be public opinions that are voiced concerning competition which may be anything from statements to opinions in the media. Actors that support the ideas of competition can include decision-makers in politics and business, theoreticians and intellectuals that give the idea of competition legitimacy, framers in the sense of spin doctors and pollsters, and supporting groups of trade organizations and interest groups. A competition strategy involves a framework of problems, policy and politics that may or may not combine in different 'streams' (Kingdon 1995). Competition is seen as a solution to the problem of inefficiency and too much bureaucratization. The competition strategy is put forward as a viable alternative to bureaucracy and hierarchy. Introducing and implementing the competition strategy into the public sector and to public service delivery meet with a certain amount of resistance.

Peters (1996) has summarized the competition models as follows. A distrust of monopoly in public service provision, decentralization as the preferred structure of organization, pay-for-performance and other private sector techniques for management, and internal markets and market incentives for public service provision. Hood (1998: 98) finds that the most important characteristic for an individualized style of public management is that:

> it starts from the assumption that the world is populated by rational egoists who are bent on outsmarting each other to get something for nothing. Rivalry and competition are central to the individualist view of what the world of public management is and should be like.

Walsh (1995: 2) notes how:

> a central purpose of the institutional changes that are being introduced is that purposes should be clearer, and standards objectively defined, and that there should be more explicit approaches to the assessment of the extent to which they are being achieved with payment and reward being tied to output. The attempt is to introduce the market disciplines that operate in the public sector into the private sector.

Contracting, it should remembered, is only one element out of several elements that make up a competition strategy for public service delivery. Other elements include vouchers, public–private partnerships, privatization of public assets, deregulation and consumer choice. (Savas 2000). The theoretical rationale behind contracting is important for its implementation success rate (Romzek and Johnston 2002: 429).

Countries have adopted various approaches to the competition strategy. Denmark has a competition strategy as part of the government's modernization programme. The competition strategy was first introduced with a Conservative government's moderniza-tion programme in the 1980s. The model was gradually extended and revised throughout the decade. The policy document in 1992 was called *Choice of Welfare*, indicating a far-reaching consumer-oriented policy coupled with recommendations for a purchaser–provider split in public service delivery. The Social Democratic-led government continued the policy, focusing on argumentative persuasion through the issue of best practice reports and focusing on the human relations aspect of contracting out. When a Liberal-Conservative government was elected in 2001, the competition strategy was strengthened. More focus on consumer choice and more legislation to introduce contracting out were initiated. The Danish approach to public management reform has generally been more towards 'modernizing' than towards 'marketizing' (Greve 2006), but competition has always been an important element in the strategy for improved public service delivery. The competition strategy in Denmark has gained a more coherent form since 2001, but it built on the previous decades' experiences.

The UK policy shifted from competitive compulsory tendering (CCT) under the Thatcher and Major governments to the best practice approach when New Labour came to power in 1997. CCT was widely unpopular as it forced local governments to use contracting out even if a local government was politically against it. Here, the power relations between central government and local government are visible. The strong UK central government put pressure on the weaker local governments to force the government's policy through. In more consensual countries, such as Scandinavia, the same kind of pressure was always more difficult. The CCT policy was superseded by the best value approach (Vincent-Jones 1999). Best value was seen as more nuanced, and more suited to the needs of local government. The Best Value performance management framework required a rethink of local governments' activities over a five-year period, and local councils had to compare themselves to other local authorities, private for-profit providers and non-profit voluntary organizations with the aim of securing a 'mixed economy of services' (Martin and Hartley 2000: 44).

The best value policy encouraged public sector organizations to look for strategic partners in both for-profit companies and voluntary companies, and approach toned down competition as a central value. Most important of all, the best value policy was implemented through a pilot programme and there was not the same kind of central control over the practice that the CCT policy required. The English Local Government Association encouraged its members to follow the best value policy. An empirical assess-ment through a survey of local governments showed that best value was received well by the local governments:

31

> The survey findings provide convincing evidence that, in contrast to the CCT regime, Best Value has, initially at least, enjoyed widespread support among local authorities. A majority of councils clearly intended to put in place initiatives which they believed reflected the principles of Best Value almost two years in advance of any legal requirement for them to do so.
>
> (Martin and Hartley 2000: 53)

Instead of competition, the government encouraged local governments to think of private sector actors as partners. The Office of the Deputy Prime Minister (2003) issued a report on strategic service partnerships between local governments and private actors. In general, the policy of the New Labour government has been to emphasize partnership and collaboration rather than competition (Entwhistle and Martin 2005).

Contracting out was an important element in the efforts to make the Australian public sector more efficient and effective in the 1990s (Hodge 2005; Makin 2003). Australia practised a competition strategy under the Kennett government in Victoria. The Kennett government of the 1990s set a target of 50 per cent of tasks to be competitively tendered (Hodge 2000: 31). Contracting out was essential to the New Zealand experience, of course, as one of the 'leading' NPM countries in the world (Barzelay 2001). Contracting out rested on a clearly understood applicability of principal–agent theory and transaction cost theory in the New Zealand case (Boston 1999; Boston *et al.* 1996). The purchaser–provider split was part of New Zealand's well-known feature of public management reform. Sweden used the competition strategy when the Conservative-Liberal governments were in office and as part of its response to an economic crisis (Almqvist 2001). Contracting out was considered to be one of the 'icons' of NPM in Sweden. Contracting out blossomed under a Conservative government in the 1990s in Sweden. A major reason behind the contracting policy was Sweden's severe economic crisis at the time. The City of Stockholm was among the key innovators towards contracting out (Almqvist and Högberg 2005). Stockholm administered a managed competition programme that encouraged competition. Public sector employees were encouraged to break out of the public sector and form their own company (a practice known as 'afknopning'). In the 2000s, however, the bigger companies were dominant in the market, since many of the smaller companies had been absorbed by the major companies.

Institutionalizing a general contracting out policy involves politics. In each country, the political process has been played out differently. One variable is whether countries have a Westminster, winer-takes-all political system that gives governments a majority in Parliament, or whether countries have a more consensual system that requires coalitions and negations before political action can be taken. It seems plausible that the Westminster-type systems were able to move more quickly to contracting out policy. Certainly, the British experience was that little formal objections were made to the contracting out policy. It was a political action to change the policy from the CCT version to the best value approach when the New Labour government came to power. In consensual democracies, the political process has played out over decades with negotiations and persuasive argumentation going on. In a country like Denmark, there may have been overall political agreement about the idea of contracting out and market testing, but the legislation that followed the idea has been the subject of much controversy each time it has been introduced.

STRATEGIC PURCHASING AND COMMUNICATION

The second part of the model concerns strategic purchasing and communication. In the literature on contracting out, 'purchasing' is the key concept for public sector managers. Kettl (1993) calls this 'smart buying'. The purpose of smart buying is that governments know what they want from their relationship between providers (Box 2.1). Brown and Potoski (2003) refer to the process of knowing what governments want and going through the steps of preparing the contracting process for feasibility capacity. Romzek and Johnston (2002) talk about having enough resources (broadly conceived), to having in-depth planning for contractor performance measurement, intensive training for state contract management staff, evaluation of contractor staff capacity, and evaluation of contractor financial management capacity; all factors that are associated with the field of strategic purchasing.

BOX 2.1 THE SMART BUYER PROBLEM

Donald F. Kettl (1993) first formulated what has become known as the 'smart buyer problem'. Kettl's original analysis was based on case studies of contracting in the US government. On the basis of his studies, he found that governments were not sufficiently prepared to meet the challenges of contracting. The key problem he singled out was that the markets for public service provision are likely to be imperfect markets. To help prepare public managers for what was at stake in contracting, he identified the smart buyer problem:

> The higher the level of imperfections in the markets in which it buys, the greater the burden of the government to behave as a *smart buyer*. Government must know what it wants to buy. It must know how to buy its goods and services. And it must be able to determine what it has bought.
>
> (Kettl 1993: 17; emphasis in original)

Subsequent research has confirmed that Kettl was on the right track. Brown and Potoski (2003) today talk about contract management capacity, and Steven Kelman (2002) wants to see a strengthened strategic contracting management approach where contract capacity is anchored strategically in public organizations.

33

A formal decision has to be taken about wanting to contract out. This is often a political decision that stems from the ruling coalition's beliefs. But a decision to contract out is often based on pragmatic reasoning where a government decides it wants to have value for money and to achieve the best service for the least cost, which makes the government want to try contracting out. Collecting information is often, but not always, a part of the process prior to the decision of contracting out. Some states form commissions (this is very widespread in the USA, for example). Denmark had a commission in the early 1990s made up of representatives from business, labour unions and experts. The commission came up with recommendations after having made a thorough analysis.

Designing the contract is about setting performance targets for public service delivery (Romzek and Johnston 2002: 435–437) (Box 2.2). When a government decides to contract out for public service delivery, it has to be sure it knows what it is going to buy. In most governments, this means setting up performance targets. Performance-based management (De Bruijn 2002) is about establishing clear and achievable goals for the provider organizations. The clearer the targets are, the more likely the success of imple-

BOX 2.2 ROMZEK AND JOHNSTON'S PRELIMINARY MODEL OF EFFECTIVE CONTRACT IMPLEMENTATION AND MANAGEMENT

American researchers Barbara Romzek and Jocelyn Johnston (2002) have conducted intensive case studies on contracting out in Kansas. They studied five contracting cases: (1) Case management for elderly Medicaid clients; (2) Medicaid managed care for welfare families; (3) Employment preparation services for welfare recipients (statewide); (4) Employment preparation services for welfare recipients (pilot project), and (5) foster care and adoption services for children legally under state custody due to child abuse or neglect. On the basis of their studies, they have come up with a number of key factors that influence the effectiveness of contracts.

Factors with positive impact:

- level of competition among providers;
- resource adequacy;
- planning for performance measurement;
- training for state contract managers;
- evaluation of contractor staffing capacity;
- evaluation of contractor financial management capacity; and
- theoretical rationale for reform.

Factors with negative impact:

- Political strength of client advocates;
- complexity for subcontractor relationships; and
- risk shifting to the contractor.

mentation in the end. Targets can vary, but they need to be ready to implement and be possible for the provider to handle.

Involving stakeholders is about how to start a process where input will come from various sources: politicians, citizens, the business world. One possibility is to make a task force that deals only with the contracting issue. Another strategy is to make an open process from the beginning and to invite input from the key stakeholders that are going to be affected by the contracting decision. Van Slyke (2003) mentions how non-profit organizations were sometimes consulted on how and what to contract out. His example is from New York State. A lobby activity on the part of non-profit organizations would suggest to public managers new areas that could be contracted out in the future. Because public managers do not always have a sufficient overview of the market and the opportunities it provides, such suggestions may sometimes come in handy and save the political decision-makers some time in scanning the market.

Creating a communication strategy for contracting issues

Contracting is not a trivial matter in most cases. Contracting will affect groups in the environment. Public managers therefore need to have a clear communication strategy where the implications of contracting are spelled out. A communication strategy must last for the duration of the contracting process. The question of a communication element to the contracting process is perhaps one of the most overlooked issues both in the literature and the practice of contracting out. Often, policy-makers and public managers seem to assume that contracting is a technical matter once the political decision to contract out has been taken. Nothing could be more wrong, as stakeholders in the organizational environment are eager to know in what direction the government is moving. Securing a clear communication strategy seems to be of high importance to modern public managers. In the literature, the argument often goes that contracting out cannot be separated from its political context (see e.g. Van Slyke 2003). If politics is a part of the game, then communicating to the key stakeholders and other organizational groups in the larger environment is a key challenge facing contract managers.

Communication can change for different phases in the process. First, it is necessary to know about the immediate consequences. Sending information to staff is of particular importance. Second, the citizens ('customers') who are going to be affected by a potential change of provider must be notified and informed. Third, businesses and interest groups must be informed about the process that is about to begin. Fourth, citizens at large must be informed about a potential change in the way the government delivers a service.

Awarding the contract is perhaps the most important part of the process. The government has to decide which companies or organizations are going to be chosen to be providers of public services in a particular geographic area. The decision will affect both citizens and the government itself if the contract does not turn out as expected (and ends in the courts), so the award question is of great importance. There are several formal ways in which awarding a contract can take place. The government may make an 'open round of bids' where everyone can send in their application. The government may also choose a method where there are a 'select number of bids' involved. Potential providers are asked to bid. After all the bids are in, the government will then makes its decision based on a number of criteria already spelled out beforehand. The final decision is always based on some judgement. If two or three bids offer roughly the same conditions, then the decision can be tough for the government. An awarding process is a highly regulated affair. In the European Union, there are clear rules for the tendering process that all governments must follow. Governments must not favour one of the bidders for any subtle reasons. The awarding has to be based on open principles. In reality this is not always so easy. The government may also take into consideration the local commercial environment and may want to give the contract to well-known providers. If there are not enough providers in the market this may pose a particular problem. In New York State's social services, many contracts are simply awarded to the sole provider. Van Slyke (2003) found that only 60 per cent of the contracts he examined were competitively tendered.

THE CONTRACT

A contract is an agreement between a purchaser and a provider (buyer and seller) which states the terms of delivery of a service or product (Domberger 1998: 12). Contracting is 'the design and implementation of contractual relationships between purchasers and suppliers' (Domberger 1998: 12). A contract is a written agreement stating a desired end purpose of a relationship between two or more parties. A contract is entered into voluntarily and has clearly specified enforceable sanctions. Contracts must not be entered into against one of the parties' will. If that is the case, then a contract may be declared illegal.

In the literature, there is the usual distinction between neoclassical contracts and relational contracts. A neoclassical contract has clearly specified targets, specified outputs and is clear about sanctions. In a neoclassical contract, it is assumed that many demands and safeguards can be built into the contract. Uncertainty should be minimized. In a relational contract, the situation is different. In a relational contract, not all targets and objectives can be specified beforehand, nor can all outputs be anticipated. The relational contract will therefore specify procedures that will allow parties to deal with problems and challenges as they arise. In a relational contract, uncertainty is accepted as we cannot know everything beforehand. This is also known as incomplete contracting.

There is a certain time difference to the contractual definitions. A neoclassical contract is what people used to perceive as a proper contract: clearly written, clear goals, easily enforceable. Yet research showed that writing up a contract for future transactions which cover all eventualities is not so easy done; sometimes services (especially public services) are hard to describe in detail, and monitoring and evaluation do entail hard work that results in added costs to the production of the service.

In more detail a neoclassical contract has the following characteristics:

- Length between three and seven years.
- Detailed, legally binding and specific contract document/specification.
- Contract contains detailed performance provisions for control.
- Limited flexibility, but contract may specify additional service delivery against payment.
- Mechanisms spelled out in contract document for dispute resolution.

(Domberger 1998: 131)

A relational contract has the following characteristics:

- Length is variable. Duration from ten to fifteen years is common.
- Agreement between the parties spells out general purpose in contract document.
- Control is achieved through cooperation. Penalties omitted. Sharing of benefits encouraged.
- Flexibility as the key issue based on full sharing of information.
- No formal mechanisms for dispute resolution. Potential disputes resolved before conflict.
- Joint venturing as contractors and the purchaser may form joint company to pursue goals.

(Domberger 1998: 131)

Risk shifting is a part of the contracting process (Romzek and Johnston 2002: 429–430). If a contractor is paid a certain amount of money for handling a client who is actively seeking work, and the conditions under which the programme operates changes, and which is not foreseen in the contract, then it is up to the contractor to find new ways of getting the job done, or face a loss in profit.

The dominant paradigm in the literature comes from the new institutional economics, and within that framework principal–agent theory and transaction costs theory, but there is also a growing interest in trust in contractual relationships, to which we return in Chapter 7 on public–private partnerships. It is important to note that it is not a complete and coherent theory about contracting. The literature consists of different approaches to contracting rather than forming a fully developed theoretical framework. Principal–agent theory is concerned with questions of governance and control while transaction cost theory is more concerned with efficiency and the proper institutional form of governance, given the transaction costs involved.

Principal–agent theory focuses on the relationship between a principal and an agent. In a classic formulation, Jensen and Meckling (1976) explain the problem:

> We define an agency relationship as a contract under which one or more persons (the principal/s) engage another person (the agent) to perform some service on their behalf which involves delegating some decision making authority to the agent. If both parties to the relationship are utility maximisers, there is good reason to believe that the agent will not always act in the best interests of the principal.

The agent has several possible reasons for not complying with the principal's wishes. This is due to the 'moral hazard' problem and 'adverse selection'. These two terms are more easily understood as hidden action and hidden information (Pratt and Zeckhauser 1992):

- hidden action (the agent hides actions from the principal); and
- hidden information (the agent hides information from the principal).

The background to principal–agent theory comes from economics and insurance science:

> Principal–agent theory was developed in economics in order to state the difficulties for two parties to arrive at an efficient contract in the private sector as soon as the interaction lasts longer than the elementary market interaction between buyers and sellers.
>
> (Lane 2000: 185)

Lane sees principal–agent theory as informing a theory of contracting in the public sector:

> One can look at the arrival of New Public Management and the extensive public sector reforms inspired by this theory from many angles. Here we examine the shift from long-term contracting, typical of bureaucracy and traditional enterprise, to short-term contracting, borrowed from private sector governance methods. Short-term contracting has three principal uses in the governance of the public sector: (1) contracting with service providers after a tendering/bidding process; (2) contracting with CEOs [chief executive officers] of the incorporated public enterprises; and (3) contracting with executive agencies about what they should deliver.
>
> (Lane 2000: 129)

The principal–agent framework is relevant to the public sector and to contracting for public service delivery:

> The key problem in agency relationships is to devise a contract that motivates the agent to work for the principal at the same time as the principal pays a compensation that corresponds to the effort of the agency. Since effort tends to be non-observable there arises the problem of fully and correctly specifying the contract guiding the interaction. Post-contractual difficulties can occur when an agent shirks – moral hazard problems – concerning hidden action. Or pre-contractual opportunism can occur when an agent hides information that is relevant to the negotiation and signing of a contract – adverse selection problems – resulting from asymmetric knowledge.
>
> (Lane 2000: 132)

What can principals do about the situation when agents do not necessarily follow orders from the outset? The following statement summarizes the opportunities for principals:

> Agents are perceived as having distinct tastes (such as the desire to limit risk taking or costly effort), which they pursue as rational maximising individuals. The principal's job is to anticipate the rational responses of the agents and to design a set of incentives such that the agents find it in their own interests (given the incentive system) to take the best possible set of actions.
>
> (Miller 1992: 2, quoted from Milward and Provan 1998)

Transaction cost theory is concerned with efficiency of governance structures. Tasks should be organized in the governance structure with the least transaction costs. Transaction costs are the costs associated with formulating, writing, monitoring and evaluating contracts (Williamson 1985). Williamson sees transaction costs as the costs of running a contractual system. The transaction costs have been difficult to measure precisely. They are relational, not absolute figures. Transaction costs must always be seen from a comparative perspective. In much reporting on contracting for public services, transaction costs are mentioned as a concept, but they are not always specified in terms of financial implications for the parties to the contract. Hodge (2000) estimated 'a few percentage points' for transaction costs when he surveyed the effectiveness of contracting out. Domberger (1998: 61) cited '5 percentage points' in his estimation in the 1990s. Transaction costs are:

> The ex-ante costs of drafting, negotiating, and safeguarding an agreement, and more especially, the ex-post costs of maladaptation and adjustment that arise when contract execution is misaligned as a result of gaps, errors, omissions, and unanticipated disturbances; the costs of running the economic system.
>
> (Willamson 1996: 379)

39

Williamson's analysis also carries some implicit recommendations for the organization of public service delivery. To Williamson, production will be carried out where the lowest transaction costs are. The arguments from transaction cost theory have sometimes been used to support those for contracting out public services to providers, but this is a misunderstanding. The institutional framework of public service production should, in Williamson's account, take place where transaction costs are minimized, and if that is in the public sector, then a public sector solution may be preferred. In other words, there is no inherent argument about private sector service provision in Williamson's theory of transaction costs.

Critics of the new institutional economics paradigm point out several drawbacks to the theory and the use of theory in questions of public service delivery. First, the institutional environments where principal–agent relationships take place are often neglected. Second, do all agents connected to public service delivery really act opportunistically, as the theory suggests? Third, the consequences of thinking of public service delivery as a chain of principal–agent relations distorts the notion of mutual public sector values.

The new institutional economics approach has been the basic building block for much theory in public sector contracting in recent years (Lane 2000). Lane finds the approach useful towards public service delivery. However, the more basic problem of 'multiple principals' is one aspect to be aware of. Public service organizations seldom attend to just one principal, but to several.

PUBLIC SERVICE PROVISION

This part is what Kettl (1993) refers to as 'whom to buy from', what Romzek and Johnston (2002) refer to as 'healthy levels of provider competition' and the 'complexity of subcontractor relationships', and Brown and Potoski (2003) label 'implementation capacity'.

Providers have to interpret the contract, hire the correct people, set in motion all the procedures promised in the contract, and start to communicate with citizens who are going to receive the service. The government withdraws somewhat during this part of the contracting process. Now the implementers must take over.

If the company is already a well-known provider with established routines, the basic task is to accommodate the new employees in an already well-oiled machine. If the provider has started its business recently, or it has not been in that area of business before, then it is a new project which demands the setting up of an entirely new organization.

Providers may also be different types of organizations. In the literature, it is common to distinguish between at least three types of providers: for-profit providers (firms), non-profit providers (voluntary organizations, not-for-organizations in the USA), and finally other public providers. It varies from country to country as to how far other public providers are allowed to bid competitively.

A fourth possibility is a provider network or coalition. Network relationships have to be negotiated and worked out.

For-profit providers

This is perhaps the most well-known category of providers of public services in alternative delivery arrangements. The for-profit company is often portrayed as the profit maximizer out to make a quick buck on providing public services. While not wholly incorrect, this is also a distortion of the argument that does not take into account the purpose of companies operating in competitive markets. At the outset, it is true, of course, that:

> the goal of such organizations [i.e. companies] is, by definition, to produce a profit, which makes it fundamentally different from the public agencies with which they are contracting. Firms are responsible not to the taxpayer but to their stockholder, if they are publicly traded businesses.
>
> (Cooper 2003: 60)

Companies have other goals too. Fligstein and Mara-Drita (1996) emphasize how companies' long-term goal is survival. Companies do not always go for a quick profit, but are just as keen to secure their place in the market in the long run. This fact will also influence companies' relations to public sector organizations. Companies may follow a strategy of building up a long-term delivery partnership with the public sector, which leaves the option of securing short-term contracts less attractive.

There are a huge variety of companies that do deals with the public sector. There are small, 'mom-and-pops' companies which perform tasks in cleaning and maintenance for governments at the local level, while there are companies with many thousands of employees that may also deal with the government. There is a huge variety in terms of services. Helping the elderly in their own homes may be a task for a locally based company, while cleaning government buildings may be done on the basis of a centrally agreed contract that covers many public organizations and involves thousands of workers. Companies' relationships with government can also vary in time. Consider the 100-year history of the Falck company in Denmark that has delivered fire-fighting and ambulance services to the Danish public sector, with a newly started up IT company that is setting up a homepage for a ministerial department. Huge differences in the size, history and capability of the company exist, as do the types of relationships which companies may establish with public sector organizations.

Non-profit providers

Governments have pursued relations with non-profit organizations for a long time. Non-profit organizations have a number of pluses to which governments are attracted:

flexibility, access to specialized groups of citizens, innovative ideas and practices, and above all legitimacy. Legitimacy is important, both in the eyes of the user, but also in the eyes of the surrounding community. Non-profit organizations have proliferated in the co-production of public services over the past two decades.

There is a huge variety in the forms of non-profit organizations. A typical non-profit organization may be a voluntary organization that provides certain trusted services as part of its remit which the public sector finds useful. Examples could be the many areas of social work or elderly care services that non-profit organizations such as the Red Cross are operating. An example in Denmark is the Diakonissestiftelsen which runs day centres for the nearby local government. These organizations will often be a part of a nation-wide organization, or even an international voluntary organization (The Red Cross again serves as an example). Non-profit organizations can also be very close to company-like structures. This is the case with many American non-profit organizations which actually resemble huge corporations, except that they do not earn a profit for shareholders on their investments.

There has been a trend towards formalizing the relationship between the government and non-profit organizations. This is where 'contracts' enter the picture. In many instances, governments used non-profit organizations as public service providers in informal ways and through understated agreements. There was not always a formalized bidding process where non-profit organizations would have to submit their offers in brown envelopes. Relationships instead formed as problems arose and therein lay the flexibility so adored by public sector organizations and non-profit organizations alike. In the area of social policy, non-profit organizations have witnessed a renewed interest from government organizations. In the USA, George W. Bush recommended further use of faith-based organizations in the provision of public services as an alternative delivery mechanism to traditional public sector organizations.

Other public providers

This is an interesting, if underdeveloped, aspect of the whole contracting out debate. In some countries, governments have the option to choose a public provider as an alternative private provider. The rules in different countries vary as to how other public sector organizations are allowed to bid for contracts, or can be given contracts by public purchasers. Van Slyke (2003) reports on how public purchasers formed public–public partnerships in New York State as an alternative to a traditional contracting out approach. The reason was that there were not enough capable private providers that responded to the request for proposals. In the Scandinavian countries, other public sector organizations are in some instances allowed to bid for contracts, although the rule set is not fully developed. Potential purchasers should therefore seek out the rules in their own country to find out if other public bodies are allowed to bid for public service delivery.

Provider networks

A fairly recent phenomenon is the provider network (or provider consortium). As such the idea is not new, and it has been known to the building industry for years. In a building or construction project, there is a main partner responsible for the contract relationship with the purchaser, and a host of sub-providers. In the debate about contracting out for public service delivery, the option of many sub-providers has not played a prominent part. This is about to change. Public purchasers can see the benefits of getting not only one, but several providers to deliver the services. A well-known example is the consortium formed to provide employment services in Wisconsin, USA. Sanger (2002) has described in detail how the provider was actually a consortium of both for-profit companies and non-profit organizations. Each contributed with their own individual organizational strengths. The result according to the public purchaser was a more elaborated and sophisticated service delivery system. In information technology service systems, the same practice may be identified. A public purchaser may enter a contract with a main provider, but the provider, an IT company, may have links with several sub-providers from the IT industry that delivers the various components of the system.

Level: local, national, global

Providers operate at different levels of government too. A stylized picture of a provider of public services might depict a locally based company that, in competition with other locally based companies, wins the contract to provide, for example, social services to a district within a local government. This could well be the reality, but there are other types of providers as well. One may be the national provider in the form of a national company or a national voluntary organization. These providers will not enter a local government market only to stay in one particular area. The strategy of the provider is more likely to be oriented towards capturing market shares. If a company enters a local government market, it may want to use this market as a trampoline to move to other markets in the future. One example could be a national IT company that enters an agreement with a local government on how to develop a new IT-based pay scheme. The IT company wants to see the IT system spread out to all the local governments potentially, while the particular local government may only be interested in the IT system to improve its own pay scheme administration. An increasingly visible phenomenon is the global provider; that is, the provider that operates across borders, many of them across many borders. There are few truly global actors in public service delivery, but many that criss-cross borders. And yet, think of Microsoft, the world's premier provider of computer software. Think about how many governments around the world use Microsoft's computer software or the internet browser on a daily basis! Another example is the company Group 4 Securicor which operates prison services in many countries around the world. Group 4 Securicor is a British-based company that came out of the merger between Group 4

Falck and Securicor, a truly global company that provides services to a variety of governments (see the elaboration of this example in Chapter 6). Alasdair Roberts (2004) has referred to these companies as transborder service provider networks. He sees a trend towards more of these global companies becoming providers of public services. The point is that the local purchaser, or even the national purchaser, will experience different power relations with the global provider than with a local or nationally based provider. The purchaser will not have such an easy task in setting the terms of the contracts, as the providers possess the expertise and ability to choose not to provide the services, since there are plenty of spaces to sell goods and services in other places.

CONSUMER CHOICE

The next part of the model emphasizes consumer choice. There is a general movement in public management where the role of citizens is being challenged by the role of the consumer or the customer (we use the terms interchangeably). A market-oriented organization is an organization that collects information on customer preferences, disseminates this information internally, and responds to this information through action. NPM advocates that 'the users of public services should be treated as customers rather than merely passive recipients and that the function of service providers is to serve and satisfy users' needs' (Advani and Borins 2001: 93). Aberbach and Christensen (2005) have noted the increased attention to consumer affairs in public management. The 'consumer knows best' has long been a mantra in the private sector, and as the public sector is trying more and more to look like the private sector, it seems only natural that governments should begin to think of their citizens also as consumers.

There are a number of unresolved issues related to the idea of citizens as customers. One issue is whether consumers in the public sector can be treated differently according to their tastes and the size of their wallets. Fountain (2001) discusses how the private sector separates customers into different 'market segments' and adjusts their services to the different segments. Would that be equally accepted in public service delivery? Another concern from Fountain is that customers will think of public service delivery as precisely services, and that the customers must be compensated if services are not up to the expected standard. The advent of citizens' charters (which perhaps should be termed customer charters) touches on the issue of what citizens/customers may expect in terms of the quality of service delivery (Drewry 2005).

There are less empirical investigations as to how citizens perceive themselves as customers, and how they shift between different roles of being 'users', 'citizens' and 'customers' than might be expected. A recent body of work comes from the Creating Citizens as Customers project in the UK. Researchers found, by interviewing citizens and public sector staff and examining policy documents, that the mindset of citizens had not changed completely to that of being a customer. A common response in the project was that 'It's not like shopping'. People did seem to want to distinguish between shopping in the nearby supermarket, and receiving or ordering public services such as elderly care, childcare or social services (Clarke and Newman 2006).

REGULATION

The regulatory challenge is eminent in contracting for public service delivery. The contracting process is meant to lead to better performance. Knowing if that objective has been reached is one of the key elements in the regulation of public service delivery. Kettl (1993) notes how governments must ask themselves 'what has been bought?' once the providers have delivered the services to the citizens and/or customers. Romzek and Johnston (2002) call for intensive training for contract management staff so that they can conduct contract oversight and monitor the progress of service delivery. Brown and Potoski (2003) talk about 'evaluation capacity' as the capacity to evaluate the contractor's performance (examples include procedures for collecting performance information and staff to conduct project audits).

The regulation is predominantly concerned with the contract oversight of the purchasing organization. The purchaser must know what has been bought, it must train contract oversight managers and it must possess the ability to evaluate the performance data.

The regulation approach goes beyond the single organization's requirements. The regulation literature is preoccupied with three forms of regulation: regulation as direct control of rule or performance target compliance, regulation as a state's regulatory role in the economy at large, and finally, regulation as all forms of social control. A great deal of literature exists within each of these categories. Our purpose here is to focus on contracts more concretely, but we propose to go beyond the single organization to look at the regulatory responsibility from a government perspective.

The regulatory state is a phenomenon that purchasers and providers cannot ignore. The expression 'the regulatory state' comes from regulation research that focused on the role of the state after the New Public Management developments. Critics were concerned with the fact that rule making and rule enforcement was not diminishing, although the neo-liberal regime had promised privatization and deregulation as part of its programme. Researchers pointed to the fact that the freer market actually meant more rules (Vogel 1996). Deregulation was not what was happening. Rules did not go away, but were changed. If rules were abandoned they were soon replaced by new rules, or superseded by rules in other policy areas, making the total number of rules in the status quo.

Researchers and international organizations instead pointed to 'regulatory reform' as a better expression of what was happening with regulation. Some researchers even went so far as to talk about a new 'regulatory state', as Moran (2003) did for Britain. Regulation was not, however, only a topic for the nation state. The making of rules was a critical feature of the European Union, so the European Union was, in fact, the chief embodiment of a political unit with focus on regulation.

As these developments were being identified in the wider economy, and the areas of privatization of public enterprises more specifically, a similar phenomenon became apparent in the public sector. New Public Management was meant to let managers manage and make managers manage. Contracting was a part of the NPM. But a variety of regulatory mechanisms followed in the footsteps of NPM, although this was not recognized fully in the NPM literature where the idea of managerial freedom was celebrated. Hood and his colleagues began to examine the regulatory phenomenon after NPM more carefully, and they conducted an analysis of what they termed 'regulation inside government' (Hood *et al.* 1999). Regulation was following in the footsteps of NPM.

What does the development of regulation mean for contracts for public service delivery? It means that researchers and practitioners need to pay more attention to the regulatory aspect of contracting. Finding out 'what has been bought', as Kettl (1993) phrased it, is not a mundane task. Regulation that comes out of the contracting process, and how the contracting process proceeded, is a highly important part of any approach to contract management.

There are organizations that are devoted to regulation only. The contracting literature needs to pay attention to organizations such as national audit offices, auditors in local governments, ombudsmen, evaluation institutes, and others who focus on what governments have been buying. The literature is not yet fully developed on these issues. Most work is focused on the individual organization. In a model of contract management, attention to the regulatory framework is destined to be of the utmost importance in the future.

THE INSTITUTIONAL CONTEXT

Contracts may be seen from an institutional perspective. Following North (1990), Knight (1992) and others, institutions set formal and informal rules that enable and restrain human action. Contracts are not enacted in a vacuum. Institutional rules circumvent the contracting process.

Institutional theory has developed tremendously over the past two decades. There are various theoretical schools of institutional theory (Scott 1995). The three most influential schools are rational choice institutionalism, sociological institutionalism and historical institutionalism (Hall and Taylor 1996). One way they differ is how they see actors. Rational choice institutionalism sees actors as self-interested, and institutions are the outcome of the various struggles. Sociological institutionalism sees actors as guided by norms and by a logic of appropriateness. Institutions in this version are not necessarily efficient. Historical institutionalism has room for both self-interested behaviour and norm-following behaviour, and does not have a fixed view of the efficiency of institutional arrangements. In general, the schools agree that institutions shape people's actions, norms and cognitive schema of thought, and they do so in a variety of ways. The interest in institutions has been intense within the framework of 'the new institutionalism'.

When a contract is signed, there is more to the contract than what is written down in the single contract. The contracting process depends on the legal system, law in general and on the mechanisms connected with the enforcement of law. In short, contracts are contextualized by the formal rules which guide exchanges between organizations. These could be constitutional laws, but also laws such as contract law and competition law. Much of this legal framework is often taken as assuming to be there by the organizations entering a contract, but in some countries the legal framework surrounding the entering of contracts is far from complete. When we talk about formal rules we mean the formalized rules that structure the contracting process. This could be anything from the structure of Parliament, the structure of ministries, competition law, contract law, the structure of markets, and other formalized rules that guide the process.

The other types of institutions are those more informal ones that guide action. A contract may invoke specific images in organizations in Britain as it does in Spain. Being subjected to a contractual process may mean different things to different organizations in different countries. How people think about contracts, and what they feel obliged to do when exposed to a contractual process may differ. We must therefore allow for an examination of the norms and values associated with contracting in different institutional contexts. How much does 'breaking a rule' mean in one country compared to another? Therefore, when we talk about 'informal rules', we mean those rules that are not written down, but remain a part of the expectations and traditions surrounding a contractual process. These could be anything from compliance behaviour to interpretations of changed relations between organizations because of a written contract.

For our purpose here, a contract itself may also be seen as an institution comprising both formal rules and informal rules. The contract is an agreement between a purchaser and provider that contains enforceable formal rules guiding the behaviour of the organizations as well as informal expectations attached to the contracting process. The informal rules are not so easily sanctioned explicitly as are the formal rules.

The implications for contract management will be evident over the following pages, but let us briefly note here that contract management implies that managers and management systems must attend to both the formal rules and to the more informal rules to make contracting work (Figure 2.1).

CONCLUSIONS

This chapter has considered the various elements in the contracting process. It has done so by presenting the elements as part of a coherent contract management model. The model comprised the following elements: contracting out policy, strategic purchasing and communication, the contract itself, provision of public services, consumption/citizens as consumers, regulation and the institutional context. Many of these factors are well known in the literature. They have been presented in a variety of ways by authors on contract management such as Kettl, Cooper, Romzek and Johnston, Brown and

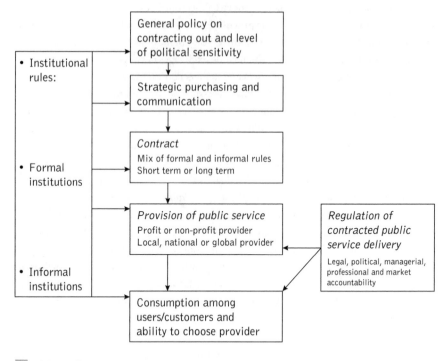

Figure 2.1 *A contract management model.*

Potoski, and others. Some of the elements have been highlighted more than in other models. The focus on communication is not something that is generally valued, although communication may be hinted at implicitly by some of the authors cited above. The focus on the institutional context is also noticeable. Again, most models of contract management tend to focus most on processes and leave the institutional context in the background. In this text, the institutional framework plays an equally important part as does the process of contracting itself.

The main purpose of this chapter has been to present the model of contract management as a heuristic device that should enable practitioners and students of contract management to think more holistically about contract management. Contract management is not only a technical process that is concerned with getting the performance measures right, but a relatively complex affair that implies focus on the strategic purchasing, the way the market is organized and so on. Attending to both the formal rules as well as the informal rules is also an essential part of contract management.

DISCUSSION QUESTIONS

1   How does the contract management model relate to your organization? Where are you placed in the model (as a purchaser, a provider, a regulator or a keeper of the institutional framework, for example)?

2   Who are the 'principals' and who are 'the agents' in the contractual relationship in your own organization? Try to make a map of the various principal–agent relationships you can identify, and then discuss the various strategies that actors can take.

3   Are there elements in the contract management model that you think are more important than others (the institutional framework over the providers, for example)? Explain your choice.

REFERENCES

Aberbach, J. and T. Christensen (2005) Citizens and customers, *Public Management Review* 7(2): 225–245.

Almqvist, R. (2001) Management by contract. A study of programmatic and technological aspects, *Public Administration* 79(3): 689–706.

Almqvist, R. and O. Högberg (2005) Public–private partnerships in social services: the example of the city of Stockholm, in G. Hodge and C. Greve (eds) *The Challenge of Public–Private Partnerships. Learning from International Experience*. Cheltenham: Edward Elgar, pp. 231–256.

Barzelay, M. (2001) *The New Public Management. Improving Research and Policy Dialogue*. Berkeley: University of California Press.

Boston, J. (1999) New models of public management. The New Zealand case, *Samfundsøkonomen* 5: 5–13.

Boston, J., J. Martin, J. Pallot and P. Walsh (1996). *Public Management – The New Zealand Model*. Oxford: Oxford University Press.

Brown, T. and M. Potoski (2003) Contract management capacity in municipal and county government, *Public Administration Review* 63(2): 153–164.

Campbell, J. (2004) *Institutional Change and Globalization* Princeton, NJ: Princeton University Press.

Clarke, J. and J. Newman (2006) The people's choice? Citizens, consumers and public services, Paper for International Workshop on Citizenship and Consumption King's College, Cambridge, 30 March to 1 April.

49

Cooper, P. (2003) *Governing by Contract. Challenges and Opportunities for Public Managers.* Washington, DC: GQ Press.

De Bruijn, H. (2002) *Managing Performance in the Public Sector.* London: Routledge.

Domberger, S. (1998) *The Contracting Organization.* Oxford: Oxford University Press.

Drewry, G. (2005) Citizens charters. Service quality chameleons, *Public Management Review* 7(3): 321–340.

Entwhistle, J. and S. Martin (2005) From competition to collaboration in public service delivery: a new agenda for research, *Public Administration* 83(1): 233–242.

Fligstein, N. and I. Mara-Drita (1996) How to make a market: reflections on the attempt to create a single market in the European Union, *American Journal of Sociology* 102(1): 1–33.

Fountain, J. (2001) Paradoxes of public sector customer services, *Governance* 14(1): 55–73.

Greve, C. (2006) Public management reform in Denmark, *Public Management Review* 8(1): 161–169.

Hall, P. and R.C. Taylor (1996) Political science and the three new institutionalisms, *Political Studies* 44: 936–957.

Hodge, G. (2000) *Privatization. An International Review of Performance.* Boulder, CO: Westview Press.

Hodge, G. (2005) Public–private partnerships: the Australasian experience with physical infrastructure, in G. Hodge and C. Greve (eds) *The Challenge of Public–Private Partnerships. Learning from International Experience.* Cheltenham: Edward Elgar, pp. 305–331.

Hood, C. (1998) *The Art of the State. Culture, Rhetoric and Public Management.* Oxford: Clarendon Press.

Hood, C., O. James, G. Jones and C. Scott (1999) *Regulation Inside Government.* Oxford: Oxford University Press.

Jensen, M.C. and W. Meckling (1976) Theory of the firm: managerial behaviour, agency costs and ownership structure, *Journal of Financial Economics* 32: 65–74.

Kelman, S. (2002) Strategic contracting management, in J. Donahue and J.S. Nye (eds) *Market-based Governance.* Washington, DC: Brookings, pp. 88–102.

Kettl, D.F. (1993) *Sharing Power. Public Governance of Private Markets.* Washington, DC: Brookings.

Kingdon, J.W. (1995) *Agendas, Alternatives and Public Policies.* New York: HarperCollins.

Knight, J. (1992) *Institutions and Social Conflict.* Cambridge: Cambridge University Press.

Lane, J-E. (2000) *New Public Management.* London: Routledge.

Makin, T. (2003) The changing public–private infrastructure mix. Economy-wide implications, *Australian Journal of Public Administration* 62(3): 32–39.

Martin, S. and J. Hartley (2000) Best value for all? An empirical analysis of local government's capacity to implement best value principles, *Public Management* 2(1): 43–56.

Milward, H.B. (2006) Book review of E.S. Savas: 'Privatization in the City', *Journal of Public Administration Research and Theory* 16(2): 319–322.

Milward, H.B. and Provan, K. (1998) Principles for controlling agents. The political economy of network structure, *Journal of Public Administration Research and Theory* 8 (April): 2–21.

Moran, M. (2003) *The British Regulatory State. High Modernism and Hyper-innovation.* Oxford: Oxford University Press.

OECD (1997) *Contracting Out. Government Services: Best Practice Guidelines and Case Studies.* Paris: OECD.

OECD (2005) *Modernising Government.* Paris: OECD.

North, D. (1990) *Institutions, Institutional Change and Economic Performance.* Cambridge: Cambridge University Press.

Office of Deputy PM (2003) *Rethinking Service Delivery. An Introduction to Strategic Service Delivery Partnerships.* London: ODPM.

Peters, B.G. (1996) *The Future of Governing. Four Emergent Models.* Lawrence: University of Kansas Press.

Pratt, J. and Zeckhauser, R. (1992) *Principals and Agents.* Cambridge, MA: Harvard University Press.

Roberts, A. (2004) *Transborder Service Systems: Pathways for Innovation or Threats to Accountability?* Arlington, VA: IBM Center for the Business of Government.

Romzek, B. and J. Johnston (2002) Effective contract management implementation and accountability: a preliminary model, *Journal of Public Administration Research and Theory* 12(3): 423–453.

Sand, V. (2004) Victoria's partly privatised prison system: an accountability report card, *Asia Pacific Journal of Public Administration* 26(2): 135–154.

Sanger, M.B. (2002) *The Welfare Marketplace.* Washington, DC: Brookings.

Savas, E.S. (1987) *Privatization: The Key to Better Government.* New Jersey: Chatham House.

Savas, E.S. (2000) *Privatization and Public–Private Partnerships.* New Jersey: Chatham House.

Scott, W.R. (1995) *Institutions and Organizations.* London: Sage.

Van Slyke, D. (2003) The mythology of privatization in contracting for social services, *Public Administration Review* 63(3): 296–315.

Vincent-Jones, P. (1999) Competition and contracting in the transition from CCT to best value: towards a more reflexive regulation?, *Public Administration* 77(2): 273–291.

Vogel, D. (1996) *Freer Market, More Rules. Regulatory Reform in Advanced Economies.* Ithaca, NY: Cornell University Press.

51

Walsh, K. (1995) *Public Services and Market Mechanisms*. London: Macmillan.

Williamson, O. (1985) *The Economic Institutions of Capitalism*. New York: The Free Press.

Williamson, O. (1996) *The Mechanisms of Governance*. Oxford: Oxford University Press.

FURTHER READING

The stages approach to contract management, where the different steps in the contracting process are laid out one after another, is covered in Phillip Cooper's (2003) work *Governing by Contract* (Washington, DC: GQ Press), although most examples and legislative details are drawn from a US context. Savas (2000) *Privatization and Public–Private Partnerships* (New Jersey: Chatham House) also has a stages model. The recent work of Trevor Brown and Matthew Potoski (see e.g., 2003) provides a good overview of the basic and emerging challenges that confront contract managers. Walsh's (1995) book *Public Services and Market Mechanisms* (London: Macmillan) remains an inspiration for its clarity and overview, although the empirical examples are now dated.

Part II

Organizing for contracting

Chapter 3

Contract management capacity

LEARNING OBJECTIVES

By the end of this chapter you should:

■ be able to identify the key capacity elements required for effective contracting;

■ be able to consider the responsibilities between different levels of government for contract management capacity; and

■ have a clear understanding of what is required of national contract management coordination.

KEY POINTS OF THIS CHAPTER

■ Contract management capacity may be divided into the process-oriented sub-elements of feasibility assessment capacity, market-making capacity, communication capacity, implementation capacity, evaluation capacity, institutional capacity and network management capacity.

■ Contract management capacity also includes institutional capacity and network management capacity.

■ Buildup of contract management capacity is enhanced by coordination at the national level.

KEY TERMS

- **Contract management capacity** – the capacities governments need when they contract with others to deliver public service (Brown and Potoski 2003: 155)/the power and resources of managers to influence contract management issues/the management imperatives necessary to develop and manage contracts successfully (Wise, in Brown and Potoski 2003: 154).
- **Market-making strategies** – the strategies governments develop to shape and/or alter existing or new markets for public service delivery.
- **National coordination of capacity building** – a central government's responsibility when assembling and disseminating knowledge about contract management capacity.

This chapter explains how public managers can build their purchasing organizations so that they will be able to get the best deals from the providers on the market. Issues include whether to make a separate purchasing division or to integrate purchasing decisions in the entire organization, how to secure adequate and up-to-date decision-making information, and how to manage the relationship with the authorizing environment in the shape of politicians and lawmakers. Are purchasers local, national – or even global?

CAPACITY FOR CONTRACT MANAGEMENT

The OECD underlined the need for contract management capacity in its recent comprehensive review of modernizing government efforts:

> There are significant management challenges for governments in moving to a market-type mechanism model, especially in separating the role of purchaser and provider of services. Traditionally, governments performed these roles concurrently. Government will have to invest in capacity for specifying services and contract management skills that they have not typically possessed in the past. It concerns both new technical skills and overall cultural change in the public service.
>
> (OECD 2005: 130)

Contract management should be relatively easy at first glance. If only contract managers had access to all relevant information and could process all that information, they could make intelligent, informed decisions. If only markets were fully competitive and enough companies were interested in providing the particular services that governments and citizens were looking for. If only evaluation and control were made possible by access to updated, accurate and interpretable performance management information. Such a perfect world of full information, real competition and control without hindrance rarely exists in public management today – and there are severe doubts that such a situation has ever existed at all. Contract management is most likely to take place in a world of limited information available, restrictions on competition and hard-to-obtain performance data which makes the public governance of private markets more often than not a real challenge (Kettl 1993).

The task of building a contract management capacity is demanding:

> Public management-capacity requires personnel with contract management experience, policy expertise, negotiation, bargaining, and mediation skills, oversight and program audit capabilities, and the necessary communication and political skills to manage programs with third parties in a complex political environment.
>
> (Van Slyke 2003: 296–297)

In this chapter we examine what it takes for government to build a contract management capacity in order to deal with this less-than-perfect contracting situation. Contract management capacity may be defined as the capacities which governments need when they contract with others to deliver a public service (Brown and Potoski 2003: 155). Government capacity is usually considered in the context of governments both ordering and producing public services. The new contract state has altered that situation, as this book is showing, and consequently, the capacity of governments today needs to include contract management capacities in addition to the traditional capacities associated with the Weberian state.

In the first section of this chapter we discuss the various elements in contract management capacity that have emerged in the literature. In the second section we discuss which level of government should be responsible for developing and maintaining the required capacities.

CAPACITIES TO MANAGE CONTRACTS STRATEGICALLY

What kinds of capacities are needed to ensure effective contract management? In the literature, this question has not been given sufficient attention until recently. Contract management was perceived to be something of a routine matter that could be left to middle managers or specialized managers once the big decision to contract out was taken (Kelman 2002). Recent work by American scholars Brown and Potoski (2003, 2004), Romzek and Johnston (2002), Van Slyke (2003) and Kelman (2002) has remedied that situation. The situation is neatly summed up by Van Slyke in his review of the need for contract management capacity:

> If a smaller, more results-oriented government is what citizens and elected officials desire, then the answer is not that all bureaucrats are opportunistic agents who create market failures for their own interest, and the answer is not to destroy competition by encouraging non-profits to collectively organize with a single voice

of opposition to a public monopoly. Rather, the issue appears, strictly from a cost-benefit perspective, to be that rigorous contracting requirements and public management capacity are more efficient investments because these resources can be invested in public management and agency capacity toward creating smart buyers.

(Van Slyke 2003: 308)

Brown and Potoski (2003: 155) link the question of capacity to the contract management process. They identify three forms of capacities that are linked to the process: feasibility capacity (the capacity to determine whether to make or buy the good or service); implementation capacity (the capacity to bid the contract, select a provider and negotiate a contract); and evaluation capacity (the capacity to evaluate the contractor's performance).

In a later work they also consider two additional capacities; the capacity to make or shape markets, and the capacity to share information about contracting with other purchasers in networks (Brown and Potoski 2004).

Kelman (2002) makes a key distinction between contracting as a routine, bureaucratic undertaking, and the role of shaping an organization's strategy around the concept of contracting, which he refers to as 'strategic contracting'. We may assume that there are different capacities connected to the two ways of dealing with contracts; thus there is a bureaucratic capacity to manage contracts and the relationships between the public purchaser and the private providers, and there is a strategic capacity to construct the strategy around the contracting vision.

In relation to the previous chapter, Brown and Potoski's initial suggestions for forms of capacities are interesting, but not sufficient. They need to be supplemented with other capacities. One additional capacity is the need to communicate decisions about contracting and to relate to stakeholders in government, the market and among civil society organizations. The task of communication cannot be left to a crisis situation if the contracting process is to be successful. Communication must be integrated into the strategy from the beginning. A second, additional capacity is making and shaping markets. Brown and Potoski (2004) have discussed this capacity themselves in some of their later work. Often there are not markets for particular kinds of services that governments are interested in. This could be in areas such as care for the elderly or childcare. If companies or other private providers do not exploit the market situation themselves, governments may be forced to be midwife to new market opportunities. Shaping an already existing market in a slightly different way is another means of influencing markets. Governments do not always sit quietly and wait for companies to develop new products, but governments may actively call for new products in particular markets. That capacity must also be included in a contract management capacity discussion. A third additional capacity is the capacity to share information and form new alliances with other governments that adopt contracting strategies, and to make alliances with specific private sector companies in public–private partnerships (Brown and Potoski 2004) (for the latter point, see Chapter 7 on Contracting through public–private partnerships). The final part of

Brown and Potoski's capacities – evaluation capacity – can also include controlling throughout the contract period, as performance data are typically discussed on a rolling basis and not just *ex-post*. The evaluation requirement may also be extended to cover the government's performance in purchasing. This expansion would include a discussion on the wider public accountability issues, and suggests there is a need for independent arm's-length evaluation besides the initial evaluation of performance data from the provider.

Having discussed additional process capacities, we might suggest that the following elements are needed in a contract management capacity that takes its point of departure as the process of contract management:

- *Feasibility assessment capacity*: the capacity to determine whether to make or buy the good or service and to find out whether performance targets can be formulated.
- *Communication capacity*: the capacity to communicate the decision about contracting and to plan a strategy for stakeholder involvement, including employees.
- *Implementation capacity*: the capacity to bid the contract, select the provider, negotiate a contract and to make the transition of the task from one provider to the next as smooth as possible.
- *Market making and shaping capacity*: if not enough providers respond to the bids, or too few providers are in existence, the government may try to encourage companies to enter the marketplace.
- *Network management capacity*: the capacity to share information with other purchasers and to form alliances with private sector companies.
- *Evaluation and controlling capacity*: the capacity to evaluate the provider's performance.
- *Accountability capacity*: the capacity to conduct an independent arm's-length evaluation of both the provider performance and the performance of the government as purchaser.

INSTITUTIONS AND CONTRACT MANAGEMENT CAPACITY

Contract management does not exist in a vacuum, but will always be situated in a particular institutional context. Additional institutional variables are therefore needed to complete the characterization of contract management capacities. Brown and Potoski (2003: 155–157; 2004) only focus on the process variables in their analysis, and they seem to neglect the institutional variables (see, however, their recent work in Brown *et al.* 2006). In their work, they only refer to institutional variables as explanations as to why governments may or may not want to invest in contract management capacities. In this section we take a closer look at the need for institutional capacities.

Following the customary division in institutional theory (Knight 1992), we might say that there exist both informal and formal norms and rules. A contract management capacity perspective needs to include a capacity to influence the informal norms that surround the contracting process. Employees, potential providers and the wider stake-holders must be convinced that governments are serious about contracting. This means that new norms of contracting instead of producing in-house must be actively dealt with. Shaping norms and expectations can be a part of the communication strategy capacity envisaged in the discussion in the previous section. Shaping formal rules and regulations is a different matter. Some of the rule making is within the jurisdiction of local government. This would include the internal guidelines that local governments use when they want to engage in a contracting process. But formal rules are also formulated and decided in central government or in international bodies such as the European Union, and that process of formal rule making can be far away from local governments' zone of influence. Rules also come with a history and they are embedded in historical-institutional development. Some of the rules are therefore likely to set the context for any action a local government might take. The room for choice and independent decision-making is limited. Recognizing this kind limitation of formal rules is often painful, but necessary in contract management.

Finally, there are the institutional features of particular countries' governments, and the historically developed organizational structures in which contract management takes place (Christensen and Lægreid 2001). A country's institutions can be more or less sup-portive of contract management. In Denmark, there is no central government regulation that forces local governments to contract out. However, there is a rule that private providers might pose a challenge to local governments if the private provider thinks a company can produce the service or good cheaper and with the same or better quality than the public provider.

Are governments organized so that strategic contracting is possible? Kelman (2002) has coined the concept 'strategic contracting' as opposed to routine or bureaucratic contracting. Strategic contracting means that the major part of the organizational strategy is built around contracting. Consequently, contracting needs to be addressed at the highest level of the organization, and high-level public managers and the key part of their organizations need to know about contracting themselves. If contracting is given a prominent place in the strategic thinking, then there needs either to be a section close to the chief executive that is responsible for contracting, and/or contracting has to be wired into every aspect of the organizational structure. In a routine-based public organization, contracting will be left to a particular department or section of govern-ment. If we take the network argument above and add the organizational element, we might also say that governments must be embedded in interorganizational contracting networks that ease access to information. A suggestion for a place for contracting in the organizational structure could be the following:

■ contracting is considered a key part of the organizational strategy and is located at the top (and wired into the rest of the organization);

■ contract management is part of the network alliances that governments build;

60

■ contract management capacity is assembled in specialized units, but those units are placed in a peripheral part of the organization; and

■ contract management capacity is only employed periodically when a section of the organization decides to contract with others for public service delivery.

In all these forms of organizing contract management capacity, governments may rely on outside help from consultants. Consultants can give advice on strategic management, on how to structure routine tasks and, for example, how to prepare the bid in the implementation phase, and on how to use contracting in a specific policy area.

The above discussion suggests that there are four additional institutional variables connected to contract management capacity:

■ *Norm capacity*: the capacity to influence norms and (organizational) culture of contracting, including shaping expectations of what contract management can deliver.

■ *Rule capacity*: the capacity to make and enforce rules of importance to contract management.

■ *Historical-institutional capacity*: the capacity to interpret and understand the historically shaped conditions, including the historical-institutional features of a particular country that form the basis for contemporary and future contract management.

■ *Organizational structure capacity*: the capacity to place responsibility for contract management in the structure of the organization, including the interorganizational network relationships to which the organization is connected.

The combined perspective of both process variables and institutional variables forms the basic blocks of a framework for contract management capacity.

CONTRACT MANAGEMENT CAPACITY AND LEVELS OF GOVERNMENT

Contract management capacity may not only be built within single organizations, but may also apply to various levels of government. Normally, contract management capacity is discussed in the context of what single organizations can do (Brown and Potoski 2003; Kettl 1993). This need not be so. Contract management capacity can also be built into interorganizational networks, the central government – or even into globalized organizations. We therefore need to discuss at which level of government each of the contract management capacities are best suited.

A first attempt would be to locate most of the process variables at the local level or even at the individual organizational level, and then the institutional variables at the interorganizational or national level of government. Individual organizations are responsible for getting the process right, while national governments are primarily responsible for getting the institutions right. A more detailed look might reveal that local governments can influence some of the institutional variables, and networks and central governments can influence the process variables.

BOX 3.1 CONTRACT MANAGEMENT CAPACITY

Process variables:

- *Feasibility assessment capacity*: the capacity to determine whether to make or buy the good or service and to find out whether performance targets can be formulated.
- *Communication capacity*: the capacity to communicate the decision about contracting and to plan a strategy for stakeholder involvement, including employees.
- *Implementation capacity*: the capacity to bid the contract, select the provider, negotiate a contract and to make the transition of the task from one provider to the next as smooth as possible.
- *Market making and shaping capacity*: if not enough providers respond to the bids, or too few providers are forthcoming, the government may try to encourage companies to enter the marketplace.
- *Network management capacity*: the capacity to share information with other purchasers and form alliances with private sector companies.
- *Evaluation and controlling capacity*: the capacity to evaluate the provider's performance.
- *Accountability capacity*: the capacity to conduct an independent arm's-length evaluation of both the provider performance and the performance of the government as purchaser.

Institutional variables:

- *Norm capacity*: the capacity to influence norms and (organizational) culture of contracting, including shaping expectations of what contract management can deliver.
- *Rule capacity*: the capacity to make and enforce rules of importance to contract management.
- *Historical-institutional capacity*: the capacity to interpret and understand the historically shaped conditions, including the historical-institutional features of a particular country, that form the basis for contemporary and future contract management.

- *Organizational structure capacity*: the capacity to place responsibility for contract management in the structure of the organization, including the interorganizational network relationships to which the organization is connected.

DISCUSSION

Brown and Potoski's (2003) findings are interesting because they suggest governments can address the problems and actually improve the capacity. They find that governments can respond to problems by building their contract management capacities. There are exceptions: governments with lower per capita revenues, governments with small populations, and/or governments isolated from metropolitian areas (Brown and Potoski 2003: 161). These last arguments are interesting in a public sector reform context because structural reforms often form new, larger local governments at the expense of smaller, less populated local governments, and this trend might boost interest in contract management. The problems that the concept of contract management capacity address include 'dissatisfaction with previous contract outcomes, contracting for the provision of public goods and services with high transaction costs, contracting with private firms more than with nonprofits or other governments, and contracting in the presence of significant political opposition from important constituent groups' (Brown and Potoski 2003: 161).

Will an improved contract management capacity also improve organizational (and economic) performance of both purchasers and providers? There is not sufficient knowledge to establish that link effectively, but Brown and Potoski (2003) argue that even though problems with preparing contracts and managing markets cannot be eliminated, governments are better suited to facing the challenges:

> Governments that invest in feasibility assessment, implementation and evaluation capacity are not immune to the problems that can undermine contract performance. Rather, these governments will be better positioned to avoid these threats and to prevent full-scale contracting disasters.
>
> (Brown and Potoski 2003: 162)

Contract management capacity can be built by governments. Governments can make decisions about structuring their organizations around a strategic contracting concept, and thereby be willing to invest resources in the area. Investment can also take place even if governments do not go for the full contracting strategy, but choose to set up a separate unit that is dedicated to contract management. Opponents of this strategy will wonder if it is all too 'rational' to adopt such a strategy and that politics will disturb the

63

organizational initiatives. This may well be so, but the illustrations in this chapter show that many governments can do more than they do at present.

CONCLUSIONS

This chapter has shown how governments can build a contract management capacity in their own organization. Both process variables and institutional variables have been identified for building contract management capacity. Among the process variables are feasibility assessment capacity, communication capacity, implementation capacity, the capacity to make and shape markets, network management capacity, evaluation and control capacity and accountability capacity. Among the institutional variables are capacities to influence norms and expectations, the capacity to make and enforce rules, the capacity to interpret historical institutional contexts and the capacity to place responsibility for contract management in the organization. Contract management takes place at various levels in the public sector: at the individual organizational level, at the interorganizational level and at the national (central government) level. Building and maintaining contract management capacity is a task that includes, but also goes beyond, the individual organization in local government.

DISCUSSION QUESTIONS

1   Consider the contract management capacity in an organization with which you are familiar. Does the organization have sufficient capacities, or do you need to expand them in any area?
2   How do institutions (formal and informal rules) relate to contract management capacity in the organizations with which you are familiar?
3   In your assessment, to what extent is cooperation between levels of government necessary to build a robust contract management capacity for the future?

REFERENCES

Brown, T. and M. Potoski (2003) Contract management capacity in municipal and county governments, *Public Administration Review* 63: 153–164.

Brown, T. and M. Potoski (2004) Managing the public service market, *Public Administration Review* 64: 656–668.

Brown, T., M. Potoski and D. Van Slyke (2006) Managing contracted public services, *Public Administration Review* 66(3): 323–331.

Christensen, T. and P. Lægreid (eds) (2001) *New Public Management*. Aldershot: Ashgate.

Kelman, S. (2002) Strategic contracting management, in J.D. Donahue and J.S. Nye (eds) *Market-based Governance*. Washington DC: Brookings.

Kettl, D.F. (1993) *Sharing Power. Public Governance of Private Markets*. Washington, DC: Brookings.

Knight, J. (1992) *Institutions and Social Conflict*. Cambridge: Cambridge University Press.

Organization for Economic Cooperation and Development (OECD) (2005) *Modernising Government*. Paris: OECD.

Romzek, B. and J.M. Johnston (2002) Effective contract management and implementation, *Journal of Public Administration Research and Theory* 12: 423–453.

Van Slyke, D. (2003) The mythology of privatization in contracting for social services, *Public Administration Review* 63(5): 296–315.

FURTHER READING

For literature on contract management capacity, readers are encouraged to seek out American researchers Brown and Potoski's (2003, 2004) recent work cited above. There is a wider literature on how to build and design government institutions of which Robert Goodin's (1996) *Institutions and Their Design* (Cambridge: Cambridge University Press) is a good starting point. The general literature on the optimalization of the management and governance process is huge, but a constructive approach may be found in L. Lynn, C. Heinrich and C. Hill's *Improving Governance* (Washington, DC: Georgetown University Press 2001).

Chapter 4

Using information technology in contract management

LEARNING OBJECTIVES

By the end of this chapter you should:

- understand the recent trends in information technology in public organizations;
- be able to assess the promises of a governance form called digital-era governance;
- evaluate how information technology is influenced and influences institutional structures;
- have developed a knowledge of how information technology relates to government contracting; and
- be prepared to consider new ways of contracting with the aid of information technology.

KEY POINTS OF THIS CHAPTER

- Information technology plays an important part in the effort to modernize governments through, for example, use of the internet, use of e-mail, web portals, interactive communication with citizens, digital infrastructures with shared databases among public organizations and so on.
- Some authors claim that we are entering an age of digital-era governance that supersedes the New Public Management era of the 1980s and 1990s.

- There is no determinism in how information technology shapes public service delivery because information technology is introduced and enacted in an institutionalized public sector, and the use of institutional theory (on formal and informal rules) can help us to understand differentiated responses to information technology development.
- Information technology relates to the different areas of contract management as they are presented in the contract management model in Chapter 2: contracting out policy, strategic purchasing and communication, the contract, public service provision, regulation, customers, and the institutional context.
- Information technology is used to match purchasers and providers better, disseminate information about contracting out quickly and efficiently, and establish an overview of potential providers, and information-based control mechanisms, but there are many other possibilities for information technology influence contracting that need to be explored.

KEY TERMS

- **Information technology** – technologies that allow for digital communication, including the internet, e-mail, web portals, information systems and so on.
- **Enacted information technology** – perception of users as well as design and use of information technology in particular settings (Fountain 2001: 10).
- **Digital-era governance** – the central role that information technology and information systems play in a wide-ranging series of alterations to how public services are organized as business processes and delivered to citizens or customers (Dunleavy *et al*. 2006: 468).
- **Institutionalized information technology** – how information technology is influenced by formal rules and informal rules, and how information technology influences institutions.
- **Information technology for contract management** – tools of information technologies specifically relating to managing contracts, and contractual relationships between purchasers and providers and others in the contractual context.

Information technology (IT) has long been recognized as having an essential role in public sector modernization. IT can speed up routine administrative processes, create efficiency gains by computerizing previous manual service work, and thereby create savings and challenges for public managers (Schedler and Schmidt 2004). The other role for IT is to open up new kinds of services, and new kinds of government–citizen interactions. This debate has mainly been taking place as a question of electronic democracy. Together this trend has been known as e-government in many 'global rating' publications by consultancy companies and other institutions (Rambøll Management 2004; West 2006).

Although IT strategies have become an important element of modernization strategies for governments, e-government has not been at centre stage until now. IT has nearly always been implemented in the name of modernization strategies. IT was a main part of the New Public Management (NPM) movement. Hood (1991) labelled 'automatization' as one of the key mega-trends he identified alongside the NPM movement in public management reform.

New developments have occurred in the knowledge of IT in the public sector (West 2005). Dunleavy *et al.* (2006) see a trend towards what they term 'digital-era governance' (DEG). The authors claim that DEG might be an alternative to NPM. They suggest that DEG is about reintegration, needs-based holism and 'digitazation' changes (Dunleavy *et al.* 2006: 481).

The relationship between IT and contracting has been seen in the light of NPM, but it has not been a prominent part of the contracting framework. Developments in IT have been taken for granted or have simply been ignored. There is hardly a reference to the role of IT in some of the more prominent works on contracting such as Lane (2000),

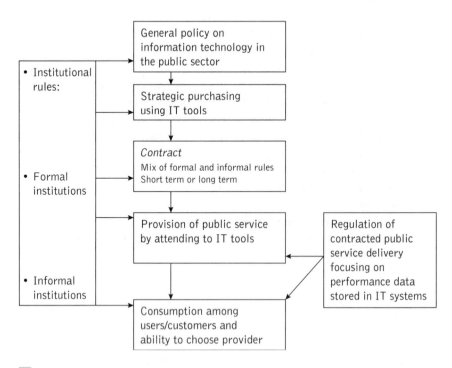

Figure 4.1 *Using IT in contract management.*

Romzek and Johnston (2002) or Brown and Potoski (2003, 2004). 'Privatization guru' E.S. Savas (2000) does not make any reference to IT, and in Graeme Hodge's (2000) meta-analysis, IT does not feature prominently either.

DIGITAL-ERA GOVERNANCE

The introduction of the internet and other IT-related mechanisms has profound consequences for the way government operates. The virtues of the IT revolution are well known and need no repetition here in detail. The consequences for government are perhaps less explored. According to Fountain (2001: 22):

> the Internet and a growing array of information and communications technologies fundamentally modify possibilities for organization communication, work, business, and government. These technologies influence society and economy in ways reminiscent of the printing press, and . . . the steam engine, railroad and electricity.

Fountain (2001: 23) continues:

> As a medium that currently supports extremely low cost communication among millions, the Internet, and the access it provides to the web, differs markedly from other communications media. Its ability to enable many-to-many communication, or communication within and among groups of individuals, separates it from one-to-many (broadcast) media, including newspapers, magazines, television and radio.

In the Gore Report on *Creating a Government that Works Better and Costs Less*, an accompanying report on IT, *Reengineering through Information Technology*, zoomed in on leadership (strengthen leadership in information technology), electronic government (develop integrated electronic access to government information and services, among other issues), and support mechanisms for electronic government (improve government's information infrastructure, improve methods of IT acquisition, among other issues) (Fountain 2001: 21).

For some time now, there has been a discussion on 'government in the information age' as one early publication named it (Bellamy and Taylor 1998). The extent of the 'IT revolution' has yet to be grasped, according to Dunleavy and colleagues. They see information technology, and more broadly digital governance, as the real successor to the NPM reform paradigm in the public sector. Digital-era governance is understood in the following way:

> Our take here highlights the central importance of Information technology (IT)-based changes in management changes and in acting with citizens and other service-users in civil society in the underpinning and integration of current bureaucratic

adaptations. We see this influence as having effects not in any technologically deter-mined way but via a wide range of cognitive, behavioural, organizational, political, and cultural changes that are linked to information systems, broadly construed. We term this constellation of ideas and reform changes digital era governance (DEG for short). The label highlights the central role that IT and information system changes now play in a wide-ranging series of alterations of how public services are organized as business processes and delivered to citizens or customers.

(Dunleavy *et al*. 2006: 468)

These authors claim that NPM has exhausted its agenda of disaggreation, competition and incentivization, and that a new agenda is taking over. This claim is controversial, and not all public management scholars are likely to agree with it (see e.g. Pollitt 2003). While their claim may be disputed, the areas of interest they point to seems relevant in a discussion of IT and contracting. Dunleavy *et al*. (2006) point to three areas that characterize digital-era governance:

- reintegration;
- needs-based holism;
- 'digitization' changes.

They understand reintegration as 'the key opportunities for exploiting digital-era technologies lie in putting back together many of the elements that NPM separated out into discrete corporate hierarchies, off-loading onto citizens and other civil society actors the burden of integrating public services into usable packages'. They understand 'needs-based holism' as 'holistic reforms seek to simplify and change the entire relationship between agencies and their clients'. And they see 'digitization changes' as the way 'to realize contemporary productivity gains from IT and related organizational changes requires a far more fundamental take-up of the opportunities opened up by a transition to fully digital operations' (the trend towards a ministry becoming its website is men-tioned as an example) (Dunleavy *et al*. 2006: 480).

The approach of digital-era governance is fascinating, but it also warrants some remarks. A key question is if one sees changes as 'inevitable' and something that is going to happen no matter what public managers say or do. In their definition and concluding remarks, Dunleavy *et al*. (2006) claim they do not expect the process towards an IT-based public service delivery system to go smoothly, but the arguments are rather eclectic and based on listing mainly 'unintended consequences'.

A substantiated analysis, fully grounded in the social science literature on institu-tions, is the analysis by Harvard Professor Jane E. Fountain (2001). Fountain sees a trend towards 'a virtual state' by which she means 'a government that is organized increasingly in terms of virtual agencies, cross-agency and public–private networks whose structure and capacity depend on the Internet and web' (Fountain 2001: 4). The 'virtual agency . . . is organized by client – for example, students, seniors, small-business owners, or veterans; each site is designed to provide all of the government's services and information from any agency as well as links to relevant organzations outside government.'

Unlike IT enthusiasts more widely, Fountain is not content with simply heralding the new technology. She sees the implementation of a virtual state strategy as one which is influenced by the institutions, including the institutional structure of the state up until now. Fountain wants to apply insights from institutional theory to the area of IT and internet issues for the public sector:

> The analytical framework I [Fountain] advance extends and refines institutional theory to encompass recent fundamental developments in information technologies. . . . As the use of the Internet unfolds, questions central to institutional thought persist with increasing force: How are bureaucratic policymakers using networked computing? Are they negotiating new institutional arrangements as a consequence? To what extent and in what ways are they constrained by current institutional arrangements? What extensions of institutional theory are necessary to take account of fundamental change in organizational communication, coordination and control?
>
> (Fountain 2001: 4)

She continues:

> An institutional perspective alerts us to the fact that government is likely to use the Internet differently than firms in the economy use it. The development of the virtual state is not likely to resemble the growth of electronic commerce.
>
> (Fountain 2001: 13)

Fountain also makes an important distinction between 'objective technology' and 'enacted technology' where enacted technology 'consists of the perception of users as well as designs and uses in particular settings' (Fountain 2001: 10).

The conclusion Fountain reaches from her empirical analysis of institutional enactment of IT in the US public sector is as follows:

> Information technologies are not simply purchased and plugged in, even when off-the-shelf products and services are procured for government organizations. They are always subject to extensive design of their use within an organization and must be integrated with work processes, communication channels, means of coordination, culture authority structures – every central element of an organization.
>
> (Fountain 2001: 195)

Fountain assigns a special role for public managers: 'It is public managers who puzzle over structural and process arrangements, new technologies, and the implementation of policy within institutions' (Fountain 2001: 198), and she continues:

> Public managers in a networked environment are the central enactors of technology in the state. They can no longer afford the luxury of relegating technological matters to technical staff. . . . In some instances enactment furthers agency or program mission. In others technology plays a transformative role that leads to the expansion, contraction or rethinking of a mission.
>
> (Fountain 2001: 199)

We may conclude from this brief review of some of the important changes linked to the use of information technology seen from an institutional perspective that information technology is set to play an even larger role in the world of public organizations, one that will eventually perhaps constitute a new digital-era governance distinct from the NPM framework but will be mediated by the institutions connected to the public sector, and that the trend is likely to influence the way public managers manage in day-to-day business. The question is now how the use of IT can make an impact on contract management more specifically.

USE OF IT AND CONTRACTS: AN ILLUSTRATION

This section will explore the possibilities and constraints in the use of IT in contract management. When Fountain wrote *Building the Virtual State*, she stated that her book filled a gap in the literature rather than standing in opposition to well-developed approaches because 'there are no well-developed approaches'. This chapter has the same feel to it, as there is a scarcity of literature that deals in depth with the relationship between information technology and contracting.

The approach in this section is therefore to describe some of the recent action taken by governments and contractors in using IT when delivering contracted public services. The illustrations are taken from Denmark where the public sector organizations are experimenting with information technology. Denmark is meant to be an illustration, as it is not assumed that countries are either very far behind or very far ahead of Denmark. All OECD countries are assumed to face the same challenges in this area, as countries must all relate to the digital-era governance challenges identified by Dunleavy *et al.* (2006). This section takes its point of departure in the model of contract management presented in Chapter 2 of this book.

The relationship between contracting policy and IT policy is not always clearly established. The government's IT policy has been incorporated into the modernization programme since the early 1980s, but the two have never influenced each other explicitly. To encourage government organizations to make more use of IT possibilities, the government has established a 'digital task force' together with Local Government Denmark, the interested organization behind local government in Denmark. The digital task force has been an active player in promoting an IT strategy, but it has not dealt with government contracting specifically. Some of its proposals have a direct influence on contracting however. The move towards electronic invoices will have an effect on the way business relates to government. The digital task force has forced providers to be more up-to-date and to use digital communication channels whenever possible.

Strategic purchasing and communication, the second aspect of the contract management model, implies that governments use IT in strategic purchasing. This has been the case in several ways. First, tenders are now announced digitally, also from the European Union. The tenders that governments put out are on the web and there for anyone to see. The information about possible tenders is spread more easily due to the use of IT. The Danish government has an agency, SKI, that has been established to make procurement more efficient. SKI agrees to 'framework contracts' with providers on behalf of the whole of government. SKI does not sign the contracts, but acts as a broker between providers and public purchasers. Public purchasers may make use of the framework contracts that SKI has negotiated. The content of the framework documents is available digitally. It is easy for a potential purchaser in local government to look up on the web which contracts SKI has negotiated. Some local governments are likely to use these contracts as an indicator of what the potential market price is – and then go on to negotiate their own deals, but the overall system of framework contracts is in place. The spread of digitalized information about contracts and about the deals that purchasers have negotiated with providers is of immense importance to the contracting process.

Communication through the web is another important aspect. The Danish government and Local Government Denmark have launched a web portal called 'The Contracting Out Portal'. On this web portal, much of available and relevant material connected to contracts is assembled. Potential providers can look for tools to contract out. Providers can look up information on the legal requirements and the previous experience with contracting out. There is information on legal issues, political issues, process issues and regulatory issues. There is information for potential purchasers, providers, consultants and governments. The web portal is designed to be a digital meeting place for purchasers and providers. It is also designed to share information and experiences about contracting out at one place on the web.

Of course, there are also individual websites of purchasers, providers and government organizations alike. The Council for Contracing Out, a council within the Danish Ministry of Finance, has its own website with information on the legal aspects of contracting out and earlier practices with contracting out. Reports that the Council has financed are available on the website. The Danish Competition Agency also has an extensive website with details on contracting out. If you go to some of the providers, for example, Falck (the ambulance company), they will have a host of information on the services they can offer to local governments and documents of their own history in providing public services.

The contract itself – or the material connected with the contract – can be made available digitally. It will sometimes feature on the purchaser's website – with the secret clauses not revealed. The contractual partners are listed digitally, creating the possibility of a quick overview of the parties to the contract.

Providers can use IT to communicate with purchasers. This may be done through e-mail, of course, but also, in more closed intranet sites, the purchaser and provider can establish mutual places where they can exchange information and keep each other abreast of what is happening in the primary service delivery function. Providers can of course also advertise their own strengths on their websites as an information tool to potential providers. Providers can be visible on lists and databases over potential providers. The Danish government maintains a database of providers of cars for the elderly through the consumer choice scheme ('frit valgs-databasen'). This gives information on how many employees the provider has, what the financial situation is for the provider and so on. A wealth of official information on the size and structure of providers is available for potential purchasers to inspect and make decisions.

Regulation is supposed to be easier and more streamlined when using IT in contracting for public service delivery. Many governments rely on performance measurement and performance-based management. IT can help in gaining information on how the performance targets are met by provider organizations:

> Information technology cannot determine the appropriate performance measures or standards for agencies. But once those are established, software analysts can embed routines, rules, and standards in programs and procedures to make data collection easier, data collection automatic, and the generation of reports simple. Information technologies that rationalize and standardize elements more powerfully than standard operating procedures and supervisors.
>
> (Fountain 2001: 41–42)

Regulators can use the performance targets to see how well providers perform. In the local government of Solrød in Denmark, for example, this is done systematically. In another local government, all workers who look after elderly people carry their own personal digital assistant (PDA) with them on work assignments, and this allows them to record their performance instantly. When they get back to their office, they feed the information from the PDA into the local government's information system. The performance report is fed into a system that allows for the sharing of knowledge and benchmarking against other providers because the system is one that is developed by Local Government Denmark's own IT company, KMD. KMD is a powerful player in the Danish market for software supplied to Danish local government – and sometimes purchasers require providers to adapt to the KMD system.

The challenge for regulators is to use all this available information consistently and with great care to ensure that meeting the performance targets is accomplished. This opens up a new world to the regulators because it means they can get detailed information almost instantaniously if they so wish. The National Audit Office usually notes in its reports whether adequate information-gathering systems are in place in service delivery organizations, and whose responsibility it is to maintain those systems. There is little legislation on which kind of performance data a delivery organization is required to keep.

The Competition Agency and other authorities publishes annual reports on the state of competition, including the use of market mechanisms in public service delivery, which also examines the use of performance indicators and the way local governments have made efforts to provide or purchase efficient service delivery. Publication of these reports is also seen to have a regulatory purpose because it sustains an overview and progress of the contracting out policy in Denmark compared with other countries.

The institutional context of the relationship between IT and contracting is underdeveloped, if one does not consider the contracting out of IT systems themselves. In some parts of the process, IT is institutionalized (digital announcements of tender, the web portal on information about contracting out and public–private partnerships), but in other areas it is weak (institutionalized provider–purchaser communication in individual agreements) or not yet systematically applied (the use of IT in control of performance data). However, it would seem that building an IT infrastructure around contracting is one important challenge that governments could rise to and to which providers could contribute.

DISCUSSION

The use of IT in contracting is still in its early stages, despite some illustrative early best practices. One way to think about the use of IT in contracting is to consider the new business relations that occur. There is talk about business-to-business (B2B) relationships in the private sector, and Fountain (2001: 6) identifies government-to-citizens (G2C) relationships, government-to-business (G2B) relationships and government-to-government (G2G) connectivity. With contracts, the relationships are more complex. Contracts add an extra element, so it should rightfully be a 'G2B2C relationship': government-to-business-to-citizen when the focus is on contracting. The contract itself is the mediating institution that regulates the relationship between the government purchaser and the private (or public) provider of services to citizens.

It is important to recognize the complexity of the use of IT in contracting. Rather than a direct causal chain between information technology and change in contractual arrangements, practice must be prepared to see the causal chain go both ways:

> Information technologies and organizational/institutional arrangements are connected reciprocally. Both function in this framework as dependent and independent variables. Each one has causal effects over the other. Institutions and organizations shape the enactment of information technology. Technology, in turn, may reshape organizations and institutions to better conform to its logic. New information technologies are enacted – made sense of, designed, and used (when they are used) – through the mediation of existing organizational and institutional arrangements with their internal logics or tendencies.
>
> (Fountain 2001: 12)

75

Institutionalizing IT is a huge task. It has to be taken seriously. Like contract management, managing IT projects can no longer be considered a technical task but one that has strategic and political aspects, and therefore must be a question for public organization leaders as well as private organization leaders. The many stories of large IT projects gone wrong is evidence of this perspective. Public sector managers have been used to donating extra money to IT projects in the hope that somehow the projects will get back on the right track. When a project eventually fails, the senior leadership figures find out how little integrated the project was in the overall decision-making process. In recent years there has been a tendency to improve by learning from earlier mistakes. The chairman of a Danish report on IT projects in the public sector observed that government IT projects may also be more vulnerable to critique than private sector projects because the private sector is good at keeping a low profile concerning ill-fated projects, while the same is not possible for an accountable and open modern government today.

CONCLUSIONS

This chapter has first identified a move towards digital-era governance that focuses on reintegration, new holism in public service delivery and digitalization of services. Making use of IT is influenced by the institutional structure of the state and how institutions facilitate but also constrain change in public sector organization must not be forgotten. IT is used in many areas of contracting, including formulating a policy, strategic purchasing, providing and regulation. The key lessons of this chapter are that the use of IT has to be taken into account when designing a contract for public service delivery, and when managing the contractual relationship. IT can be of particular help in matching the purchasers and providers and it is also useful in disseminating information about contracting.

DISCUSSION QUESTIONS

1   How compelling is the evidence for the digital-era governance revolution? Do you agree with Dunleavy *et al.* that digital governance constitutes an independent alternative to the New Public Management movement?

2   Choose an area of contract management within which you specialize. Consider which improvements, if any, to contract management, the use of IT has made in your area.

3   In your judgement, how well is the policy on IT integrated or coordinated with the policy for contracting out in your country? Try to give examples of where you see the connection.

4   What are the institutional factors (formal and informal rules) that constrain or facilitate use of IT in contracting in your own organization? What may be done to overcome any institutional obstacles?

5   Think of a recent information technology device with which you are familiar. Could that device be used in relation to government contracting?

REFERENCES

Bellamy, C. and J. Taylor (1998) *Government in the Information Age*. Buckingham: Open University Press.

Brown, T. and M. Potoski (2004) Managing the public service market, *Public Administration Review* 64(6): 656–668.

Dunleavy, P., H. Margetts, S., Bastow and J. Tinkler (2006) New public management is dead – long live digital era governance, *Journal of Public Administration Theory and Practice* 16(3): 467–494.

Fountain, J. (2001) *Building a Virtual State. Information Technology and Institutional Change*. Washtington, DC: Brookings.

Hodge, G. (2000) *Privatization*. Boulder, CO: Westview Press.

Hood, C. (1991) A public management for all seasons? *Public Administration* (spring): 3–19.

Lane, J-E. (2000) *New Public Management*. London: Routledge.

Pollitt, C. (2003) *The Essential Public Manager*. Buckingham: Open University Press.

Rambøll Management (2004) *Top of the Web. User Satisfaction and Usage. Survey of E-government Services*. Report prepared for the eGovernment Unit. DG Information Society, European Commission.

Romzek, B. and J. Johnston (2002) Effective contract management implementation and accountability: a preliminary model, *Journal of Public Administration Research and Theory* 12(3): 423–453.

Schedler, K. and B. Schmidt (2004) Managing the e-government organization, *International Public Management Review* 5(1): 1–20.

West, D. (2005) *Digital Government. Technology and Public Sector Performance*. Princeton, NJ: Princeton University Press.

West, D. (2006) *Global E-government, 2006*. Rhode Island, NE: Brown University, Center for Public Policy.

www.udbudsportalen.dk (Danish website disseminating contracting out information to purchasers and providers).

FURTHER READING

Jane Fountain's *Building a Virtual State* (2001) is one of the best introductions to information technology in a social science perspective. Fountain employs institutional theory to the changes that information technology brings with it. She does not fall for easy amazement of the information technology revolution, but carefully examines through empirical studies how institutions influence information technology and visa versa. Patrick Dunleavy and colleagues published their book-length treatment of digital-era governance in late 2006 which provides an interesting elaboration of the arguments of how influential the digital revolution is in public service delivery. Readers are also encouraged to seek out the earlier work of Richard Heeks (1999) *Reinventing Government in the Information Age* (London: Routledge). A variety of survey reports from the major consulting companies of the latest trends in digital-era governance are also available on the internet.

Chapter 5

Training and educating contract managers

LEARNING OBJECTIVES

By the end of this chapter you should:

- have a clear understanding of the specific challenges for contract managers;
- be able to distinguish between routine contract management and strategic contract management; and
- understand why the responsibility for strategic management must be shared between different levels of the organization, including the political leadership.

KEY POINTS OF THIS CHAPTER

- To be a contract manager requires specific skills related to contracting.
- Strategic contracting management places contracting at the apex of the organization.
- Strategic contracting management must be shared among the chief executive officer, the political leader and the rest of the organization.

KEY TERMS

- **Contract manager** – the title of the position specifically devoted to formulating, implementing and evaluating managing public service contracts.

- ■ **Contract management competencies** – the competencies relating to specific contract management skills (as opposed to more general management skills).
- ■ **Strategic contracting management** – when contracting is used to promote central agency goals.

Contract managers need specific skills that include the way to write a contract, to clarify performance targets, to manage budgets for contracting purposes, to negotiate contracts, and to monitor and evaluate contractors' performance. This chapter will also discuss how to mix on-job training with more customized courses on contract management and will look at the requirements for contracted employees. The issues include how to motivate employees who are hired by contract to perform for limited periods of time, how to handle transition of employees from one provider to another, and how to keep and develop the human resource potential of employees working for different providers.

The way the chapter proceeds is to first discuss two contributions from outstanding researchers on the topic. The American professor, Donald Kettl, addressed the issue of contract managers in his seminal work *Sharing Power. Public Governance and Private Markets* (Kettl 1993). In a later contribution, another American professor, Steven Kelman, has argued for the need to 'go beyond' the requirements identified by Kettl a decade ago (Kelman 2002). Kelman was responsible for overseen contracting or outsourcing policy in the Clinton administration in the US in the 1990s. The second part of the chapter discusses who the contract managers are and tries to come up with a classification. By way of a conclusion, the third and final part discusses what kinds of challenges contract managers are likely to meet in the future.

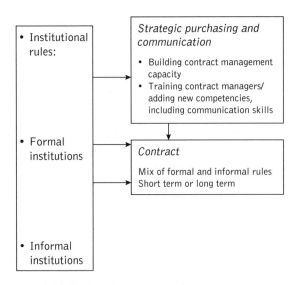

Figure 5.1 *Contract management capacity and training contract managers.*

CHALLENGES IN CONTRACT TRAINING IN PUBLIC MANAGEMENT

In a recent book on contract management, American professor Phillip Cooper (2003: 13) remarks how public officials are becoming dependent on contract management for delivery of services to citizens. He goes on to observe that 'it makes no sense to speak of effective public policy of professional public management, or even informed citizenship, without an awareness of the nature and operation of public contract management'. Cooper sees the problem of contract management at the intersection between the hierarchical government model and the horizontal (market-based) model.

On contract management as part of the operation stage of contracting, Cooper (2003: 169) notes how 'contract management is as intensive as any other public management enterprise', and that 'it is extremely dangerous to have top public management believe they can contract something out and forget it'. He also notes how contract management is 'more than audit and control' and involves 'performance contracting'.

The well-known American public management scholar from Harvard, Mark Moore (2002: 88), agrees:

> It is tempting to believe that when government makes the decision that something for which it is paying should be provided by private organizations, it has removed one item from its agenda of worries. . . . A moment's reflection will suffice to remind anyone who might hold such fond hopes that though the decision to contract changes the nature of government's worries, it does not eliminate them.

The question of what contract managers should do was addressed most forcefully by Donald Kettl (1993) in his work on public governance of private markets. Kettl's core question, it will be recalled, was how governments could learn to be 'smart buyers', and know what to buy, who to buy from and finding out what it has bought. He gave his own advice on what it would require to create a smart buyer (Kettl 1993: 208–211):

- front-line bureaucrats must be hired and rewarded;
- mid-level bureaucrats must be retrained;
- political appointees must be aware of issues involved in contracting;
- political rhetoric must be toned down;
- core governmental functions must not be contracted out;
- it must be recognized that market mechanisms raise new issues for governance; and
- create political leadership can make and win the case for investing in contract management.

The above list shows how governments must build the organization around contract managers, invest in their training and education, and pay them enough political attention so that they will not be left in the dark and unable to perform their duties. In Kettl's study there lies a warning, also visible in Cooper's contribution, that contract management is not likely to work if it is either just left to itself or placed in some remote part of the organization without the sufficient resources and competencies to do the job at hand. Of course, one premise that both writers make is that organizations actively choose the contracting route. Alternative views of public organizations might view organizations as still performing all the key tasks themselves and leaving the fringe tasks to contracting. Clearly, contracting itself remains in focus for both Kettl and Cooper's view of organizations.

This image of contract managers is recognizable from other writings on contract management. The organization must transform itself to become more geared towards contract management. In a tale on contracting in Charlotte, North Carolina, it is argued how the organization had to master new skills such as overseeing the market and making sure it could check the output of the service delivery correctly (Sizer 2001). Others have told of their experience with negotiating skills, especially if the service providers know they enjoy a *de facto* monopoly on service delivery. Sometimes service providers are able to activate a political network if the contract managers press them too hard on a matter. Providers may have good channels of communication to political leaders directly, and this can make the work of the contract manager stressful. Besides having economic competencies, negotiation competency is also important. Overseeing the contractual process calls for a competency to master a great variety of often quite technical information, requiring the contract manager to have a good education or formidable work experience to cope with the challenges he or she faces.

BOX 5.1 CONTRACT SKILLS ACCORDING TO KETTL

Contracts need able and foresighted public management to work. American professor Donald F. Kettl sees a place for contract management in the current 'transformation of governance'. He emphasizes that 'contracts do not manage themselves'. Kettl (2000: 162) lists four factors in contract management where new skills are needed:

- skills to specify programme goals;
- skills to negotiate good contracts;
- skills to oversee the results; and
- skills to develop markets that supply goods and services for governments to buy.

Strategic contract management

In a recent contribution to the literature, Harvard's Steven Kelman has made a critique of the view exposed by Kettl and others about the tasks and responsibilities of contract managers. He is not critical of the work per se, but he simply states that Kettl's book is now over ten years old, and that both the literature and real-world experience have moved on since the early 1990s:

> Because so much of what agencies do and deliver has increasingly come to depend on contracts with third parties, successful contracting has become a central part of agency success. A number of agencies such as the Departement of Defense, the Department of Energy, and the National Aeronautics and Space Administration, spend much of their budgets on contracted products and service – 46, 94, and 78 per cent respectively.
>
> (Kelman, 2002: 89)

Kelman is making the point that contracting is now an essential function for government organizations to master. It is no longer a task that can be relegated to the youngest employee in the organization. It is no longer a task that public managers do not need to know anything about. The time when public managers could only be trained in law, political science or economics without having studied contracting as a subject is no longer relevant. In 2004, the director of NASA, Sean O'Keefe, was asked at the American Society for Public Administration's conference if the recent Columbia disaster had altered views on contracting and if he wanted to produce 'in-house' again. His reaction was one of amazement. He told the audience that NASA was working with contractors not only in America but all over the world, and the whole world was providing parts or spare parts for NASA's equipment. Going back to the old in-house production was simply not an option he considered realistic. Kelman has summed up the challenge as one where 'the ability to manage contracting must be considered a core competency of the organization' (Kelman 2002: 89).

'Competence' according to the *Oxford Advance Learners Dictionary* is 'having the ability, power, authority, skill, knowledge etc to do what is needed'. The phrase used by Kelman to capture the importance of contracting to the organization is 'strategic contracting', and he sees that as the situation when 'contracting should be used aggressively to promote central agency goals' (Kelman 2002: 89). First, Kelman expresses scepticism towards journalistic accounts of fraud and waste in contract management which projects the image of a disorderly state that has led researchers to talk about a hollow state. This image is overblown to Kelman's mind and is not representative of the empirical case material of which he is aware.

The point in Kelman's view is to first recognize that contract management is more than just a routine job function, and that the job encompasses many of the competencies normally associated with managing generally in the public sector. This means that public

83

managers who are responsible for contracts adopt a strategic perspective to contract management. Kelman (2002: 92) lists the competencies that a strategic contract manager must possess:

- strategy and goal-setting;
- the ability to inspire those doing the work, including contractors, with enthusiasm and public purpose;
- performance management;
- management of horizontal interfaces between the contractor and end users;
- management of vertical interfaces with higher levels of the organization; and
- managing relations with the external environment, including attending professional meetings.

What should be done to help contract managers become strategic contract managers and develop the necessary competencies for the future? Kelman (2002: 94) points to three requirements: governments must 'define and provide training for the job, split off lower-level tasks from the executive-type tasks, and make an investment in performance measurement as a discipline'. Contract management should be just that, management, and not just routine-based administration. What is considered boring is just monitoring contract compliance in a fairly mechanical way. Mastering performance measurement seems particularly important to today's and tomorrow's contract managers. Performance management is being noted in the contemporary contract. De Bruijn (2002) has researched both the constructive sides to performance management and the down sides. Connecting contracting and performance management is a crucial matter in a strategic contract management framework in both theory and practice.

Being good at performance management may to some extent make the need for keeping some parts of service provision 'in-house' obsolete. Kelman (2002: 97) argues against the widespread view in the contract literature that governments risk becoming too 'hollow' for their own good. Going back to Kettl's original work, he was thinking about how governments could learn to be 'smart buyers'. In Kelman's opinion, it is possible to just concentrate on being good strategic contract managers and to leave the actual production of services to other (private) providers. The chief reason is that governments will still have relationships with providers, know the markets, evaluate bids and so on, and this way they will acquire and keep important knowledge on production that does not have to imply that they do actual production work themselves. Governments can also develop a strategy of hiring the best people from the provider organizations to make them keep up with current production knowledge. Former employees of providers can become contract managers who work for the government. In addition, governments acquire intimate knowledge on providers' capabilities when providers are asked to supply a 'statement of objectives' in early rounds of competitive bidding (Kelman 2002: 99). The future of strategic management is a problem of 'human resources management – of people and job design' (ibid.: 99).

Other authors are in line with the need facing adequate contract management training:

> Public managers' ability to act as smart buyers of goods and services is compromised when there is a shortage of public managers trained in contract management and substantive policy areas. In addition, the issues of goal diversity, competing incentives, and political and bureaucratic realities further inhibit a public manager's ability to manage contract relationships and provide meaningful oversight that mitigates against fraud, waste and abuse.
>
> (Van Slyke 2003: 307)

The implications for governments of Kelman's critique are that they need to think a lot more about making contract management jobs exciting and giving contract managers challenging objectives. Governments then need to supply the contract managers with the necessary competencies, including strategy, goal-setting, the capability to inspire and motivate, and performance-based management techniques. The competencies of negotiating and managing external relationships are also crucial. To these requirements we could add the points discussed by Cooper (2003). These points are about being aware of the legal contract aspects and having knowledge of the institutional context in which that contract takes place, and the role of government in society, the history of the state and the democratic values that uphold, and, perhaps most importantly, the competency to strike a good economic deal.

WHAT COMPETENCIES DO CONTRACT MANAGERS NEED?

One critique of Kelman might be that he only talks about formal contract managers who have 'contract manager' as their primary job description. Like the term 'public manager', there could be more discussion about who the public managers – and here the contract managers – are. In Lawrence Lynn's work on public management, he at one time defined public management simply as 'the executive part of government' (Lynn 1996). In Mark H. Moore's (1995) widely read work on public management as the power to 'create public value', he has a good discussion about who the public managers are. Contract management is then how to create public value through contracts. In Moore's, and also Lynn's view, many people contribute to the practice of public management, and more people than those who are simply officially 'public managers' contribute. Moore sees politicians and government ministers as helping to define and execute public management. Employees and consultants may also perform duties related to public management and could therefore be called 'public managers' in some respect. Yet the group of people normally associated with public managers is the group of public managers at the top of the hierarchy. Moore also ends up writing primarily about the top executive personnel in charge of formal organizations, but the themes, the functions and the competencies could also be relevant to others.

85

In contract management, the discussion on who are the contract managers is becoming important. The contract is the institution binding the purchaser and the provider together. While most texts refer to the government contract managers, it should not be forgotten that, of course, there are contract managers on the private sector side too. These people should also be referred to as contract managers. Private sector provider managers need to understand contract management too. They almost always do, of course, because they are dependent on getting contracts with purchasers in both the public and private sector. In the following part of this section, we will try to find out who the contract managers are and how we can make a classification of them.

A first step would be to consider the politicians – government ministers, local government councillors – who make decisions about entering into the contracts. Are these people contract managers? In a way, they are. They have to think about the public services they are purchasing, and how the users of the services, who are also voters, will value the services they receive. They have to think about their reputation if the contract is messed up and if a scandal hits the newspaper headlines. Politicians have to think carefully about signing contracts with private providers. A messed-up contract could easily cost the politicians their careers.

The next group is the top executives in the public sector – the permanent secretaries in the ministries and the chief executive officers in local government. Are they contract managers? They collaborate closely with politicians in all-important areas of their work. They too have to be sensitive to issues that can harm their political masters. At the same time, the top executive of an organization has to run the organization and to manage relationships with external organizations. No longer can they afford to be ignorant of contract matters if we are to believe the argument of Kelman and others. Contract management must be a core competency of theirs along with the other attributes that are considered to be part of top executives' portfolios.

The third group of people would be those who are perhaps normally associated with the term 'contract managers'. These are the people who have a specific programmatic or organizational responsibility. They are at the second level of the organization and negotiate with provider organizations, and are responsible for the day-to-day relationships when the contract is being implemented. This responsibility involves human resource management. These people should now, in Kelman's view, receive more training and education in 'normal' strategic public management competencies than they have in the past.

The fourth group of people make sure that contract compliance from the providers is achieved. They carry out the more routine-based tasks of contract management. They may not have a formal education, but could be trained internally in the organization, or as a secretary or clerk. In some contexts they may be called 'contract administrators' or 'controllers' more than contract managers per se.

The fifth group of contract managers would be the top executive level of the provider organizations. These people are strategically forming and managing the relationships with the purchaser organizations, but on behalf of the providers. In the language of

Table 5.1 *Competency and contract managers*

	Politicians: mayors and ministers	Top executives	Mid-level managers	Controllers	Strategic private sector managers	Street-level private sector managers
Political competency	X					
Strategic competency		X	X		X	
Controlling competency			X	X		
Street level competency						X

principal–agent theory, they are the agents. Yet they are also managers responsible for managing their own organizations and for delivering the services that are in the contract.

The sixth group of contract managers are responsible for programmes or specific parts of the organizations in the provider organizations. They are the most direct overseers of the people actually doing the work, whether it is street cleaning, childcare, care for the elderly, maintaining an ICT system and so on. This group of people will often be in close contact with their counterparts or overseers in the purchaser organizations. They clear up day-to-day matters and clarify work responsibilities, deal with stories in the press and generally keep in touch with how the service delivery is progressing. Finally, there are the people who actually carry out the work: firemen, ambulance drivers, nurses, social workers, garbage collectors and so on.

It could be debated whether more groups should come under the already expanding heading of 'contract managers'. What about interest group representatives, ordinary citizens or consultants? A case could probably be made for each of these groups, but it is perhaps more wise to keep the 'manager' term closely related to the people that bear some sort of formal responsibility for carrying out the service provision. There are also the people who control the actions of the contract managers, such as national audit officers or lawyers and legal experts of different kinds. These people should be considered as, auditors and legal experts, and should probably not be termed contract managers either.

It should be clear by now that when the talk is about competencies, we are, in all likelihood, talking about different sets of competencies for each group. The competencies for the politicians are not necessarily the same as the competencies for the 'street-level contract managers' who oversee the actual service delivery on a daily basis.

Let me then try to develop Kelman's 'strategic contracting' concept and to outline some types of competencies that are required for contracting for public services:

- *Political contracting competency* (Who should the organization contract with? What partner fits the organization well? What are the political risks of entering a contract? How is political accountability secured?). Core competencies: strategic outlook, knowledge of politics and policy, hiring top contract managers.
- *Strategic contracting competency* (How do you build relationships with provider organizations? How is the organization going to be responsible and accountable for its actions?). Core competencies: strategic organizational outlook, negotiation and managing relationships/external relations.
- *Controlling contracting competency* (How is information about services promised in contracts stored and retrieved? Who should have access to what type of contract management information? How is information about progress and results best presented to internal and external accountability institutions?). Core competencies: information and communication management competency, economics training.
- *Street-level contracting competency* (How is the job affecting the customer performed best? How can we change the day-to-day routines if necessary without violating the contract?). Core competencies: understand the contractual framework, make sense of contractual obligations, make decisions about specific situations and incidents.

Support competencies include:

- *Legal contracting competency* (What is the legal requirements of the contract? What kinds of threats do politicians, managers and staff face when they sign a contract? How can the organization be held legally responsible for its actions?). Core competency: detailed and thorough knowledge and practice of contract law.
- *Human resource competency* (How are people motivated? How are people and managers in organizations working for you under contract motivated? What kinds of opportunities can be provided for both the organization's own contract managers and the provider organization's contract managers?). Core competency: knowledge of how to deal with and manage human resources to explore the full potential of employees.
- *Consultancy competency* (How do governments get advice on what they should buy and who they should buy it from? How can advice be given effectively to minimize both cost and time for purchasers?). Core competency: ability to give required and correct advice.

CONCLUSIONS

This chapter has looked at the competencies and the various roles of contract managers. How does the picture fit with the themes in contemporary contracting literature?

Recent efforts in research have been directed at finding a way to 'effective contract management and implementation' (Romzek and Johnston 2002). In relation to that research, more attention should be paid to how contract managers can help facilitate effective contracting implementation. Political competencies should be clarified in their model. Strategic contracting competency and controlling competency are obviously very important. Another aspect is that contracting, even strategic contracting, is a joint effort between several types of people. This is in addition to the type of analysis that only focuses on special contracting units in the purchaser organizations. In addition, the 'support' groups of legal experts, human resource experts and consultants must not be forgotten. Consultants will often provide exactly those kinds of services: legal expertise and human resource insight as well as giving general advice on management practice.

There is a need to look even more at how contract management is carried out for different services and in different countries. There are a lot of impressive research results out there already, and we need to build on those to focus specifically on management competencies.

One of the key challenges of the future is to make the different levels of contractual competency work together more efficiently. Too often, the three tasks are seen as separate. If governments are better at realizing what competencies they need, they will be more able to meet the challenges that a successful contracting process requires. If, on the other hand, governments continue to view contracting as a 'side order', something they presume is present in the organization, then contracting will not proceed as smoothly as it should. The implications of this view are, as both Kettl and Kelman pointed out, that there needs to be much more focused training of contracting managers in all the different types of competency. A training course for contract managers must refer to all of the competencies raised above and probably more too. Contracting should be considered a core competency in the same way as strategic management and performance-based management and communication ability must be in every public manager's toolbox. If the current trend with contracting continues, as we have witnessed in the military, in space exploration and in providing services for ordinary citizens, then the time has come for governments to pay more attention to the competencies of contract managers.

DISCUSSION QUESTIONS

1   How have the challenges facing contract managers changed over time?

2   Is Kelman realistic in suggesting that contract management competencies will always be viewed favourably in public organizations? What factors hinder this development?

3   Do you agree with the number of competencies, or would you add other competencies you deem necessary for contract managers?

4   Who should be responsible for upgrading contract managers' competencies?

REFERENCES

Cooper, P.J. (2003) *Governing by Contract. Challenges and Opportunities for Public Managers.* Washington, DC: GQ Press.

De Bruijn, H. (2002) *Managing Performance in the Public Sector.* London: Routledge.

Kelman, S. (2002) Strategic contracting management, in J. Donahue and J. Nye Jr. (eds) *Market-based Governance. Supply Side, Demand Side, Upside and Downside.* Washington, DC: Brookings.

Kettl, D.F. (1993) *Sharing Power. Public Governance and Private Markets.* Washington, DC: Brookings.

Kettl, D.F. (2000) *The Transformation of Governance.* Baltimore, MD: Johns Hopkins University Press.

Lynn, L. Jr. (1996) *Public Management as Art, Science and Profession.* New Jersey: Chatham House.

Moore, M.H. (1995) *Creating Public Value. Strategic Management in Government.* Cambridge, MA: Harvard University Press.

Moore, M.H. (2002) Privatizing public management, in J. Donahue and J. Nye Jr. (eds) *Market-based Governance. Supply Side, Demand Side, Upside and Downside.* Washington, DC: Brookings.

Romzek, B. and J. Johnston (2002) Effective contract management and implementation. A preliminary model, *Journal of Public Administration Research and Theory* 12: 423–453.

Sizer, E. (2001) Impact on public organizational structure and behaviour: managed competition and privatization, in R.A. Johnson and N. Walzer (eds) *Local Government Innovation: Issues and Trends in Privatization and Managed Competition.* Westport, CT: Quorum Books.

Van Slyke, D. (2003) The mythology of privatization in contracting for social services, *Public Administration Review* 63(3): 296–315.

FURTHER READING

A good edited volume on the challenges of contracting for public managers is John Donahue and Joseph Nye's *Market-based Governance* (Washington, DC: Brookings, 2002). The difference in public managers and private managers' approach to contracting is captured well in Simon Domberger's *The Contracting Organization* (Oxford: Oxford University Press, 1998). On the broader challenges of innovation and new ideas in the public sector, see S. Osborne and K. Brown's *Managing Challenge and Innovation in Public Service Organizations* (London: Routledge, 2005).

Part III

Contracting and public service delivery systems

Chapter 6

Private providers of public services

LEARNING OBJECTIVES

By the end of this chapter you should:

- have a knowledge of what a public service delivery system is;
- gain an insight into the nature of the providers of public services; and
- be able to understand the challenges that globalization of markets present to public service delivery.

KEY POINTS OF THIS CHAPTER

- Public service markets are social constructs which are always changing.
- Providers of public services involve both incumbents and challengers.
- Public service provision is increasingly also a global business with global providers.

KEY TERMS

- **Provider** – an organization that provides public services under a contractual agreement with a public purchaser. The organization may be a for-profit company, a non-profit voluntary organization, another public organization, or any combination.
- **Markets as politics** – the idea that markets are created by states and involve dynamics between firms fighting for market control, and internal struggle within

firms for strategic direction/social constructions reflecting political-cultural constructions of firms and nations.

■ **Public service providers** – organizations that provide services to the public sector on a contractual basis. These organizations include for-profit companies, non-profit voluntary organizations and other public sector organizations.

■ **Public service delivery system** – the structure of the public service organizations that deliver public services, including organizations that have contracts with public purchasers.

■ **Global/transborder service systems** – the notion that public service provision has a global dimension where providers are active in several countries with standardized products.

This chapter examines markets for public service delivery, the profile of the providers and the various levels (local, national, global) of today's public service marketplace. I argue that providers are a mixed bunch of organizations that together make up 'the public service delivery systems'. Providers vary according to their origin (public or private) and their age and size (incumbents, challengers). Increasingly, public service providers today operate in international or global markets, and purchasers become dependent on the current providers' supply of goods and services. While contract managers are used to being able to 'get the best deal' from local or national providers, the trend towards more globally oriented providers poses challenges for still locally based purchasers.

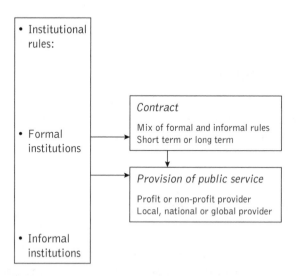

Figure 6.1 *The providers of public services.*

HOW POLITICS SHAPES MARKETS

Economic theory views markets as arenas where goods and services are traded through a monetary medium and where there is fierce competition among different providers to offer services. The market model is characterized by the following factors. The principal diagnosis of what is wrong with the current public sector is that public organizations enjoy a monopoly in their service production. Instead the public sector must be decentralized to allow for local initiative to flourish. Management is influenced by pay-for-performance schemes and other private sector techniques. Market incentives are the main drivers for change (Peters 1996). Installing market mechanisms in the public sector is not easy, because it requires institutional change as well. Walsh (1995: 54) observes how 'the creation of an effective market-based system of management within the public service depends upon the development of an appropriate institutional frame-work within which it can operate'. Kettl (1993) views markets for public services as mainly imperfect markets.

The notion that markets are inherently political and embedded in social institutions has been argued most strongly by Fligstein (1996). Fligstein sees markets as politics as a metaphor for understanding the way the social structures of markets are organized. First, markets are part of the way states are formed and organized. Second, the dynamics of markets are influenced by political struggles: a struggle between firms to control markets, and a struggle within companies for direction of the strategy of those companies (Fligstein 1996: 657).

Viewed in this way, focus must be on how each country has gone about building its markets for public service delivery. Markets were not there by accident but by intentional design. A first task in understanding how public service markets operate is to understand how they were formed. Many markets for public service delivery are relatively new. It is only recently that private prisons have begun to be built in the UK and Australia (Sands 2004), although the USA has had them for a number of years. Markets must be designed and constructed. The process of market structuring and designing involves establishing property rights (who has the right to profits?), governance structures (which rules define the rules for competition and other company-related institutions?), conceptions of con-trol (what is the perception of markets by key actors?), and rules of exchange (who can transact with whom?) (Fligstein 1996: 658).

A recent example would be the construction of a competitive market for railway services in the UK, where the old British Rail system has been abandoned and replaced by a number of commercial train operators (Terry 2001). The system was later changed again, perhaps because the market structure was not thought through sufficiently. Was there a sense of which company must profit from railway privatization? Were there enough reliable rules that market investors felt comfortable with? Was there a common understanding between the railway authorities, the new providers and the local cus-tomers about what the market was about? Was it clear how a railway provider could contract with sub-providers or with other rail companies? Many of these questions were

97

left unanswered when railway privatization was first implemented in the UK (Terry 2001).

A similar example would be the construction of the market for welfare services in the Scandinavian countries. In these countries (Norway, Sweden, Denmark), most public service delivery is traditionally handled by public sector organizations. There is no clear market for welfare services. Only an emergent market may be said to exist. The property rights are not clearly divided, and local governments still think of themselves as the main providers of services. They have no incentive to let private providers enter the markets in care for the elderly or childcare. If private providers make a huge return on their investment, would that be socially and politically acceptable? These matters have not been thought through. The institutionalized rules that should designate the welfare market are implemented sporadically, not through a coherent policy. In Denmark there is a new set of rules for consumer choice, a new set of rules for contracting out, and a new set of rules for how public employees may 'break out' and form their own company. On each proposal's own terms they probably make sense, and individual companies might adapt to the rules. But the overall picture is more blurred. There is no holistic or proven set of rules that will give companies enough certainty for them to enter the market. That is why private providers stay away from markets for welfare services in the Scandinavian context. There is no common understanding of what a market for welfare services is. The government seems to think that providers are innovative risk-takers, and they are excited about the new market possibilities about to open up. But providers want security and strive for survival, and they are too risk-prone to enter into public service markets where the conditions may change again after the next general election. Finally, the rules for who providers can sell their services to are also up for debate. The newly enacted legislation on consumer choice in care for the elderly allows an elderly person to change provider within a short period of time (sometimes only to three days, while in other places it may take a month). The flexibility of this policy is great for the customer but not for the provider, who cannot plan for a steady provision of services, and a steady income from the sale of those services.

How politics create and shape markets is, of course, a recurring theme within the field of political economy and has been the subject of many treaties. Here we are especially concerned with the rise of public service markets. New research is emerging in this area. Sanger (2003) has studied the creation of markets for welfare services in selected states in the USA. She notes how government programmes, and change in government programmes, can emphasize the involvement of private companies, for example, in the TANF programme, and also in Medicaid programmes (see Romzek and Johnston 2002). The analysis by Sanger shows that new types of providers are driving other providers out, and that some providers are putting their identity at risk:

> Public capacity is waning under increasing contracting. The future of mission-driven nonprofits is uncertain and worrisome. While systems of managed competition with the private sector are clearly improving the management, capacity, and

performance of many fiscally sound nonprofits, many others are in danger of 'losing their souls', and distorting their mission. Still others, living on the brink, are in danger of extinction.

(Sanger 2003: 106)

Central governments both try to force local governments to use private service providers, and also encourage private providers to explore the new business opportunities that arise when governments create markets. An example is the Danish government's decision to allow private companies to 'challenge' public organizations on service delivery. If private organizations can show that they can produce a service better, cheaper and more efficiently, then the public organization (a local government, for example) must consider the challenge formally. If the challenge is rejected, the local government has to declare the reasons for the rejection. There are several ways that governments can actively create and shape markets. One of the more spectacular initiatives was the effort of the European Union (then the European Community) to create the single European market where goods and services should be produced without national hindrances.

Fligstein (1996: 663) has identified three phases in marketplaces: emergence, stability and crisis. What is the situation after the market has been created or (re-)shaped? Fligstein (1996: 663) suggests that the market is viewed as a place where companies strive for control. In the first instance this involves a struggle between those that are already in the marketplace (incumbents) and the companies that are outside the particular market, but want to enter the market (challengers). Incumbents are usually bigger in size and have an intimate knowledge of the market, while challengers are smaller and have limited knowledge of the market, but it is not always size that is the essential issue (bigger companies from another country or another sector might challenge a big company in a particular public service market). Furthermore, Fligstein distinguishes between stable markets and new markets:

A stable market is defined as a market in which the identities and status hierarchy of firms . . . are well known and a conception of control that guides actors who lead firms is shared. Firms resemble one another in tactics and organizational structure. Politics will reproduce the position of advantaged groups. In new markets, the politics resemble social movements. Actors in different firms are trying to convince other firms to go along with their conception of the market.

(Fligstein 1996: 663)

Let us concentrate for a moment on the emergence of markets that characterize many public service delivery systems. One proposition regarding new markets is: 'At the beginning of a new market, the largest firms are the most likely to be able to create a conception of control and a political coalition to control competition' (Fligstein 1996: 664). An example of a stable market would be the market for soft drinks, where Coca-Cola and Pepsi Cola are the two largest providers globally. Any company that wants to

BOX 6.1 TYPES OF PUBLIC SERVICE MARKETS

Emerging markets: markets are created and shaped by the state that define property rights, create governance structures and set the rules of exchange – and subsequently regulate the companies.

Stable markets: when incumbents rule the market, and the status and hierarchy of the main actors are understood and accepted by all actors, including challengers.

Crisis markets: when incumbents begin to fail, or when an exogenous shock, such as an economic crisis or a state intervention, influences the market.

(Fligstein 1996: 656–673)

produce and sell a soft drink in any market has to consider the market power of the two global leaders.

The examples of the railway market and the market for welfare services are instances of new markets, or markets that have to be created before they can operate on a full basis. They resemble 'social movements', in Fligstein's words. New market actors have to persuade other market actors what the market is supposed to look like. The other example is the market for welfare services. In some areas of this market, the incumbents – the ones that are already in the marketplace – are the public providers themselves. And as 'politics reproduce the position of advantaged groups', according to Fligstein, we might expect that the politics of welfare service delivery will tend to shelter the dominant, public providers from the challengers in the private sector.

One vibrant market internationally has been the market for employment services (training and finding jobs for unemployed people). In some areas of the world, the welfare service delivery has involved private providers (Considine 2001; Considine and Lewis 1999, 2003). Employment services used to be provided by public providers. The reason to contract with private providers in this field is due to the usual reasons given for involving the private sector: that they are faster, more efficient, and it is more flexible for the public purchaser to use. Here we may speak of an emergent market that is gradually turning into a more stable market. In this stable market, there are already a few dominant firms in the marketplace. The public sector as a purchaser of services may be able to shape the market for employment services. In other areas this may not be so easy because the public providers will know the service intimately, and will not necessarily be interested in giving up their market power as dominant providers.

What happens when markets are stable? The market for ambulance services in Denmark is quite a stable market, largely dominated by the private company Falck. This observation concurs with Fligstein's (1996: 667) proposition that 'in markets with stable conceptions of control, there is a great deal of agreement by market participants on the conception of control and that status of hierarchies and strategies it implies'. Only a few companies challenge Falck's dominant position. Some challenge Falck in road assistance. Only a few local governments themselves challenge Falck in the area of ambulance driving and fire-fighting. Falck remains the incumbent actor in that marketplace.

What happens when there is a crisis in the public service market? There are not endless examples of crises in public service markets, partly because governments are prone to enter to prevent a crisis in a delivery system of great importance to citizens. The example of the railway system in the UK could be considered to be a crisis in some sense, as there is general agreement that the system did not work as commercially viable as was intended in the first place. Fligstein (1996: 668–669) attributes the crisis both to an incumbent's beginning failure and to exogenous forces such as invasion of other companies, economic crises or state intervention. The crisis of public service delivery systems is an interesting topic that warrants closer observation in the future, but there are not many vivid examples where failure has meant a disappearance of a particular public service.

Summing up on how politics shape markets, we can say that markets are not given for many public services. Markets have to be created. If the markets are stable it is usually in the form of dominant (incumbent) public providers that want to keep private providers (challengers) away from the market. The government faces a huge task in making room for market entry, and to regulate markets once they become more stable to ensure that competition still exists. The main lesson from the markets-as-politics approach is that providers seek stability. Providers are not risk-inspired businesses that will do anything to get into a new marketplace. The markets are dominated by some bigger providers that set the tone for how competition will unfold.

A PROFILE OF THE PROVIDERS

Who are the providers that deliver public service? In many treaties of contracting, providers are almost taken as given; as organizations which are out there in the marketplace, but do not achieve further consideration. This section of the chapter is based on the notion that it is essential to know about the providers themselves, and the public service delivery system of which they are a part. Providers come in many shapes and sizes. Providers also differ in terms of their origin. Are they private companies that have always been private and with a background in providing services to the private sector? Or are they companies that have been privatized recently, and bring with them a history of public service delivery from when they were public enterprises or government organzations? One could argue that recently privatized companies have an advantage because they know the purchasers and the customers intimately. But then again the opposite could also be true. Recently privatized companies may never have conducted customer surveys before, and may not possess that knowledge of the customers which private companies are quick to assemble and process so that the

101

difference between recently privatized companies and real private companies may not be that big after all. Everyone seems to agree that the variety of providers and the variety of markets are now greater than ever:

> The ecology of non-profit and for-profit service providers has proved over time to be far from stable. Business activity has expanded in many fields dominated by non-profit organizations. Large for-profit corporations are now providing job training, child care and rehabilitation services at ever greater levels. In health care, for-profit hospitals and health maintenance organizations are buying out non-profit institutions and moving into new markets. In education, publicly traded firms have actively staked out a significant portion of the expanding charter-school market in states from Arizona to Florida. In welfare-to-work services, several large defense contractors have begun to compete for and win contracts. As these and many other sectoral boundary incursions have occurred and as for-profit providers have gained ground, non-profit advocates have argued that it is now necessary to counter some of the real advantages that business firms possess to allow both non-profit and for-profit providers to take part in the delivery of complex human services.
>
> (Frumkin 2002: 67)

The for-profit provider

One type of provider is the for-profit private company. In Wisconsin, New York City and Phoenix, Arizona, USA, private contractors have been active in the new emerging 'welfare services markets' that have been created and shaped in the USA in recent times (Sanger 2003). Providers are here both bigger companies, like Maximus Inc that operates in several states, and the smaller for-profit companies that stick to their local market. In Denmark, the part of the welfare service marketplace that has been contracted out to private providers is dominated by larger firms such as Falck (which provides ambulance services and puts out fires) and International Service Systems (which cleans buildings and provides services for the elderly). In Sweden, there are several private for-profit companies that run public service in the capital city of Stockholm (Almqvist and Högberg 2005). In Melbourne, Australia, the tram and transport system is run by a private company under contract to the city council. The buses in Copenhagen, Denmark, are run by private contractors. Prisons are operated by for-profit companies in many countries, and they have been surrounded by some controversy (Sands 2004).

The bigger private for-profit providers are increasingly entering markets that previously 'belonged' to either public sector organizations or non-profit organizations:

> Market forces alone are likely to drive the large national for-profits to arenas where their comparative advantages make them dominant. When caseloads decline

and easier-to-place clients are scarce, the for-profits are likely to move on to other human service areas where they can increase their market share, economies, and profits.

(Sanger 2003: 106)

The health sector is one where private for-profits operate visibly. There are private hospitals in many countries, for example, in the UK. The UK has a long tradition of creating markets for health services. In the labour market, many companies are competing in job-seeking courses and assistance to unemployed people. In several countries (e.g. Australia, the Netherlands, the UK, Denmark) this has been big business for a number of years.

The non-profit provider

Another type of provider is the non-profit organization with contracts for public service delivery. Many of the UK's voluntary organizations provide services to the public on contract with local governments. In Denmark, many schools are run by private organizations. In Germany, there is a tradition of involving organizations in the delivery of public services in ways that transcend the border between the public and the private sector (Oppen *et al.* 2005). Romzek and Johnston (2002) also refer to a more complex organizational design concerning non-profit providers in their account of contracting out in Kansas. The non-profits face special challenges:

> Outsourcing and new public sector management techniques also have important effects on the voluntary sector itself, particularly in relation to partnerships and the resulting commercial pressure. The community services sector is diffuse, with large and small organisations supported by diverse funding from governments, grants, fees and donations, and a substantial volunteer base. . . . We see this uneasy alliance between tendering for government work and older norms of social services in the discomfort of churches and traditional providers as they are forced to compete for government contracts. Such competitive allocation of resources raises awkward problems for peak bodies, committed as they are to different, community-focussed values.

(Chalmers and Davis 2001: 83)

In some of the literature, the non-profit providers have been termed 'third party government' (Salamon 1995). Salamon has pointed out how the non-profit sector has developed alongside the expansion of the welfare state, but that the role of the non-profit sector has often been overlooked. Non-profit organizations are highly efficient organizations, although their image is often associated with what Salamon (1995: 261–264) calls the 'myth of pure virtue' and the 'myth of voluntarism'. The non-profit sector in the US had more than ten million jobs in 1996 (Light 2000: 8).

103

The use of non-profit organizations in delivering public services has a long history behind it. Salamon (1995) writes about the US in the following, but the quote could easily be about other countries:

> In short, the extensive pattern of government support of nonprofit institutions can be viewed as just one manifestation of a much broader pattern of third-party government that reflects deep-seated American traditions of governance as well as more recent concerns about service cost and quality. Instead of the hierarchic, bureaucratic apparatus pictured in conventional images, the concept of third-party government emphasizes the extensive sharing of responsibilities among public and private roles that is characteristic of the American welfare state. Because a number of different institutions must act together to achieve a given program goal, this pattern of government action seriously complicates the task of public management and involves real problems of accountability. . . . But it also has much to recommend it. It makes it possible to set priorities for the expenditure of societal resources through a democratic political process while leaving the actual operation of the resulting public programs to smaller-scale organizations closer to the problems being addressed. It thus creates a public presence without creating a monstrous public bureaucracy. And it permits a degree of diversity and competition in the provision of publicly funded services that can improve efficiency and reduce costs.
>
> (Salamon 1995: 43)

Networks or consortia of providers

A more hybrid form of provider is where organizations combine in interorganizational networks or form consortia to provide public services. An example of a consortium is described in Sanger's (2003) tale of private providers in Wisconsin, USA, where for-profit companies have joined forces with not-for-profit organizations to provide services. A recent and well-described case is the interorganizational network that provides services to the mentally ill in Arizona which has formed the basis of Milward and Provan's (2000) version of governance theory. When providers contract with sub-providers to ensure service provision to the public, then complex relationships arise, which may have a negative impact upon contract implementation and management precisely because of the complexity that can cause bewilderment for the provider and contract manager in the public sector. Salamon (1995: 220–242) has noted the 'marketization of the non-profit sector' where commercial providers enter the non-profit sector territory, and where non-profit organizations become more commercial in their orientation, drawing more revenue from sale of services than cash-in-kind contributions.

Other public providers

Another possibility is to contract out to another public provider. Van Slyke (2003) mentions how public purchasers contracted with other public providers in public–public partnerships because there were too few competitive contractors available in social services in New York State.

The possibility that public providers may engage in competitive behaviour is welcomed by Harvard's prominent public management professor Mark Moore:

> Once the commitment to the use of competition had been made, there is no use to restrict that competition to private suppliers. If former government bureaucrats are able to form enterprises that can do the job more efficiently, effectively, and fairly than private firms, then it would be to the public's advantage to allow them to compete. This would have the additional virtue of being fairer to government employees, who would otherwise be arbitrarily excluded from employment opportunities.
>
> (Moore 2002: 318)

The best value scheme in the UK allowed a more competitive environment that not only focused on private for-profit providers, but also allowed local governments to engage in a number of ways that would pursue the objective of delivering public value to the citizens (Entwhistle and Martin 2005; Martin 2000).

In Sweden and Denmark, public employees were encouraged to form their own enterprises to engage in competition for public service delivery bids (Almqvist and Högberg 2005; Erhvervs og Byggestyrelsen 2006).

Incumbents and challengers

Fligstein (1996) has reminded us to distinguish between incumbents and challengers. There are those companies that have been on the market for ages, and then there are the new kids on the block; providers that want to get into the market and achieve a share of the market for themselves. Incumbent providers in service markets are the well-known and established players. In the electricity markets there have been attempts to generate fierce competition, but the main players still rule (Hodge *et al.* 2004). In the market for telecommunications, many former monopolies are now the main player, such as the case in Denmark where the company TDC (formerly Tele Denmark) still has the majority of the market (Greve and Viborg Andersen 2001). Challengers in public service markets could include new telecommunication companies (e.g. Telia in Denmark, which is, in fact, owned by the Swedish state – so really the challenger is supported by another state). In markets for services to the elderly, private companies are often the challengers and public organizations the incumbents.

105

GLOBAL PROVIDERS OF PUBLIC SERVICES?

We perhaps customarily think of providers as localized providers to local governments. This may be the case of a small company providing cleaning services or help to elderly people in the local community. The other main illustration is the national service provider that caters for a large number of customers across many local governments' jurisdictions. The for-profit provider, Falck in Denmark, provides ambulance and fire-fighting services to a number of local governments. The standard of the service is the same everywhere.

Public services are not only provided by local or national providers. New global challengers are entering the marketplace and threatening national incumbents on the market. Global service providers can compete in terms of volume and the standards of their products and services. This trend has been termed 'transborder service systems' or global provider network organizations by Roberts (2004). Transborder service systems are described as follows:

> Companies have expanded their reach, entering newly opened markets to exploit opportunities created by outsourcing and privatization. . . . These processes of expansion and consolidation have created enterprises dedicated to the private provision of public services that are more geographically dispersed, and local in more culturally and politically diverse jurisdictions than ever before.
>
> (Roberts 2004: 11)

These transborder service systems are found in a number of sectors. Roberts (2004) mentions correctional systems, water systems, healthcare systems, social services, airports, toll highways and electricity. As Roberts (2004: 16) observes, these new transborder service systems challenge the traditional (national) way in which services are delivered:

> Transborder service systems constitute a potentially radical innovation in the design of administrative apparatus of government. These enterprises create hard, structural links between entities that are responsible for the provision of public services in multiple jurisdictions. . . . Each of these transborder service systems can be thought of as a boundary-spanning network of service providers, and the expansion of these systems can be regarded as the evolution of a form of networked governance.

Globalization of public service production was also a topic for Dunleavy (1997) in an earlier analysis. Dunleavy argued that governments wanted to be 'best in the world' as a result of the New Public Management reforms which emphasized efficiency and effectiveness of public service production, but that the organizations which could provide the economies of scale that were needed were global private companies. These global companies could turn out standardized products and services that they could sell all over the world. Selling of burgers and colas in this way is a well-known phenomenon, but some

106

may wonder if the same trend can apply to public service production. Global providers do in fact turn their attention to the public service market. Consider the computer industry where computer hardware and software are provided to governments by private companies.

When a Ministry of Defence is buying military equipment, the Ministry is often up against global providers of military equipment. One example is helicopters. The Danish Ministry of Defence was buying helicopters, and it tried to specify requirements to the product, being a strategic purchaser. The providers were reluctant to make additional changes to the helicopters they regarded as a standardized product that governments could buy or not buy. The Danish Ministry of Defence came to realize that it would not be able to impose its national views on helicopter specifications in a global provider's product range.

Another example would be when governments are shopping for computer software, where they have only a limited number of software packages from which to choose. In many cases, governments end up with buying Microsoft's software packages: A national purchaser buys from a global provider where little choice of the overall style and substance of the product is available to the 'strategic' purchaser.

A local government purchasing playground tools for kindergartens will face the same challenges. A number of producers have specialized in making tools for playgrounds in kindergartens. The local purchaser can only buy from a limited range when there is a small number of dominant providers and the providers may be reluctant to make alterations to their products just because one or two kindergartens ask for specific features.

The implication of a global provision of public services is that the providers set the terms of what is going to be produced. Of course, they will want to engage in dialogue with their customers at some stage, but it is not the individual local government purchaser that will be able to influence the range of the global provider's product lines. The global provider will carry a big responsibility in producing the 'right' services that governments want, but governments cannot, in fact, be sure of that. Often the global provider will have a number of markets to sell to (Microsoft sells the same kind of computer software to private companies, non-profit organizations and individual customers).

BOX 6.2 THE RISE OF A GLOBAL SERVICE PROVIDER

Group 4 Securicor is now the second largest provider of security services in the world. The company is a merger between Group 4 Falck and the British company Securicor. Group 4 Falck was itself a merger between the Danish company Falck and the British company Group 4 Securicor. Falck was an old Danish family-owned firm before it became listed on the Danish stock exchange in the late 1980s. In the 1990s Falck expanded its operations and activities to several other countries. When Falck merged with Group 4, the services were expanded to include security on a large scale. Group 4 Falck was responsible for security services in Iraq and Israel, and bought the American prison company Wackenhut. Today, Group 4 Securicor provides security in more than a hundred countries and has 230,000 employees worldwide.

(Roberts (2004), Greve and Ejersbo (2005) and www.falck.com, www.group4secuicor.com)

MANAGING THE ECOLOGY OF PROVIDERS

It is one thing to manage the direct contractual relationship between a purchaser and provider. As we have seen in this book, this might be a complex affair. It is another matter to make sure that there continue to be sufficient providers in the marketplace, and that one type of provider does not dominate the others. Frumkin (2002) refers to this challenge as preserving a mixed organizational ecology. One would think that the market itself took care of that, but Frumkin sees it as a special part of contract management to develop and maintain a solid ecology of providers:

> Preserving room for both non-profit and for-profit service providers across a range of fields, at least for now, must be viewed as a managerial imperative, given the generally poor state of current knowledge about when and under what circumstances one kind of provider is likely to serve the public interest better than the other.
>
> (Frumkin 2002: 67)

Non-profit and for-profit providers differ in a number of ways. Non-profits may enjoy the legitimacy connected to their mission and to their organizational history, but for-profit companies often have the resources with which to underline their arguments. According to Frumkin, non-profits and for-profits differ on availability of capital (for-profits have lots of it, non-profits do not), access to power (for-profits engage in lobbying, non-profits hold back on this and are also prohibited by legislation in some instances), compensation and human resources (for-profits can hire whom they want because they are able to pay a competitive salary, non-profits do not have the same possibilities), and normative constraints (non-profits have a clear identity and strong commitment from staff while for-profits are more oriented towards efficiency and effectiveness) (Frumkin 2002: 68–76).

There is a real challenge in managing the organizational ecology of provider organizations. For local government, the challenge may be overwhelming. A local government purchaser will have enough to cope with if it just wants to get an overview of, say, a social service market. There may be non-profit providers, but also a challenger from the for-profit provider side. Keeping an eye on providers in a single area may be a daunting task in itself, so how can local government be expected to think ahead and plan for the provider situation in a few years' time? The answer may lie in the appropriate level of government for taking on such a responsibility. Individual local governments (let alone individual contract managers) may not be sufficiently capable of overseeing markets of providers, so the responsibility must be placed somewhere else. The main responsibility could lie with the National Competition Agency: to oversee the stock of providers, and to make sure that an appropriate institutional framework for competition exists. International organizations, such as the European Union, are, of course, also concerned with the level of competition and the number of areas where competition exists. Interest groups, especially industry interest groups, also show a natural interest in maintaining the level of competition – and an appropriate level of competitors. Sometimes it is the smaller businesses' associations that are most on the edge of thinking in creating competition, as they represent the 'challengers' in Fligstein's term.

Global providers need not be only large for-profit companies. Some of the well-known international relief organizations are, in fact, global non-profit providers, such as the Red Cross.

Managing the organizational ecology of providers is about preserving a healthy level of competition continuously, and to aware if any of the types of providers are either being too dominant (e.g. large global providers) or risk becoming extinct (e.g. small and local non-profit providers).

CONCLUSIONS

This chapter has examined the market side of public service provision. Markets are made and shaped politically. The markets as a politics metaphor has been put forward by Fligstein, who argues that politics create markets (through property rights, governance structures and rules of exchange), and political struggle within the marketplace – both as struggles to control the marketplace and as struggles within firms on strategy and direction – forms the ways markets are institutionalized.

Providers are both for-profit private companies, but also not-for-profit social organizations that deliver public services through contracting arrangements. Private providers may be divided into 'incumbents', organizations that are already in the marketplace; and 'challengers', organizations wanting to enter the market. There is also a distinction between recently privatized companies, and companies that have been in the private sector for a long time and know the rules of the game.

Global public service provision is on the rise. Roberts (2004) has described the trend towards 'transborder service systems' where global companies deliver standardized products to different public sectors all over the world. The trend equals the much

109

discussed McDonaldization in the private sector, where standardized products are sold all over the world. In some industries, for example, in IT hardware and software, globalization is already familiar to the public sector, but in other sectors the age of the global service provider of public services has only just begun.

DISCUSSION QUESTIONS

1   Try to name the most vivid providers in your area of expertise. How are the providers structured? Is it a local provider, a national provider, a global provider?
2   Compare the market for employment services to the market for childcare services. What kind of a market is it? A stable market, a new market, a crisis market?
3   What would you consider to be the optimal mix of providers (for-profit, non-profit, public, network) in your area of expertise?
4   Can you think of a strategy for managing the ecology of providers, as suggested by Frumkin (2002), in social areas compared to markets for care of the elderly?
5   What are the main contract management challenges in stable markets as opposed to new markets (or crisis markets)?
6   What are the strategies for maintaining a healthy level of competition and a vibrant organizational ecology of providers in your policy area(s)?

REFERENCES

Almqvist, R. and O. Högberg (2005) Public–private partnerships in social services: the example of the city of Stockholm, in G. Hodge and C. Greve (eds) *The Challenge of Public–Private Partnerships. Learning from International Experience*. Cheltenham: Edward Elgar.

Chalmers, J. and G. Davis (2001) Rediscovering implementation: public sector contracting and human services, *Australian Journal of Public Administration* 60(2): 74–85.

Considine, M. (2001) *Enterprising States*. Melbourne: Cambridge University Press.

Considine, M. and J. Lewis (1999) Governance at the ground level: the front-line bureaucrat in the age of markets and networks, *Public Administration Review* 59(6): 467–480.

Considine, M. and J. Lewis (2003) Bureaucracy, network, or enterprise? Comparing models of governance in Australia, Britain, the Netherlands, and New Zealand, *Public Administration Review* 63(2): 131–140.

Dunleavy, P. (1997) 'The globalization of public services production: can governments be "best in the world?"', in A. Massey (ed.) *Globalization and Marketization of Public Services*. London: Macmillan.

Entwhistle, J. and S. Martin (2005) From competition to collaboration in public service delivery: a new agenda for research, *Public Administration* 83(1): 233–245.

Erhvervs og Byggestyrelsen (2006) *Guide til afknopning*. Copenhagen: Erhvervs og Byggestyrelsen.

Fligstein, N. (1996) Markets as politics: a political-cultural approach to market institutions, *American Sociological Review* 61(4): 656–673.

Fligstein, N. (2001) *The Architecture of Markets*. Princeton, NJ: Princeton University Press.

Frumkin, P. (2002) Service contracting with nonprofit and for-profit providers: on preserving a mixed organizational ecology, in J. Donahue and J. Nye (eds) *Market-based Governance. Supply Side, Demand Side, Upside and Downside*. Washington, DC: Brookings.

Greve, C. and N. Ejersbo (2005) From local partnering to global partnering?, in G. Hodge and C. Greve (eds) *The Challenge of Public–Private Partnerships. Learning from International Experience*. Cheltenham: Edward Elgar.

Greve, C. and K. Viborg Andersen (2001) Management of telecommunication service provision: an analysis of the Tele Denmark company 1990–1998, *Public Management Review. An International Journal of Research and Theory* 3(1): 35–52.

Hodge, G. *et al.* (eds) (2004) *Power Progress*. Monash: Monash University Press.

Kettl, D.F. (1993) *Sharing Power, Public Governance and Private Markets*. Washington, DC: Brookings.

Light, P.C. (2000) *Making Nonprofits Work. A Report on The Tides of Nonprofit Management Reform*. Washington DC: Brookings.

Martin, S. (2000) Implementing best value. Local public services in transition, *Public Administration* 78(1): 209–227.

Milward, H.B. and K.G. Provan (2000) Governing the hollow state, *Journal of Public Administration Research and Theory* 10(2): 359–379.

Moore, M. (2002) Privatized public management, in J. Donahue and J.S. Nye (eds) *Market-based Governance*. Washington, DC: Brookings.

Oppen, M., D. Sack and A. Wegener (2005) German public–private partnerships in personal social services: new directions in a corporatist environment, in G. Hodge and C. Greve (eds) *The Challenge of Public–Private Partnerships. Learning from International Experience*. Cheltenham: Edward Elgar.

Peters, B.G. (1996) *The Future of Governance. Four Emergent Models*. Lawrence: University of Kansas Press.

Roberts, A. (2004) *Transborder Service Systems: Pathways for Innovation or Threats to Acccountability?* Arlington, VA: IBM Center for the Business of Government.

Romzek, B. and Johnston, J.M. (2002) Effective contract implementation and management. A preliminary model, *Journal of Public Administration Research and Theory* 12(3): 423–453.

Salamon, L.M. (1995) *Partners in Public Service. Government–Nonprofit Relations in the Modern Welfare State*. Baltimore, MD: Johns Hopkins University Press.

Sands, V. (2004) Victoria's partly-privatized prison system. An acountability report card, *Asia Pacific Journal of Public Administration* 26(2): 135–154.

Sanger, M.B. (2003) *The Welfare Marketplace*. Washington, DC: Brookings.

Terry, F. (2001) The nemesis of privatization. Railway policy in retrospect, *Public Money and Management* 21(1): 2–4.

Van Slyke, D. (2003) The mythology of privatization in contracting for social services, *Public Administration Review* 63(3): 296–315.

Walsh, K. (1995) *Public Services and Market Mechanisms*. London: Macmillan.

FURTHER READING

Peters' *The Future of Governing* (Kansas: University of Kansas Press, 1996) provides a good overview of 'the market model' for public service delivery. Fligstein's (2001) *The Architecture of Markets* sociological work on markets from an institutional perspective makes an interesting addition to the voluminous literature on markets for service delivery. Sanger (2002) *The Welfare Marketplace* gives a good description of the dynamics behind private companies wanting to gain access to markets for public services. Lester Salamon has written extensively on non-profit organizations and third party government. The volume by Salamon, *Partners in Public Service* (Baltimore: Johns Hopkins University Press, 1995) is a collection of his many important articles. The work by Roberts, *Transborder Service Systems: Pathways for Innovation or Threats to Accountability?* (IBM Center for the Business of Government, 2004) needs to be studied as a case of transborder service systems for public service organizations.

Chapter 7

Public–private partnerships

LEARNING OBJECTIVES

By the end of this chapter you should:

■ be aware of the different meanings of public–private partnerships;

■ be able to distinguish between different forms of partnerships;

■ understand the relationship between (traditional) contracting and (new) partnerships; and

■ have a clear sense of the evidence related to the empirical experience with partnerships.

KEY POINTS OF THIS CHAPTER

■ Public–private partnerships are best viewed as a continuation of the policy of integrating the private sector in public service delivery.

■ The focus on risk-sharing and organizational innovation is what separates public–private partnerships from traditional contracting.

■ Public–private partnerships are best seen as a smart way of contracting rather than a completely new alternative to contracting.

KEY TERMS

■ **Public–private partnerships** – cooperation of some sort of durability between public and private actors in which they jointly develop products and services and share risk, cost and resources which are connected with these products (Van Ham and Koppenjan 2001: 598).

■ **Economic partnerships or private finance initiative (PFI) partnerships** – models for cooperation between public sector and private sector actors over construction, finance and maintenance of infrastructure projects such as building and running a hospital, a school, a prison or a transport facility.

■ **Social partnerships** – partnerships in a variety of policy areas between public sector actors and private sector actors that have some durability (i.e. not a short-term contract) and that involve joint service production or development as well as some element of risk management.

■ **Public–private partnership policy** – the activities and strategies which governments and other organizations undertake in order to promote and implement public–private partnerships.

This chapter examines the increasing use of 'partnering' and public–private partnerships (PPPs) between the public sector and the private sector and between groups of provider organizations in consortiums. While traditional contracting for public services has often been associated with hard, principal–agent contracting with emphasis on narrow performance targets, the movement towards softer, relational contracts has emphasized mutual trust and cooperation as essential features – and an extension of this kind of contract may be found in the debate on PPPs. This chapter explores how contract managers can facilitate and encourage partnering between purchasers and providers, and between providers internally. Partnerships pose some of the biggest challenges to contracting for public services because – ideally – it is about building long-lasting relationships based on trust and mutual dependencies. There are many questions that arise from the introduction of PPPs. Some of the key questions include why PPPs occurred and what value they bring with them (Broadbent *et al.* 2003). 'Why establish PPPs?' seems to be an important question because the contracting phenomenon was already there, so why invent something new or similar? In other words, there has to be a special reason to talk about partnering instead of just talking plainly about contracting. Second, what value they bring with them (the other part of Broadbent's question) is also of high importance since there has to be a special added value that the partnership form can bring with it that traditional contracting could not deliver. That special purpose is what we are looking to explore more in this chapter.

The chapter is divided into the following sections. The first section defines PPPs. The second discusses PPPs in the perspective of the contract management model presented in Chapter 2. The third section evaluates the empirical findings on PPPs. The fourth section describes the current discussions in the PPP literature. The fifth section concludes if PPPs are a real alternative to traditional contracting out. The sixth section summarizes the findings.

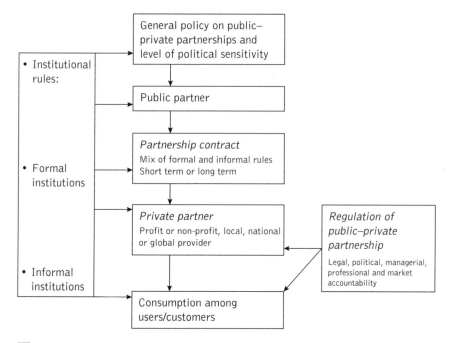

Figure 7.1 *Partnering for public service delivery.*

DEFINING PUBLIC—PRIVATE PARTNERSHIPS

Public—private partnerships are 'cooperation of some sort of durability between public and private actors in which they jointly develop products and services or products and share risk, cost and resources which are connected with these products' (Van Ham and Koppenjan 2001: 598). This is one definition (out of many) to start off with. The definition tells us that PPPs are new because:

■ *Cooperation*: PPPs involve cooperation. The relationship is not one that is formed around competition as was traditional contracting. Cooperation is the keyword in any definition of partnerships. Cooperation means that we have to look for other types of relationships than principal—agent relationships to begin with. One may say that both the public partner and the private partner are 'principals' in some sense, because they both have something to contribute to the partnership. They are also 'agents' in theory because they will both be expected to be engaged in the implementation process one way or another. The usual principal—agent relationship where a principal directs an agent to perform certain tasks does not apply to a PPP. The partnership joint production is sometimes portrayed as building on some form of a trust-based relationship between organizations, a more visible risk-sharing, and a

115

focus on mutual innovation between the public and the private sector. Most importantly, perhaps, organizations are seen as partners that share a specific objective. The
division between a purchaser that wants a service delivered, and a provider that
delivers the service, is dissolved in a way. Instead of competition, cooperation is very
much the focus in PPPs.

- *Durability*: Cooperation is supposed to take place over a certain period of time. PPP
  contracts are expected to last for 'a longer period of time'. Theoretically, there is
  no fixed period that could define a PPP. Empirically, PPP contracts typically run
  from 15 to 20 years up to 50 to 60 years, but in the UK they can also be of shorter
  duration. There is a huge variety in the durability of PPP contracts. Why this length
  of time? Because one of the key reasons for PPPs is that private capital becomes
  available for building public projects, and in writing off debt and paying an interest
  rate, there has to be a sufficient time period in which to do that. So the 'durability'
  is more empirically than theoretically defined.

- *Joint production and/or development*: Public and private actors commit themselves to
  do a project that could not be done by one of them alone. There is much talk about
  'synergy effects' and 'innovation' in the literature on PPPs. In traditional contracting, the purchaser is supposed to know what to buy and to specify exact performance
  targets. It is then up to the provider (the agent) to carry out the task as envisaged
  by the principal. There is little room for independent improvement and independent
  action because most of the relevant targets will be specified in the contract. In a PPP
  there is no such absolute certainty about the targets from the beginning. Rather, the
  performance targets are up for some negotiation. Public partners want to find out
  if the private partners have any ideas on how to make improvements, and they want
  to incorporate those improvements into the contracts.

- *Sharing of costs and resources*: 'Sharing' is here really about altering the ways in which
  purchasers and providers split the bill or find out about the financial arrangements.
  In a traditional contract the purchaser pays for the service and the provider delivers.
  The purchaser has already got the money (usually from collecting taxes). Payments
  can vary according to the amount and quality of services delivered, but that is mostly
  up to the purchaser to decide the terms of the payment process. In PPPs (what we
  refer to as economic PPPs or PFI-type partnerships), the government requires
  private finance to build a new piece of infrastructure (e.g. a school, a hospital, a
  prison). The private partner provides the capital, builds the infrastructure and
  sometimes manages the infrastructure afterwards (facility management), and the
  role of the government is more of an 'arranger' of services and as a dialogue partner.
  The 'sharing of resources' in most economic partnerships is related to the private
  partner providing the financing, and the government is coming up with the initial
  project outline and the loose specifications for what the final product or service
  might look like. In other types of partnerships (social partnerships), the public and
  the private partner may inject resources into a common project organization or a
  mutual company. Here both will provide financial resources, and both will commit

staff to work on the project side by side. It is important to note that the government (or the public) will pay for the project eventually. It is not as though PPP projects are paid for by the private sector. The private sector delivers financial resources, but the money has to paid back over the 30-year period or so. This is similar to when you buy a new car the bank will lend you the money, but you have to pay for the car yourself ultimately through a regular pay-back of the money the bank lent to you. Private sector companies often claim that they have a lot to offer in terms of innovation, but they are not allowed to divulge their knowledge to the public sector due to the strict performance measures. In PPPs, the private sector can get into a dialogue with public sector organizations. Cooperation goes on through other phases of the policy process, especially the implementation process. Public sector organizations and private sector organizations continue to work together on issues of implementation matters in partnership arrangements whereas that is not always the case in traditional contracting. Innovation concerns both new organizational processes, and also the services themselves. New ways of delivering services are at the heart of the PPP approach. Saving money is not always important, but making innovation in public service is.

■ *Risk*: Sharing risks is one of the key characteristics associated with PPPs. Risks may be anything from financial risks, to construction risks, to governance risks (see Box 7.3 for examples of risk types from Victoria, Australia). There is also the wider perspective on 'governance' risks (Hodge 2005). It is not as though there was not any risk in traditional contracting. It is more the case that the risks were recognized silently beforehand, ignored or not focused upon as much. With PPPs, identifying and managing risks have become a key part of the partnering process. Who should bear the risks associated with a large PPP project of designing, financing, building and operating a new hospital? The common answer is that the risks should be borne by the parties most appropriate to bear those risks. In practice that is not always so easy to identify. The government is often likely to assume a number of risks that could be shared or perhaps transferred to the private sector. A good example is the construction of the metro extension project in Copenhagen, Denmark, where the government and the city of Copenhagen have openly committed themselves to bear 'all other relevant risks associated with building the metro', which could be an almost endless list of possible things that could go wrong with the metro (e.g. flooding, erosion of tunnels). The risks also tell you something about the partners that can enter a PPP contract. A small and newly started company may have more difficulty sharing big risks than would a major global company. The government's shoulders are likely to act as a bulwark against most risks, but the private partner may vary a lot in how much risk-sharing he or she can engage in.

■ *Gain-sharing or blame-sharing*: Implicit in the above definition is that both parties have a stake in the final result which also means that they must assume responsibility. If the project turns out to be successful, both parties should be able to show visible gains. If the project goes wrong, both parties should be prepared to take some of

117

the blame. What is not often remembered in PPP definitions is that there may be a need for an outside arbitrator or a regulatory system that backs up the partnership agreement (see the extended discussion below).

It is not as though a number of these elements were not found in the contracting literature previously. This is also what people refer to when they claim that there is nothing 'new' in PPPs and that PPPs are merely a new concept for a very old idea of collaborative arrangements between the public and the private sector (Wettenhall 2003, 2005). There is some merit to that argument (which we discuss further in this chapter), but the main argument for PPPs has been that PPPs then highlight these elements in combination – contrary to traditional contracting where there may be some cooperation and trust concerning individual contracts, but where most contractual relationships were formed in a context of competition and privatization. What is new about PPPs is that coherent policies are beginning to be designed and implemented on public–private interaction. Where previously there were individual organizational arrangements (as in Wettenhall's many historical examples), there are now government-sponsored policies that suggest actions and set-up institutions to deal with PPPs. And that's new!

Table 7.1 *Contracting out and public–private partnerships*

	Contracting out	Public–private partnerships
Theme	Competition	Cooperation
Roles of public and private actors	Purchasers and providers	Partners
Main driver	Cost reductions, ideology, innovation	Cost reductions, innovation
Contract duration	Short-term contracts	Long-term contracts
Service delivery	Full responsibility of the provider once contract is signed	Mutual responsibility for joint service production
Resources	Allocation of resources from public purchaser to private provider	Use of private finance in order to establish service or infrastructure
Risk	If risk is acknowledged, it is transferred to provider	Sharing of risk, allocation of particular forms of risk to the most adequate partner
Results	Key innovations in the hands of the provider unless otherwise stated in contract	Key innovations shared according to agreement in partnership contract

Sources: Klijn and Teisman (2002) and own development.

FORMS OF PUBLIC–PRIVATE PARTNERSHIPS

PPPs come in many shapes and forms. There seems to be two major types of partnerships discussed in the literature and experience in practice: economic partnerships and social partnerships (Hodge and Greve 2005). They have each come to signify a special type of partnering relationship (see Box 7.1).

In recent years, economic partnerships have tended to dominate much of the writing of PPPs. By economic partnerships I here refer to partnerships where private sector actors participate in designing, financing, building and operating a service or an infra-structure project (i.e. a new school building, a hospital, a prison, a motorway, a bridge) together with public sector actors. They include variations of:

- design
- build
- finance
- own
- operate
- manage
- transfer

In the UK, economic partnerships have come to be known as private finance initiative (PFI) partnerships. The UK experience with financial PPPs is perhaps the most developed in all nations. The British Treasury defines a PFI-type partnership as an arrangement where:

> the public sector contracts to purchase quality services on a long-term basis so as to take advantage of private sector management skills, incentivised by having private

BOX 7.1 FORMS OF PUBLIC–PRIVATE PARTNERSHIPS

- DBO: Design, build, operate.
- DFBO: Design, finance, build, operate.
- BOO: Build, own, operate
- BOOT: Build, own, operate, transfer
- O&M: Operate, maintenance
- LBO: Lease, build, operate
- BBO: Buy, build, operate

(Savas 2000: 246)

119

finance at risk. This includes concessions and franchises where a private sector partner takes on the responsibility for providing a public service, including maintaining, enhancing or constructing the necessary infrastructure.

(HM Treasury 2003)

In October 2005 there were signed contracts for more than 700 PFI-type partnerships in the UK according to Partnerships UK (HM Treasury 2006: 3). Around 450 of the projects were in their operational phase or completed. In 2006, the UK Treasury mentioned that 200 projects were in the pipeline over the following five years, and that the projects were worth 26 billion GBP in capital value (HM Treasury 2006: 1).

According to the UK Treasury itself, the results of the PFI policy have meant that the users are satisfied (79 per cent say that projects are delivered to satisfaction always, or nearly always), that public authorities are reporting good overall performance, that the services contracted for are appropriate, and that incentivizations within PFI projects are working (HM Treasury 2006: 1).

Much of the literature in UK public administration and public management is about PFI-type partnerships where governments contract with a private partner to finance or build a new hospital, for example, or some form of government infrastructure. The early experience was analysed by Francis Terry (1996) among others. Terry concluded that PFIs posed risks for the government, that private organizations are not always inherently more efficient than public organzations in all areas, that the transfer of risks is complicated and not easy to judge for the government, and that the total sum of the projects might not be cheaper than they were in the public sector. Later Broadbent and Laughlin (2005) saw the PFI as an integral part of the UK modernization programme for the public sector, and they concluded that PFI could best be seen as a 'modernity' plan for the public sector with the justification often being sought in macro-economic terms. The contracts in UK PFI deals are highly complex, and the 'private partner' may, in fact, be a consortium of a number of providers and sub-providers engaged in constructing new infrastructure. The 'finance' part is usually very important in these types of PPPs. Gaining access to private finance has been regarded in this literature as the key added value to PPPs compared to previous public–private interorganizational forms. The process of using private finance to achieve public ends in the UK has been analysed extensively by Rob Ball and colleagues (Ball et al. 2000, 2003). They found that innovation was more the exception than the rule, and that more local community participation and consultation was needed in PFI projects. They also found that there is an asymmetry in the risk transfer question, and that the private sector seems to be getting all the benefits while the public sector people have difficulty imposing penalties on private sector firms if anything goes wrong.

Another strand of partnerships is social partnerships. By social partnerships I mean partnerships where public and private actors come together to jointly produce goods and services for a longer period of time and in doing so share risks and resources and gains. The exact organizational form of this cooperation is very much an open question. The

120

Table 7.2 *Typology of public–private partnerships*

Finance and organization/ policy area	Finance important, organizational structure less important and not so different from traditional infrastructure contracts	Finance less important, organizational relations in networks important
Infrastructure (building of schools, hospitals, prisons)	Economic/PFI-type partnerships	'Partnership light' model (collaboration with traditional government financing behind)
Other policy areas (social policy, housing policy)	Joint financing of new areas	Social partnerships

'project organization' is the preferred organizational tool in many forms of collaboration. One extreme is to form a joint company together and commit to a common destiny. Another extreme is to cooperate more loosely and not commit organizationally, but more spiritually to each other around a common core of ideas or policies, and let a loose network be the only organizational basis that binds the partners to the contract (broadly understood) together. Many of the recent experiments in networks between public and private actors may be seen as PPPs. The network perspective on PPPs has recently been developed in the literature by authors such as Klijn and Teisman (2005) and Skelcher (2004). The network perspective has been promoted at the local governance level and OECD has established a Forum on Partnerships and Local Governance. Here PPPs are a more loose configuration that can accommodate many concrete forms of collaboration between public sector and private sector actors.

Sometimes it is as if there are two literatures and two practices. The PFI discussions have moved on from deciding how private finance may be obtained to how complex contracts may be operated, and how sub-provider (the operations part) will be managed. The social partnership literature and practice has progressed from discussion about how joint organizations could be formed to meet new needs to how networks can be designed and operated innovatively at various levels of government. Obviously there are different contractual challenges involved in the two discussions. One challenge is how the government can oversee a complex set of sub-providers and write robust contracts that will take into consideration all the legal and financial implications in dealing with a financial and construction consortium. Another challenge is to write contracts that will allow a multi-member network organization and leave space for an anticipated innovative capability.

Contracting does not go away because there is a PPP. Most PPPs are not simply established by a close encounter between a public partner and a private partner, but instead PPP contracts have been competitively tendered – and the private actor that wins the contract receives the right to form a partnership with the government.

121

PUBLIC–PRIVATE PARTNERSHIPS AND THE CONTRACT MANAGEMENT MODEL

In terms of the model of contract management presented in Chapter 2, how does partnering for public action differ from the more traditional contracting out approach?

The policy perspective

PPPs began to appear on the policy in the late 1990s (Osborne 2000). They are now a part of a global spread of PPPs (Ghabedian *et al.* 2004; Hodge and Greve 2005). First, the policy can be built on the previous contracting out policy. As contracting out policies became exhausted, policy-makers, providers and purchasers began to look for a new label that could reinvigorate the contracting phenomenon. 'Privatization' was also an exhausted concept. Increasingly, the partnership idea began to create excitement in policy-making circles in governments around the world, in consultancy firms, and with purchasers and providers. The partnership label simply seemed more appealing than merely contracting to a broad range of stakeholders. Seen in this light, PPPs are more a fancy label to describe modern contracting practices.

Second, it may be seen as a new set of policies emphasizing the involvement of private finance in public infrastructure projects in a more systematic way. In the UK, the PPP debate began with the private finance initiative under the Conservative government in the early 1990s. In 1992 John Major's government announced plans to invite more private finance into the public service delivery and especially new public infrastructure. The Major government wanted to show a more sympathetic approach to public services than the previous Thatcher government, but it did not want to raise taxes to do so. Many British schools and hospitals needed injections of cash, but the government was not prepared to pay and raise taxes. The private finance initiative seemed an appropriate response to this dilemma: promise more and better public infrastructure and let the private sector finance the expansion – so the government could pay the money back over a longer time period. The Blair government was elected in 1997 on a 'third-way' plat-form that very much emphasized the partnership theme. The Blair government decided to carry on with the PFI scheme, but put an end to its universal and uncritical use in the public sector (Broadbent *et al.* 2003). The Blair government moved quickly to reassure the investors in the private sector that the scheme's principal ideas were to be continued. The whole partnership rhetoric emphasized cooperation much more than competition, and the policy on contracting out was changed too – from CCT to best value (Entwhistle and Martin 2005). Contracting out (best value) and PPP (PFI) policies were kept as separate policies under the New Labour government.

The policy of partnerships has a long pedigree in public policy in other countries. Organizational arrangements in the United States have often been referred to as PPPs. Donald Kettl (1993) referred to public–private partnerships in characterizing the public policy initiatives in the US after the Second World War. Research on local and urban development and governance has used the term 'PPPs' for a long time (Pierre 1998).

When the PFI debate exploded in the early part of the 2000s, the PPP was on every government's public policy agenda. International organizations began to pick up interest too. The World Bank (2004) has discussed PPPs in transport policy. The European Commission (2004) issued a Green Paper on public–private partnerships. The European Commission (2004: 3) described the PPP phenomenon in the following way:

> The term public–private partnership (PPP) is not defined at Community level. In general, the term refers to forms of cooperation between public authorities and the world of business which aim to ensure the funding, construction, renovation, management, or maintenance of an infrastructure or the provision of a service.

Note that the definition only points to 'the world of business' and that non-profit organizations' relations with government, or the more experimental partnerships where little finance is involved, seem to be downplayed in the Commission's approach to the partnership concept.

The Commission adds that the most common elements related to PPPs are the long duration of the contract, the method of funding, the important role of the economic operator, and risk management (European Commission 2004: 3).

The Commission has recently made recommendations in the area of PPPs. Its main concern is how the idea and practice of PPPs relate to the European Union rules and policies on effective competition and how it relates to 'legal clarity' (European Commission 2004: 5). The key problem is that the European Union wants to improve effective competition among firms from the member states.

The OECD discussed PPPs in its recent overview, *Modernising Government*. It refers to PPPs as:

> arrangements whereby the private sector finances, designs, builds, maintains and operates infrastructure assets traditionally provided by the public sector. PPPs can also involve the private sector purchasing already existing infrastructure assets and redevelop them. Public–private partnerships bring a single private sector entity to undertake to provide public infrastructure assets for their 'whole of life' (generally 20–30 years).
>
> (OECD 2005: 131)

As we have seen, this definition only covers some of the PPP organizational population, namely the economic partnerships.

Countries where PPP policy is most developed outside the UK include Canada, the Netherlands and Australia. Canada has the Canadian Council for Public–Private Partnerships. The Council defines PPPs as 'A cooperative venture between public and private sectors, built on the expertise of each partner, that best meets clearly defined public needs through the appropriate allocation of resources, risks and rewards' (Canadian Council for Public–Private Partnerships at www.pppcouncil.ca/aboutPPP_definition.asp accessed 23 January 2006).

All these countries have special entities devoted to the promotion of PPP policy: Kenniscentrum in the Netherlands, Partnerships UK in Britain and the Department of Treasury and Finance in Victoria. Australia has an impressive history of PPPs already. PPPs are mostly found in New South Wales and Victoria. The government of Victoria wants to see the following criteria met in PPPs:

- outputs clearly specified, including measurable performance standards;
- the government making payments only upon delivery of the specified services to the required standards;
- a relatively long-term commitment, with the term depending on the nature of the project;
- one or more private parties being fully accountable to the government for delivery of the specified services;
- risk allocation between the parties being clear and enforceable, with consequential financial outcomes;
- clear articulation of the government's responsibilities with respect to the monitoring of outcomes; and
- inclusion of mechanisms for delivering ongoing value for money throughout the life of the project.

(Department of Treasury and Finance, Victoria, Australia 2000: 5)

Countries such as Denmark, Germany, Sweden and New Zealand seem to adopt a more reluctant approach to PPPs. But Germany especially seems to be pursuing PFI-type PPPs (see http://www.kommunaler-wettbewerb.de/). They have not built as many economic partnerships as the leading PPP countries such as Britain, Canada and Australia.

Strategic purchasing and communication (or the public partner's perspective)

In PPPs the public role is not so much a strategic purchaser as an interested partner. The key insight from theories of PPPs is that both partners are not sure of the output they want to reach, but they want to leave some space to find out what the exact output is going to be in mutuality. It is a mutual task for public and private partners to find out what they want. Therefore, both partners are 'strategic purchasers' in a sense; it is not a role reserved for only the public part. In theory, the partners must find out in common what they want to achieve. In practice it will often be the government which has some idea for a project. Instead of trying to specify the targets beforehand, the government is supposed to be interested in what new ideas the private sector is capable of coming up with. Likewise, the private sector organization is assumed to be eager to present its ideas of improvements to the public sector. Sometimes the partners will simply team up to start work on a new project together. In practice most of the partnership agreements will only be entered after a competitive tender process where private actors can bid to become the public sector organization's preferred partner. The recent rules of 'competitive dialogue' in the European Union are supposed to support the way that governments and private sector organizations can join forces in partnerships.

The contract in partnerships

The contract at the outset is meant to be relational in theory. Partners are going to be open to discuss what the contents of the contract should be. In theory, it should be a trust-based partnership where no one wants to get too many details down on paper from the outset. In reality, things have turned out to be different. Contractual explorations exist on the basis of a neoclassical contract. I call that 'relational contract with a twist of neoclassical contracts'. Some parts of the contract may be open for further revision and negotiation, but there is still a black-letter formal contract that lays the ground for the cooperation. Lawyers on both sides make sure that many contractual clauses and details are in place. This feature has made some observers reluctant to call partnerships new because they think that many so-called partnership agreements are, in fact, familiar principal–agent type contracts. The innovation part of the cooperation is to find places other than in the concrete contract.

A main difference is the length of the contract. Many PFI-type contracts last up to 30 years or longer. This gives a new perspective to the contracting process. There is a special challenge in designing and signing a 30-year contract. The government has to examine as many contingencies as possible beforehand. This leaves a huge task for lawyers and legal experts. The government must make sure it does not do anything wrong in signing a long-term contract. During the contract period, the contract has to specify how governments may intervene or propose changes, and how the working relationship with the private partner should be conducted. The private partner has to secure some autonomy from precisely that intervention during the contract period. There must also be a clause on how to terminate the contract, a fact often overseen by the parties to a contract (Cooper 2003). A further important challenge is to specify in the contract the relationship between the main partner or contractor and the subcontractors. In highly complex PFI deals this is especially important. The subcontractors may not have the same 'close' relationship to the public partner that the main partner or contractor has, and so the subcontractor may look at the relationship in a more straightforward business perspective. That could potentially undermine the whole partnership idea, but it is a realistic challenge to be taken into account. 'Getting the contract right' is therefore a huge challenge in PPPs (Evans and Bowman 2005).

The providers (or private partners)

In a PPP, the provider is not always the private organization alone, but often fulfils its job in close cooperation with the public organization. In other instances there may still be a private provider, but one that works in cooperation and partnership with the public part. Adopting Cooper's terms, the relationship may be horizontal in its initial understanding, but the public part will still have a vertical commitment to attend to (and so it cannot be a truly horizontal public–private partnership).

Often there will be several providers and sub-providers. In a typical PFI-type contract, there will be a construction company in charge of constructing a building, a financing company in charge of financing the deal, and a facility management company that is supposed to run the project for the 30-year period. The building of a school in Trehøje in Denmark may serve as an example. The local government contracted with a consultancy company to make a feasibility study. The local government then competitively bid out the contract to design, finance, build, own and operate the school building. The bids attracted interest from 19 consortia. Five consortia were invited to participate in a competitive dialogue with the local government. On the basis of this material and the dialogue, the local government of Trehøje chose its partner. The partner consortium consisted of a Danish building company, a German bank and a Danish maintenance/operating company. The roles of these providers each has its own function. The bank provides the finance capital. The constructing company builds the school. The operating company is supposed to maintain and operate the building for the next 30 years. The company has committed itself to adapt to new ideas during the period of the contract. After the 30-year period, the responsibility for the school will be turned over to the local government again.

Customers

Customers should be indifferent to whether a partnership or a contract provider delivers the services. There are some instances where the customer could be invited into a dialogue, but that has not been a primary goal in partnerships up until now. In the case of the school in Trehøje mentioned above, the primary customers are the people who are going to use the school buildings: the teachers and the pupils. The representative for the customers is the school headmaster. The customer in a wider sense is the local government which is buying and paying for the services from the contractor. The taxpayers of the local government are also customers in a sense because their taxes will be reduced or spent better if the deal is financially superior to what the local government could have reached through a traditional construction deal (which is the main argument of the PPP advocates).

Regulation of public–private partnerships

Regulation is a challenge in economic partnerships due to the technical, economic and juridical complexity of the contracts and the partnership deals. As experiences with partnership agreements is ongoing, and few long-term contracts have reached their conclusion, the scope of the tasks of regulation has yet to be explored fully.

The objective of regulation of a partnership can be the basis for some controversy. Is it the final or medium-term – or ongoing – output that should be regulated? Is it the behaviour and the actions of the PPP that should be regulated? Or is it the process of the partnership relationship that should be the subject of the regulation? Other areas of interest could be the 'market entry' part, where governments may regulate how the process of selecting partners take place, and how it is determined by what criteria the partnership selection takes place.

Regulation is often left to regulators. These regulators could be national audit offices (see, for example, the experience of the UK National Audit Office) or auditor generals. The National Audit Office is building up a reputation for an early and professional regulation of PPPs in the UK. The auditor general in Victoria, Australia also has a good insight into the partnership agreements. Regulation is still done on a contract-by-contract basis for PPPs in many countries. Regulation of PPPs remains focused on the contract itself. There is no statutory basis for the regulation as such. There is a huge challenge in general for regulation and regulators to adjust to these new organizational forms of PPPs.

Institutional context

It tends to vary as to how well formal and informal rules on PPPs are wired into the fabric of individual countries. The UK legislative framework is perhaps the most developed. The Blair government moved quickly to commit itself to the PPP policy and to establish a credible institutional framework (Broadbent *et al.* 2003). Institutionally, the policy was run by an organizational entity in the Treasury. A government entity was established as a knowledge centre on PPPs. In 2000, this would turn into a PPP itself, as it is now owned by the private sector together with the public sector (HM Treasury) (known as 'Partnerships UK'). The purpose of Partnerships UK is 'to support and accelerate the delivery of infrastructure renewal, high quality public services, and the efficient use of public assets through better and stronger partnerships between the public sector and the private sector'. By December 2004, there were 670 PFI contracts with an estimated value of 141 billion GBP over 26 years (Pollitt 2005: 207; see also Corner 2005). The regulatory framework in the UK system is in the hands of the National Audit Office which is responsible for auditing in connection with PPPs (Corner 2005). The Public Accounts Committee follows up on reports made by the UK National Audit Office. There is also an Office of the Public–Private Arbiter mentioned in connection with the London Underground PPP (Flinders 2005: 227).

127

The Dutch institutional framework is well developed as is the Canadian framework. Australia is another country with a highly developed PPP framework. Australia's institutional framework was developed in the 'Partnership Victoria' policy described above. The Victorian government has also empowered the auditor general to review PPP policy as part of the institutional set-up. Other countries seem to lag behind. In particular this goes for the Scandinavian countries where a comprehensive and coherent PPP institutional framework is largely absent.

The European Union has recently issued a Green paper on PPPs, but there is still some clarification to be made. The EU calls for public–private partnership rules to be aligned with their focus on effective competition and legal clarity. This has not happened yet in Europe. The OECD suggests policy guidelines for PPPs (OECD 2005). The policy guidelines advocate some caution towards PPPs. Many countries – except for Britain – have not moved swiftly to legislate coherently about PPPs. The situation for developing countries is different because the World Bank generally endorses PPPs in the policy (World Bank 2004). Could it be that many countries are waiting for more authoritative European Union and OECD legal interpretation before they move to legislate and amend legislation in their own countries?

EMPIRICAL EXPERIENCE WITH PUBLIC–PRIVATE PARTNERSHIPS

How much added value do PPPs bring with them? The effects of economic PPPs ('PFIs') are the subject of some controversy. Naturally, governments want to present the effects in a prominent light.

PPPs are creating more value for money according to many official presentations. Some claim that the verdict on PPPs is mostly positive on balance. Projects are delivered on time and the economics of infrastructure building has been improved. Pollitt (2005), a Cambridge University economics professor, has analysed cases in the United Kingdom, and he argues that PFI projects are more cost-efficient, are delivered on time and make room for innovations. Pollitt (2005: 226) writes about the lessons from the UK PFI experience that:

> it seems difficult to avoid a positive overall assessment. The UK PFI seems to have been generally successful relative to what might have happened under conventional procurement. Projects are delivered on time and to budget a significantly higher percentage of time. Construction risks are generally transferred successfully and there is considerable design innovation.

Shaoul (2005), on the other hand, has argued that PPP projects are 'public funding of private profit', that the economic forecasts and calculations are murky and hard to judge for outsiders, and that there are huge democratic accountability problems with handing over responsibility to private contractors. There is evidence that PFI is 'big business'. Pollitt (2005: 207) reports that 43 billion GBP worth of capital was raised from the private sector.

There is also documentation that private involvement has improved services, for example, in prisons (Sands 2004). There was an early claim for efficiency and effectiveness in a study by Arthur Andersen and the London School of Economics which centred on a 17 per cent savings figure. That early investigation rested on few cases and was considered to be a very early assessment, according to Hodge (2005).

OECD (2005: 141) cites a report by the UK Treasury showing that 90 per cent of PPP projects were delivered on time (as opposed to 30 per cent of non-PPP projects) and that four-fifths of all PPP projects were delivered to budget (as opposed to only a quarter of non-PPP projects). PPP projects now account for one-tenth of the annual capital procurement in the UK (OECD 2005: 145).

Others claim that PPPs waste resources and are not adequately managed to ensure value for citizens (Shaoul 2005). The question of accountability has been addressed in several Australian research projects (e.g. Hodge 2005). Some countries (e.g. Denmark) have been reluctant to commit to a fully developed PPP policy.

The think-tank Institute of Public Policy Research had a Commission of Public–Private Partnerships working for two years, and this Commission came up with a balanced assessment, warning that PPPs should not be 'the only show in town' (IPPR 2001). While they recognized that PPPs could bring value to some sectors (notably the building of infrastructures), the Commission also stated that gains in other sectors (hospitals and schools) were less obvious. The commission's report was an important element in endorsing the continued use of PPPs by the Blair government in the UK in 2001.

BOX 7.2 PUBLIC–PRIVATE PARTNERSHIPS IN THE HEALTH SECTOR

Economic PPPs have been used in the health sector in the UK to a great extent. HM Treasury reports on 185 PFI contracts in the health sector (HM Treasury 2006). One example of a PFI contract is the Dartford and Gravesham NHS Trust in the UK. The PFI contract has been the subject of investigation by the National Audit Office, and by researchers Broadbent, Gil and Lauglin (2003).

The PFI contract was made possible due to a 'concession agreement' between two parties: the NHS Trust and the 'Hospital Company'. The Hospital Company was the legal entity set up to manage the PFI project. The Hospital Company signed two PFI contracts.

- One contract was with a construction company that was going to build the new hospital.
- Another contract was with the facilities management company that was going to manage the new hospital facilities.
- The contract with the bank to finance the buildings was made between the NHS Trust and a consortium of banks that provided the capital.
- Both the construction company and the facility management company contracted with sub-providers.

In the 'concession agreement' the NHS Trust required the Hospital Company to 'design and construct the new hospital to the design agreed by the Trust'. The private partners were given some leverage in the implementation process. The NHS had some experience in hospital building and was able to act as a 'smart buyer' to a certain degree. The project turned out to be a success in the sense that the new hospital building was completed on time and to budget. However, expectations of the architecture and the function of the new building were high, and there was considerable public debate about the final product.

The facility management part included services such as domestic services, window cleaning, portering, transport and internal security, linen and laundry, catering, switchboard and telecommunication, and external security and car-parking. Monitoring of service standards occurred on a regular basis and also involved some goodwill trust.

The financial part of the contract meant that penalties were invoked if services were not up to standard. Monthly payments from the Trust to the Hospital Company took place.

The risks in the partnership contract were divided into ten different areas: design and construction, operation, legislation/regulation, availability, volume, technology/obsolescence, disposal, termination, finance, employment. It was specified which of the parties was responsible for each risk type. Risks were monitored on a continuing basis, but were not made the subject of a specific evaluation after the hospital was built.

The case shows that there are complex contractual relationships involved in a PFI contract. There are more than the two obvious partners: the NHS Trust and the private partner. The NHS Trust has itself formed a company to handle the contract, and the 'private partner' is actually three different partners (banks, construction, facility) that also involve further subcontractors.

International organizations are sceptical too in terms of the promise from PPPs:

> while it is true that cooperation between the public and the private sectors can offer micro-economic benefits permitting execution of a project that provides value for money and meets public interest objectives, recourse to PPPs cannot be presented as a miracle solution for a public sector facing budget constraints. Experience shows that, for each project, it is necessary to assess whether the partnership offers real value compared with other options, such as the conclusion of a more traditional contract.
>
> (European Commission 2004: 4)

The OECD has followed the PPP debate as well. The OECD has not fully endorsed the PPP framework as a general recommendation for public sectors in all its member countries. A PPP is considered to be one out of several elements in the use of market-type mechanisms. The following mixed conclusions on PPPs are from the OECD:

> The unique efficiency gains associated with PPPs derive from the interaction of the design-build-maintain phases. The greater the maintenance and operation components, the greater the potential for efficiency gains. The appropriate allocation of risk between the government and the private partner is fundamental to the success of PPPs. A more common problem is the tendency for governments to retain the majority of the risks with PPPs. That undermines the PPP concept and may reveal that it is only being used as a vehicle to move the transaction off budget.
>
> (OECD 2005: 145)

BOX 7.3 PUBLIC–PRIVATE PARTNERSHIPS IN THE TRANSPORT SECTOR

Hodge (2005) describes the project of the Melbourne City Link in the state of Victoria in Australia. City Link was formed as a BOOT project worth AUS$ 2.1 billion. The government of Victoria formed a special organization to manage the City Link project. The project linked three major freeways in Melbourne, and more than 22 kilometres of road, tunnel and bridge works (including the road to Melbourne's airport) were completed: AUS$ 1.8 billion was financed by a private consortium. The private consortium operates the toll way for 34 years, and after that returns it to the state (Hodge 2005: 319). The City Link project is a design-build-finance-own-operate-transfer (DBFOOT) project.

City Link was subject to various controversies. Water started to leak into the tunnel at one point. There was the case of the City Link wanting to pressure for the freeway instead of a high-speed train connection to Tullamarine airport.

In evaluating the project, the City Link experience comes out favourably in terms of managing the commercial risks, while the governance risks were more open for discussion:

> Substantial risks were indeed transferred to the private sector in this project. Private contractors for instance bore almost all of the construction risks along with most of the design, construction, operating, financing and market risks based on the contract. . . . Overall then, we might conclude that most of these commercial risks were indeed borne by the private sector investors and that they deserved to earn a margin. The larger concern regarding project risks seems not to be from the commercial side, which was largely well managed, but from the perspective of political governance.
>
> (Hodge 2005: 320–321)

Hodge then goes on to name some of the risk elements: little publicly available economic or financial evaluation, exclusion of citizens' participation, no separate provision for protection of consumers, and possible prolonging of the concession period to 54 years to make sure that the project was profitable for the consortia.

The City Link project was subject to several legal battles, but most of them involved private sector organizations against other private sector organizations.

The OECD concedes – as does the European Commission – that a detailed case-by-case assessment is necessary for judging PPP projects, and that PPPs cannot be endorsed as a universal institutional innovation to be followed across nations. According to the OECD, 'a comparison of the benefits and costs of PPPs versus traditional procurement needs to be rigorously and dynamically conducted, and PPPs should be subjected to at least the same scrutiny as traditional expenditures in the public budget' (OECD 2005: 145).

BOX 7.4 LINDER'S LIST OF REASONS FOR PUBLIC–PRIVATE PARTNERSHIPS

The American scholar Stephen Linder (1999) used 'deconstructive strategy' to explore six different meanings to the term public–private partnerships which he found in the literature and in governmental practice:

1   PPP as management reform (innovative use of market forces);
2   PPP as problem conversion (a 'universal fix' for remedy of public governance problems);
3   PPP as moral regeneration (as a 'middle ground' between public and private);
4   PPP as risk-shifting (response to financial pressure of the state);
5   PPP as restructuring public service (move from public to private workforce); and
6   PPP as power-sharing (sharing control and responsibility).

Some see PPPs as a rhetorical stunt designed by governments and private for-profit firms to sweeten the already existing ideas and policies of contracting out and privatization (Linder 1999). In this perspective, PPPs are a clever set of rhetoric that makes them 'look good' in the eyes and ears of citizens, companies and public purchasers (see Box 7.3). The 'real' meaning – extended use of market mechanisms in the delivery of public service and infrastructure – is hidden underneath. Some observers have noted how PPPs become heavily contractualized and are not built on trust or a smooth cooperation mechanism (Klijn and Teisman 2005). Privatization advocate Savas (2000) conceded that PPPs sounded better than contracting out, and that the PPP concept should be used on these grounds alone.

Research has shown how arguments for PPPs have shifted over time. The argument in the early days of the Major government focused on the ability to save money, but later on it shifted towards innovation during the Blair government's reign (Flinders 2005). Partnerships are presented as something positive that governments cannot do without. Cooperation is a valuable factor for both governments and the private sector, and it is hard to be against cooperation. In reality, there can be power struggles connected to implementing partnerships (Coghill and Woodward 2005). It has to be said that there have been surprisingly few contested political battles about PPPs although there are controversies surrounding some of the British projects (see Shaoul 2005) and some of the Australian projects (see Hodge 2005).

BOX 7.5 E.S. SAVAS

The North American researcher E.S. Savas has played a prominent role in the development of the practice and research literature on contracting out. Savas was employed in New York City in the late 1960s when a snowstorm hit New York.

Savas was astounded at the public organizations' performance, and he set about finding out if private contractors could do a better job. New York City thus became one of the first to adopt a systematic contracting out policy. Savas moved into academia. He wrote on alternative service delivery mechanisms, which sounded more neutral than the term 'privatization' that is often used for contracting out in the United States. In 1987 he published the work *Privatization: The Key to Better Government* (New Jersey: Chatham House) which contained theories of contracting out and a wealth of evidence of contracting practices. He consulted widely with governments around the world, especially after the collapse of communism in Eastern Europe. Savas has never hidden his pro-privatization policy views, which has sometimes caused him to be regarded with some scepticism by the rest of academia. He does not always seem to give credit to research that empirically demonstrates the downsides of contracting out. In 2000, he revised his book on privatization/ contracting out, and included a chapter on the newly emerging public–private partnerships (PPPs). The book was then called *Privatization and Public–Private Partnerships* (New Jersey: Chatham House, 2000). Savas continues his lifelong, if sometimes controversial, interest in contracting out and privatization more generally. His most recent book is about contracting out experiences in American cities.

IS A PUBLIC–PRIVATE PARTNERSHIP AN ALTERNATIVE TO TRADITIONAL CONTRACTING OUT?

The question is if a PPP is a new institutional arrangement, or whether it is contracting that is just made to look good! Are PPPs alternatives to traditional contracting out, or should PPPs be regarded as a special way of doing contract management? There are arguments in the research literature and in the empirical findings to support both types of arguments. There are those who claim that PPPs are entirely new and that PPPs make a break with the traditional contracting. This group normally includes governments that are eager to push for PPPs and companies that are eager to enter the market for PPPs. This argument is based on the fact that the DBOO, BOOT and BOT models (the economic version of partnerships) have not been practised to the same extent as they are now. These models represent an innovation in contract management, and must be recognized as such. Certainly the models have not been used widely in the public sector previously. Governments, for example, the Victorian government in Australia, also want to promote PPP as something they have been developing themselves, and other governments acknowledge the British inspiration openly (Department of Treasury and Finance, Victoria 2004). From the perspective of 'social partnerships', the claim is that public actors and private actors are finding innovative ways of collaborating, and that this is often tied to new network structures and a more explorative approach to public policy-making where the output is not specified beforehand. This approach – associated with the broader governance and policy networks literature, and backed up by OECD projects on local governance – suggests that PPPs should be regarded as something new, and with a promising future in sight.

There are those who claim that PPPs are nothing new at all (Wettenhall 2003, 2005). The argument here is that there has been cooperation of some durability many times during history. The interconnection between the public sector and the private sector has taken many shapes and forms, and to postulate that PPPs only arrived on the policy scene in the 1990s represents a gross misinterpretation of facts. Some of the network scholars criticize the economic partnerships for being principal—agent contract relationships that have more to do with traditional contracting than with new and innovative PPPs (Klijn and Teisman 2005).

A middle position is taken up by a number of authors. While they recognize that cooperation between public and private organizations is nothing new, they also acknowl-edge that new forms, usually involving innovative ways of organizing and financing public service delivery based on risk-sharing and trust, are a step away from the principal—agent version of contracting where every precaution is taken prior to contracting to ensure that the agent is hiding its action or information (Hodge and Greve 2005).

BOX 7.6 RISKS IN PUBLIC–PRIVATE PARTNERSHIPS

The Department of Finance (2000: 9) in the state of Victoria, Australia identifies the following types of risks associated with public–private partnerships:

- design and construct risk – to cost, quality and time;
- commission and operating risk;
- service under-performance risk;
- industrial relations risk;
- maintenance risk;
- technology obsolescence risk;
- regulation and legal change risk;
- planning risk;
- price risk;
- taxation risk;
- residual value risk (where appropriate); and
- demand (or use/volume) risk.

DeHoog (1990) distinguished between three types of contracting: competitive, cooperative and relational. This division gives a good indication of where PPPs may be seen to be different from traditional contracting. Traditional contracting is here 'competitive' or adversarial while cooperative contracting more resembles the organizational and financial arrangements described in the current literature on PPPs. Seen in this light, a PPP is a special form of contracting where trust, cooperation and creating mutual benefits for each other are some of the key characteristics. PPPs may then be regarded as a special form of contracting, but not a complete alternative to contracting. This also suggests that there are different grades of partnerships. The first type is where partners cooperate, but still work from separate organizations (what is called 'loose' organizational forms in Hodge and Greve 2005). The second type is where cooperation is integrated in a common organization (what is referred to as 'tight' organizational forms in Hodge and Greve 2005).

A compromise position would acknowledge that both traditional contracting and PPPs involve some degree of contracting and some degree of cooperation. PPPs may be promoted as partnership agreements, but most PPPs will have a formal contract as the baseline for the relationship. PPPs are not 'contract-free' environments. Several authors and organizations observe how economic partnerships rest on complex contractual agreements (Broadbent *et al.* 2003; Hodge 2005). Likewise, traditional contracting is developing. Whether from a principal–agent perspective or a more trust-based contract system, the contracting techniques and approaches are developing too in order to accommodate more cooperation. Therefore, we might witness a convergence in the two forms that were supposed to be different: PPPs are becoming more formalized and adopting features normally associated with traditional contracting. Traditional contracting is becoming more flexible, and more oriented towards cooperative arrangements; features that are normally associated with PPPs. The end result is that in the future it will be harder to distinguish sharply between 'traditional contracting' and 'PPPs', and that is why it is perhaps better to talk about degrees or variants of contracting, following DeHoog's (1990) early suggestion.

CONCLUSIONS

The question is if contract management in the future will be based primarily on partnerships or if it will still be on the outskirts of public service delivery. There are those who think that partnerships are the key foundation for public service delivery. They usually build their arguments around the idea and practice of networks. The governance literature is based around the same argument. Governance takes place through and in networks. Cooperation is inevitable and there is no going back to hierarchy. Others think that partnerships are a fine part of public service delivery, but only in a marginal way. In this line of argument, PPPs are a special form of contracting that again is a means that governments can choose, but do not necessarily have to use. The hollow-state thesis is being criticized: the state is not hollow at all, it is argued, and the implications that the future of public service delivery lies with private sector organizations is misunderstood.

This chapter has examined the most recent trend in contracting: the trend towards public–private partnerships (PPPs). The first part of the chapter identified various meanings of the term PPPs. The second part of the chapter has discussed what is new about PPPs, and focused on risk-sharing and innovation as two key features of PPPs that have warranted attention from scholars and practitioners. The final part of the chapter has discussed how PPPs can be distinguished from more traditional forms of contracting out, how there are different varieties of PPPs and how a system of contract management may be based on the partnership idea.

DISCUSSION QUESTIONS

1 What constitutes an official public–private partnership in your country? Now try to compare this with the definition offered in the first section of the chapter. Do they fit or do they differ?

2 Are PPPs mainly an Anglo-Saxon phenomenon, or are there signs that it will catch on in other countries as well?

3 What are the main differences in public–private partnerships as opposed to traditional contracting in your opinion?

4 Is the 'contract management model' applicable to partnerships, or do we need a different kind of model to capture the essence of the partnership agenda?

5 How do you assess the empirical evidence for the effectiveness of partnerships in light of the discussion surrounding public–private partnership policy?

6 How well worked out is the regulatory framework and the institutional framework for PPPs compared to the situation with traditional contracting?

7 Are traditional contracting and PPPs converging (both rely on contracts, both seek cooperative arrangements and well-developed institutional frameworks), or do you think that traditional contracting and PPPs will still be seen to be different?

REFERENCES

Ball, R., M. Heafy and D. King (2000) Managing and concluding the PFI process for a new high school. Room for improvement?, *Public Management Review* 2(2): 159–179.

Ball, R., M. Heafy and D. King (2003) Risk transfer and value for money in PFI projects, *Public Management Review* 5(2): 279–290.

Boardman, A.E., F. Poschmann and A.R. Vining (2005) North American infrastructure P3s: examples and lessons learned, in G. Hodge and C. Greve (eds) *The Challenge of Public–Private Partnerships. Learning from International Experience*. Cheltenham: Edward Elgar, pp. 162–189.

Broadbent, J. and R. Laughlin (2005) The role of the PFI in the UK government's modernization agenda, *Financial Accountability and Management* 21(1): 75–97.

Broadbent, J., J. Gil and R. Laughlin (2003) The development of contracting in the context of infrastructure investment in the UK: the case of the Private Finance Initiative in the National Health Service, *International Public Management Journal* 6(2): 173–197.

Coghill, K. and Woodward, D. (2005) Political issues of public–private partnerships, in G. Hodge and C. Greve (eds) *The Challenge of Public–Private Partnerships. Learning from International Experience*. Cheltenham: Edward Elgar, pp. 81–94.

Cooper, P.J. (2003) *Governing by Contract, Challenges and Opportunities for Public Managers*. Washington, DC: GQ Press.

Corner, D. (2005) The United Kingdom Private Finance Initiative: the challenge of allocating risk, in G. Hodge and C. Greve (eds) *The Challenge of Public–Private Partnerships. Learning from International Experience*. Cheltenham; Edward Elgar, pp. 44–61.

Danish Government (2004) *Action Plan for Public–Private Partnerships*. Copenhagen: Ministry of Economics and Commerce.

Department of Treasury and Finance, Victoria (2004) *Partnerships Victoria*. Melbourne: Treasury.

DeHoog, R.H. (1990) Competition, negotiation, or cooperation. Three models for service contracting, *Administration and Society* 22(3): 317–340.

English, L. (2005) Using public–private partnerships to deliver social infrastructure: the Australian experience, in G. Hodge and C. Greve (eds) *The Challenge of Public–Private Partnerships. Learning from International Experience*. Cheltenham: Edward Elgar, pp. 290–304.

European Commission (2004) *Green Paper on Public–Private Partnerships and Community Law on Public Contracts and Concessions*. Brussels: European Commission.

Evans, J. and D. Bowman (2005) Getting the contract right, in G. Hodge and C. Greve (eds) *The Challenge of Public–Private Partnerships. Learning from International Experience*. Cheltenham: Edward Elgar, pp. 62–80.

Flinders, M. (2005) The politics of public–private partnerships, *British Journal of Politics and International Relations* 6(4): 215–239.

Ghabedian, A., N. O'Regan, D. Gallear and H. Viney (2004) *Public–Private Partnerships*. London: Palgrave.

Greve, C. and G. Hodge (2005) Introduction, in G. Hodge and C. Greve (eds) *The Challenge of Public–Private Partnerships. Learning from International Experience*. Cheltenham: Edward Elgar, pp. 1–21.

HM Treasury (2003) *PFI – Meeting the Investment Challenge*. London: HMSO.

HM Treasury (2006) *PFI – Strengthening Long Term Partnerships*. London: HMSO.

Hodge, G. (2005) Public–private partnerships: the Australasian experience with physical infrastructure, in G. Hodge and C. Greve (eds) *The Challenge of Public–Private Partnerships. Learning from International Experience*. Cheltenham: Edward Elgar, pp. 305–331.

Hodge, G. and C. Greve (eds) (2005) *The Challenge of Public–Private Partnerships. Learning from International Experience*. Cheltenham: Edward Elgar.

Institute of Public Policy Research (2001) *Building Better Partnerships*. London: IPPR.

Kettl, D.F. (1993) *Sharing Power: Public Governance and Private Markets*. Washington, DC: Brookings.

Klijn, E-H. and G.R. Teisman (2005) Public–private partnerships as the management of co-production: strategic and institutional obstacles in a difficult marriage, in G. Hodge and C. Greve (eds) *The Challenge of Public–Private Partnerships. Learning from International Experience*. Cheltenham: Edward Elgar, pp. 95–116.

KPMG (Denmark) (2005) *OPP-markedet i Danmark* 2005–2010 [The Market for Public–Private Private Partnerships 2005–2010]. Copenhagen: KPMG.

Linder, S. (1999) Coming to terms with the public–private partnership: a grammar of multiple meanings, *American Behavioral Scientist*, September.

Organisation for Economic Cooperation and Development (2005) *Modernising Government*. Paris: OECD.

Osborne, S. (ed.) (2000) *Public–Private Partnerships*. London: Routledge.

Pierre, J. (1998) *Partnerships in Urban Governance, European and American Experiences*. Basingstoke: Palgrave.

Pollitt, M. (2005) Learning from UK private finance initiative experience, in G. Hodge and C. Greve (eds) *The Challenge of Public–Private Partnerships. Learning from International Experience*. Cheltenham: Edward Elgar, pp. 207–230.

Sands, V. (2004) Victoria's partly-privatised prison system. An accountability report card, *Asia Pacific Journal of Public Administration* 26(2): 135–154.

Savas, E.S. (2000) *Privatization and Public–Private Partnerships*. New Jersey: Chatham House.

Shaoul, J. (2005) The Private Finance Initiative or the public funding of private profit?, in G. Hodge and C. Greve (eds) *The Challenge of Public–Private Partnerships. Learning from International Experience*. Cheltenham: Edward Elgar, pp. 190–206.

Skelcher, C. (2004) Public–private partnerships and hybridity, in E. Ferlie, C. Pollitt and L. Lynn (eds) *Oxford Handbook of Public Management*. Oxford: Oxford University Press.

Statskontoret (2005) *Konkurrens i gränslandet mellon offentligt og privat*. Stockholm: Statskontoret.

Teisman, G. and E-H. Klijn (2002) Partnership arrangements: governmental rhetoric or governance scheme?, *Public Administration Review* 62(2): 197–205.

139

Terry, F. (1996) The Private Finance Initiative – overdue reform or policy breakthrough?, *Public Money and Management* January–March: 9–16.

Van Ham, H. and J. Koppenjan (2001) 'Building public–private partnerships', *Public Management Review* 3(4): 593–616.

Wettenhall, R. (2003) The rhetoric and reality of public–private partnerships, *Public Organization Review: A Global Journal* 3: 77–107.

Wettenhall, R. (2005) The public–private interface: surveying the history, in G. Hodge and C. Greve (eds) *The Challenge of Public–Private Partnerships. Learning from International Experience*. Cheltenham: Edward Elgar, pp. 22–43.

World Bank (2004) Where do we stand on infrastructure deregulation and public–private partnership?, *World Bank Policy Research Working Paper 3356* (authors: A. Estache and T. Serebrisky).

FURTHER READING

There are several books that provide good overviews of the PPP literature and themes. An early collection of contributions is Osborne's *Public–Private Partnerships* (London: Routledge, 2001). A collection of the international experience with PPPs in light of several countries' experiences (including North America, the UK, Australia, Germany, the Netherlands, Sweden and Denmark) with economic partnerships and social partnerships may be found in G. Hodge and C. Greve's *The Challenge of Public–Private Partnerships. Learning from International Experience* (Cheltenham: Edward Elgar, 2005). For historical overviews of public–private partnerships, see the work by Roger Wettenhall (2003, 2005). The websites of the UK partnership agency is informative as well, as is the Canadian Institute for Public–Private Partnerships. There are special issues of journals such as the *Public Money and Management* special issue 2003. About the network approach to PPPs, readers are advised to examine the work of the Dutch scholars E.-H. Klijn, G. Teisman and J. Koppenjan (Teisman and Klijn 2002; Klijn and Teisman 2005; Van Ham and Koppenjan 2001). For questions of PPPs in Europe, the website connected to the Green paper on public–private partnerships is informative and contains documents from most European governments on PPPs.

Part IV

Conclusions

Chapter 8

Holding contractors accountable

The regulatory context

LEARNING OBJECTIVES

By the end of this chapter you should:

- be able to differentiate between accountability and regulation;
- learn to distinguish between command-and-control regulation, market-based regulation, management-based regulation and the combined model of 'regulated competition';
- gain knowledge of the role of more independent regulatory authorities; and
- learn how contractual regulation works in practice.

KEY POINTS OF THIS CHAPTER

- Regulation is useful to ensure that contractors align with public values and goals.
- Regulation remains important in public service delivery and some observers see a 'regulatory state' emerging after the decentralization of responsibility in the New Public Management period and the privatization and so-called deregulation in neo-liberalism.
- Regulation is often the responsibility of independent regulatory authorities at arm's length from central government and market actors.
- Contract managers and contractual governance designers face different options in making contracting work better: write more sophisticated contracts and set ambitious performance targets, let

the burden of regulation rest with managers and providers themselves in management-based regulatory systems, or use competition as a regulatory tool itself.

KEY TERMS

- **Regulation** – the process of setting rules and checking if the rules are kept.
- **Accountability** – the process by which actors give an account and are held to account.
- **The regulatory state** – a state that still uses regulation as a means of intervention and that has been more prominent in the aftermath of the New Public Management reforms and the privatization movement.
- **Independent regulatory bodies** – regulatory bodies established at arm's length from the government, usually headed by a chief regulator.
- **Command-and-control regulation** – direct, hierarchy-dominated regulation. The more sophisticated versions are associated with principal–agent theory.
- **Management-based regulation (or enforced self-regulation)** – regulation that gives responsibility to contractors themselves and lays the burden of proof on the contractors.
- **Market-based regulation** – regulation that relies on the use of market forces to align with public values and goals.

One of the enduring questions of contract management, and in public management more widely, is how to hold public service providers accountable for their actions. This chapter asks how public service organizations that deliver public services can be regulated and how accountability can be ensured. Regulation is here understood as sustained and focused control over public service delivery while accountability involves giving an account and being held to account.

Contracting makes the accountability issue more complex because the contract itself will stand in the way of more traditional accountability mechanisms associated with the hierarchical state. The challenge for contract managers is to write a contract that is sufficiently specific to be able to hold them to account for the promised service quality and quantity. From a principal–agent perspective, the problem is that the contractor may try to hide its actions and to conceal vital information that the purchaser needs in order to make an informed choice.

Accountability is more complex than only principal–agent relations. Accountability involves questions of accountability to whom and accountability for what. Accountability to whom is directed towards some organizational authority. Accountability for what is often associated with accountability for results in these New Public Management times (see Bardach and Lesser 1996).

> The issue of accountability also seems to be a significant sleeper. It is typically oversimplified into terms of basic financial or customer interest alone, rather than in the interest of citizens, of democratic processes, of advocacy roles for industry or local communities. Are some public sector services complex and not necessarily amenable to the simple-linear-sequential business model? I suspect so.
>
> (Hodge 2000: 241)

Recent years have meant more focus on accountability. While the view earlier was that the new forms of public organization and management were threatening accountability, there is now more optimism in general:

> The good news is that the discussion of accountability in public administration in general, and in contemporary contract operations as well, has been reinvigorated in recent years in several important respects. That discussion includes the perspectives of those actually making decisions, those concerned with management for performance, and those concerned with more traditional, though updated assessments of responsibility for official conduct.
>
> (Cooper 2003: 144)

Cooper goes on to argue:

> Two factors have become increasingly important with respect to accountability in public management in general, and contract management in particular: They concern the growing importance of market accountability and the significance of an international dimension, in no small part related to the increasing importance of the market in so many areas. The international factor has been partly a function of globalization, underwritten by the free trade policies of the United States and many other countries as well as important international lending agencies such as the World Bank and the International Monetary Fund.
>
> (Cooper 2003: 145–146)

REGULATION

The challenge of regulation of contracted services has long been recognized in the literature. Kettl (1993) spurred governments to find out 'what has been bought'. Milward and Provan (2000) pointed to the general problem of 'governing the hollowing state', and implicitly, how to control the different organizations delivering public services through contractual arrangements.

145

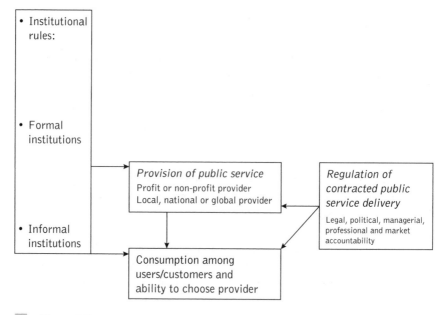

Figure 8.1 *Regulation of contracted public service delivery.*

One simple definition of regulation is that regulation means a 'sustained and focussed control exercised by a public agency over activities that are valued by a community' (Selznick quoted from Baldwin and Cave 1999). Another is that regulation is 'the promulgation of an authoritative set of rules, accompanied by some mechanism, typically a public agency, for monitoring and promoting compliance with these rules' (Baldwin *et al*. 1998: 3). A third definition of regulation of public service markets may be thought of as 'the processes by which standards and rules (whether formal or informal) are made . . ., compliance with such standards and rules are monitored, and behavioural modification sought for those who do not comply' (Baldwin *et al*. 1998: 15–16).

In the literature, there is usually a division between three forms of regulation (Baldwin *et al*. 1998: 2; Levi-Faur and Jordana 2004):

- a specific set of commands;
- a deliberate state influence;
- all forms of social control or influence.

The specific set of commands is the most concrete of the regulatory forms. Regulation as direct influence in specific cases is what people normally associate with the independent regulatory bodies. Regulation by command control is the regulatory form that is 'first base' for any regulatory understanding. A second and more abstract mode of thinking is seeing regulation as state intervention in the economy. In this respect, regulation is a way for the state to intervene in capitalism all over the world (Levi-Faur and Jordana 2004). A third form is to see regulation as nearly all forms of social control or influence in society. Admirers of the French philosopher Foucault are prone to view regulation in this light. For the purposes of this chapter though, the focus will be on the first two types of regulatory forms.

When regulation is concerned with markets and competition, a useful distinction is between regulation for competition and regulation of competition (Levi Faur and Jordana 2004: 6). Regulation for competition is mainly a concern for national competition agencies or authorities while regulation of competition is a matter mostly for sector-specific regulatory authorities (such as the telecommunications regulation agency). In relation to contracting for public service delivery, the national competition agency will usually be concerned with overseeing the rules of the transactions and questions of market entry, while a regulatory agency concerned with the quality of services to the elderly, for example, will be focused on regulation of performance in that specific service area.

Regulatory issues have gained prominence during the past ten to fifteen years. It is widely recognized that markets cannot be liberalized completely. There is still a need for some kind of regulation. That is why most observers prefer the term 'regulatory reform' to describe what is going on. It is not a case of deregulation as economists once foresaw.

Rather, the regulatory landscape is a case of 'freer markets, more rules' as in the apt phrase of Vogel (1996). Governments use market mechanisms, but establish regulatory reform to ensure that markets are regulated. There are also areas where there is a need for new regulation, for example, in environmental matters. International organizations, such as the European Union, are also producers of rules. Rules and regulations are not going to go away, but the way they are used and applied can be changed. OECD and other organizations refer to the new type of regulation as 'smart regulation'. Regulations help the government, but regulations also act as a way to tell providers that transactions are occurring in stable environments. Regulatory reform means that governments are constantly struggling to make sure that the regulations issued are fair and efficient, and that more focus on regulation follows in the footsteps of neo-liberalism:

> Governance through regulation (that is, via rule making and rule enforcement) is at the same time both constraining and encouraging the spread of neo-liberal reforms. Regulatory expansion has acquired a life of its own. Regulatory solutions that were shaped in North America and Europe are increasingly internationalized and projected globally. Deregulation proved to be a limited element of the reforms of governance and, where it occurred, it was followed either immediately or some-what later with new regulations.
>
> (Levi-Faur 2006: 11)

Within the public sector, a discussion on regulation has also evolved. An early character-ization was Michael Power's (1994) discussion of an 'audit society'. Power saw a trend towards an extended use of audit mechanisms being applied to public service delivery. At the same time, the focus on accountability followed the establishment of agencies and market-type mechanisms (Flinders 2001). Hood *et al.* (1999) and his colleagues viewed the trend as an exercise in 'regulation inside government'. They focused on the 'mirror-image' development of decentralization of management responsibility and the subsequent focus on rules and regulations. They estimated that the number of rules had not gone down, but had grown.

Regulatory reform

Regulatory reform is a subject that has been gaining wide attention in recent years. It is triggered by the fact that public management reform has decentralized services, including privatization and contracting out of public services. Competition has come in many new areas such as telecom, transport and electricity. American scholars have long been interested in regulation because of their state/market institutions, but Europeans only began to talk about regulation and regulatory reform fairly recently, as the Italian scholar Giandemenico Majone (1996) has explained:

> 'Regulatory reform' is the term used to describe the development in regulation in a number of areas and industries. Regulatory reform means that it is not deregulation, but re-regulation instead, and the freer the market gets, the more rules there will come into existence.
>
> (Vogel 1996)

Regulation has evolved dramatically during the past ten years, most notably in the telecom sector. The transport sector and the electricity sector have only recently undergone change in their regulatory regimes. The key driver in reform has been EU-initiated liberalization. The proposed liberalization of the infrastructure markets was the primary reason that the former public enterprises restructured their businesses (Greve and Andersen 2001).

Consumer organizations and voices have begun to influence policy more so than before, but there is still a long way to go. The Council for Consumers is active in speaking for consumers. A guide has been established on the internet which allows customers to compare prices for telecom services. Generally, the consumer organizations are following the newly liberalized infrastructure companies closely, and the Council makes a priority of watching the telecom companies' moves.

Consumers have got used to the increased competition on the infrastructure markets. In the telecom market, competition is welcomed by the consumers who seem to enjoy all the new telecom products and services. There is a general understanding that the competition is EU-initiated and so far the competition has only been welcomed.

The regulatory state

Regulation takes place at different levels. Much work has been done on national regulation. National regulation is supplemented by regulation from international bodies such as the EU or the World Trade Organization. Regulation for telecom services, for example, includes the International Tele Union and other bodies. The competition authority in each country also plays a role usually together with the more dedicated independent regulatory bodies. Sometimes the regulatory responsibility is delegated to independent regulatory authorities. The neo-liberal reforms of public services were followed by regulation in many countries: 'While at the ideological level neo-liberalism promotes deregulation, at the practical level it promotes, or at least is accompanied by, regulation' (Levi-Faur 2006: 13).

Majone (1994) sees a trend towards 'the regulatory state'. The term entered the vocabulary in European political science in earnest in the 1990s. Majone's main argument is that European polities are turning more towards American-style regulation as the markets are liberalized, deregulated and opened up for more competition across borders. Majone saw the primary policy function of the European Union (EU) as one that is producing regulation. Regulation is the preferred policy instrument of the EU. New 'independent' regulatory bodies are established in many policy sectors throughout Europe, working at arm's length of their government. How do these independent regulatory bodies fit into the existing institutional structures of the various nation states?

The challenge is to get the different levels of regulatory bodies to work together. Taking the telecom industry as an example, there will be regulation at the national level from an independent regulatory body, competition regulation by the competition authority, regulation at the EU level from an independent European regulator and then industry regulation worldwide by various international agreements and international organizations such as the International Tele Union. All of these regulatory bodies have an interest in pursuing regulation in their own jurisdictions. The challenge is that the jurisdictions frequently overlap.

The question of a future European 'super-regulator' instead of the national regulators has been brought up in the various sectors. Take the telecom sector as an example. The current view of the National Telecom Agencies in Europe seems to be that it is still much too early to begin discussions on a common European regulator in the different sectors. The most likely future scenario from a national point of view is that there will be some cooperation between a European regulator and national regulators. In telecom, the Danish National Telecom Agency is part of the Independent Regulators Group which meets regularly to discuss regulation issues. From the perspective of national governments, the cooperation and consultation among the national telecom regulators is probably sufficient for the moment. In a longer term perspective it seems likely that national governments and the individual telecom agencies will go constructively into negotiations if a European regulator is going to be established.

One reason why the regulatory state is becoming important is because of the problem of credible commitment. The government needs to send a signal to the markets that the

149

institutional rules and regulations governing market transactions are safe and will not suddenly be altered:

> Short-term electoral cycles, growing regulatory competition and increasing international interdependence create the basic conditions for the delegation of authority to both domestic and international institutions. . . . The issue of credible commitment is therefore intimately connected with the change in the context of regulation. Governments that are entangled with growing regulatory competition are pushed to transfer control through institutionalized forms of delegation as a way to enhance their credentials in the eyes of transnational business.
>
> (Levi-Faur and Jordana 2004: 10)

Independent regulatory authorities

The independent regulatory authorities have been highly visible in recent years (Thatcher 2005). Led by chief regulators, these bodies are placed at an arm's-length distance from the government departments, and are not usually under the direct influence of a government minister. The independence is what gives these bodies their credibility. There is a huge literature on why delegation to independent regulatory bodies can be a wise move for governments to make. Politicians can encapsulate their own preferred policy into the future, or make sure that the appointments they make will work to their advantage in the years to come.

The (Independent) Regulatory Authorities came into prominence in the 1990s. They are led by a chief regulator, they have independent status, and they usually derive some of their money from the industry they are regulating. Independent regulatory bodies vary from country to country. The UK has set up very high-profile regulatory bodies with very prolific chief regulators. Other countries around the world have followed suit. The Scandinavian cases are not always quite as independent as their British counterparts, and their chief regulators are certainly less visible to the public. Nevertheless, independent regulatory bodies have been established in Scandinavia throughout the past decade. A recent report on the Swedish experience showed that the independent regulators have fulfilled their mission towards recently privatized companies on quasi-markets (Swedish Public Management Office 2005).

In the telecom sector, a semi-independent telecom regulator was established in 1996. The inspiration for the Danish telecom regulator came from the British authority Oftel, but the idea of an independent regulator was modified to suit the Danish administrative culture (Greve 2002). The regulator was made independent of the minister in some respects, but not in others. The minister for telecom is still in charge of overall telecom policy, and formally appoints the head of the telecom regulator. The minister cannot, however, give directions or make alterations in specific telecom decisions which affect the providers of telecom services. The minister can dismiss the head of the telecom agency if he or she wishes. This has caused some observers, OECD among them, to criticize the Danish telecom regulator for not having enough independence of the ministerial level (OECD 2000).

The effectiveness of the separation between the regulatory and operational functions work well in some sectors, but less so in others. The separation works best in the telecom sector. The national telecom regulator has gained a reputation for credible commitment to regulation. The national telecom regulator has carried out its regulatory functions in accordance with the intention of the legislation and a majority in Parliament. Studies have shown that many regulatory authorities have been successful in adapting their organizations to the new task of regulating a competitive industry (Baldwin *et al.* 1998; Greve 2002).

Tension and competition exist between the different regulators. Most notably, there is tension between the individual independent regulatory authorities and the competition agency. The competition agency is likely to project a situation where the individual markets will be supervised by competition rules alone. Individual independent regulatory authorities see a role for themselves many years ahead, although the independent regulatory authorities agree on the long-term goal that the telecom market should eventually operate like a free market.

There are a number of activities that different regulators might take up. We should therefore not expect an overall regulator for all areas (unless each nation's 'competition agency' gets its way), but more a mixture of regulatory authorities with different responsibilities. One list might be as follows:

- performance data (auditors as responsible regulators);
- market entry and market rules (competition agency as responsible regulator);
- provider performance (competition agency and eventually market forces!);
- misconduct (parent ministry, parent local council, Audit Office);
- administrative standards and procedures (Ombudsman and Audit Office); and
- quality of services (Evaluation Institute, Consumer Council and Audit Office).

Scott (2006) is sceptical towards the alleged power and influence of the independent regulatory authorities. He sees a trend instead towards fragmentation of regulatory power. He writes: 'fragmentation of regulatory power is not restricted to the diffusion of formal powers amongst state actors. Formal authority is not the only source that is required to regulate companies and markets. Other key sources include information, organizational capacity, wealth, and the capacity to bestow legitimacy' (Scott 2006: 145).

Who else regulates or monitors contracts?

So far, the discussion has concerned the official regulatory bodies. There are other organizations and groups that can regulate or at least monitor what contractors are up to. The first group is the auditors who are assigned to the contractors, or work on behalf of a government or local government. Audit companies gain unique insights into the workings of contractors, and they report on these findings in public. In countries such as the UK, the Audit Commission plays an important role in gaining knowledge on the quality of public services. There are also companies that specialize in accreditation. If a contractor get accreditation, the quality is supposedly of a high standard. Last but not least, there is the public – citizens as customers who pass judgement on the services they deliver. This could be through citizens' surveys. Another well-known method is the use of vouchers or consumer choice where citizens-as-customers choose between different service delivery organizations. The choice that citizens-as-customers practice functions as a tool of regulation and monitoring of the quality of services.

FORMS OF REGULATION

This section distinguishes between three forms of regulation: regulation by hierarchy (also called command-and-control regulation), management-based regulation (or enforced self-regulation) and market-type regulation.

Regulation by hierarchy

Regulation by hierarchy focuses on the principal–agent relationship. An agent is engaged in an activity. The principal cannot see what the agent is doing, or have sufficient knowledge on what the agent is capable of. The first issue is referred to as 'hidden action', and the second issue is described as 'hidden information'. Lack of information is really the basic problem in the principal–agent theory. When regulators regulate 'from above', they will usually not have a clue about how the agent is going about its business, or have comparable information that tells the principal how the agent can perform. When regulation by hierarchy is regulation of organizations in a marketplace, Hood refers to this as the 'competition-oversight' hybrid form. The principal–agent chain of regulation will then look like this:

- ministry regulates purchaser (hierarchy–hierarchy);
- ministry sets terms for independent regulator (hierarchy–hierarchy);
- purchaser regulates provider (hierarchy–market actor);
- independent regulator regulates provider (hierarchy–market actor); and
- Audit Office regulates both purchaser and provider (hierarchy–market actor).

Models of accountability exist to accompany hierarchical regulation: parliamentary accountability, juridical accountability and managerial accountability (Flinders 2001). Public organizations have to be accountable to their politicians in the government and in Parliament both politically ('parliamentary accountability') and with regard to the legal requirements ('juridical accountability'). Managers can also be accountable both to other

152

managers and to politicians which is referred to as 'managerial accountability'. An almost similar distinction is made by American contracting scholars Romzek and Johnston (2005: 441), who point to hierarchical, legal, political and professional accountability ('parliamentary accountability' encompasses 'hierarchical' and 'political' accountabilities).

Parliamentary accountability involves:

- ministerial accountability;
- select committees;
- public accounts committees;
- national Audit Offices;
- parliamentary questions; and
- parliamentary commissioners.

Judicial accountability is about living up to the legal requirements of entering a contract. Juridical accountability can take place through a variety of means. Juridical accountability includes:

- juridical review;
- administrative law;
- codes of practice (e.g. open government);
- tribunals;
- judicial inquiries; and
- European legislation/influence.

Managerial accountability is about a group of managers (the providers) being accountable to another group of managers (purchasers or contract managers). Contracts can be the tools in which the terms for accountability are being specified. It is in contracts that providers agree to the terms on which they are delivering the services. Managerial accountability includes:

- agentification;
- contracts;
- charters;
- market mechanisms; and
- audit.

Regulation by competition

Regulation by competition (or market-type regulation) is another mode that governments can rely on. Quite simply, the price mechanisms will perform the duty of regulation. If your business goes under, then it was not strong enough to perform well in the market:

153

In its simplest and most stripped-down form, capitalism is constructed on this blueprint of highly intensive accountability. The metric of faithful stewardship is the growth of capital value through adroit commercial moves. The steward is answerable only to owners – and if he is the sole owner, only to himself. Success and failure are unambiguous. This clarity allows for simple, sturdy measures to manipulate agents' motivation and to invoke whatever consequences their performance merits. Deviations – a lost contract, a surge in costs, a dip in profits, a slip in capital value – are right seen (absent a compelling excuse) as conclusive evidence of bad performance.

(Donahue 2002: 5)

The market, in this view, is always right, and there is little ground to cast doubt on it. Price mechanism and the ratio between price/quality regulate providers' behaviour. Customers' choices regulate providers' behaviour. In the classical exposition of this perspective, its proponents would argue that even a badly functioning market is preferable to allowing the state to come in and 'second-guess' market actors' activities. Choosing a specific parameter from the benchmarking systems can be called 'randomized competition' in Hood's (1998) words.

Regulation by competition also means that providers hold each other at bay. Benchmarking – the systematic comparison of performance data from different organizations – is a way to ensure that the comparisons are made from the same basic criteria. Benchmarking by peers is good for providers because everyone is regulated from the same conditions.

Consumer choice is one element of a competition regulation mechanism. If users or consumers can be empowered to select their services from various providers, they will constitute a powerful regulatory influence (the 'exit' option in Hirshman's terms). A strategy for governments that want to use the competition model is to make consumer choices available to users, and to put pressure on both purchasers and providers 'from below'.

Regulation through randomness is another 'impersonal' mechanism that is not so often used, but can be very effective. As soldiers in some countries are recruited through a lottery (young persons draw a number that then decides if they join the forces or not), organizations may be subject to regulation at any given time. The way a national Audit Office conducts surprise inspections sometimes works from this principle. The principle is believed to be fair by the organizations subject to the control – because it could just as well have been next door's organization that had been chosen. Randomized regulation in contractual arrangements would entail regulators making surprise inspections of contracts. Regulators would select a particular contractual arrangement, and then investigate the relationship thoroughly. National Audit Offices have these kinds of powers, and will occasionally perform surprise visits in an area. In this case, 'randomized oversight' is the term used by Hood.

Christopher Hood (1998) has distinguished between four types of regulation. Inspired by 'cultural theory' in anthropology, Hood's approach assumes that there are four basic ways of organizing: the hierarchist way, the individualist way, the egalitarian way, and the fatalist way. Hood uses the categories of 'grid' and 'group' as an analytical tool. Grid describes how much behaviour is circumscribed by rules. Group describes how much action take places in a collective setting.

The regulated competition model

Combination models exist. Hood talks about 'regulated competition' as one hybrid model. Another model would be 'enforced self-regulation' or centralized decentralization' which utilizes both hierarchy and management-based regulation. In real-life institutions, some combination form of regulation is likely to be found. Few countries rely exclusively on only one form of regulation.

The regulated competition model acknowledges that competition is in focus in public service delivery. This is not a normative standpoint, but an empirical observation judging from the past 20 years of New Public Management reforms. Competition is not unfolding in an institutional void. It is dependent on policies promoting competition, and on mechanisms that regulate the competition game as well as the providers and the results they create. The institutional framework that surrounds service provision and the regulation mechanisms specifies the formal and informal rules guiding the competition. Therefore, one of the most likely regulation models is a regulated competition model.

EXPERIENCES WITH REGULATION OF CONTRACTED PUBLIC SERVICE DELIVERY

This section discusses selected empirical examples of how regulation systems work in practice: An American example shows how accountability in practice can be challenging. Romzek and Johnston (2005) find that for two of the cases in their investigation accountability effectiveness was quite high, while for three of the cases (out of five) there was only moderate accountability effectiveness. Romzek and Johnston had proposed that accountability effectiveness is enhanced by three factors: contract specifications, contract design and accountability design (2005: 444). The accountability design was built around legal accountability (compliance), professional accountability (deference) and political accountability (responsiveness). Romzek and Johnston are concerned with 'if observed accountability approaches are aligned with the managerial strategies and tasks of the contract' (2005: 445). They find that 'the contract management context – specifically, the level of political support for the state and contractors and the market environment – was often critical to effective contract accountability'. This corresponds to what we have termed 'institutional context' in the framework presented in Chapter 2. Although contracts contain clauses of mismanagement, it takes political clout to enforce the contracts and put sanctions in place.

155

Broadbent *et al.* (2003) find evidence that policy-makers in Britain tried to focus on the 'system level' of institutional rules to ensure that public–private partnership policy could continue from the Major government to the Blair government in Britain in the 1990s. For Cooper (2003), it is very important to influence the right regulatory framework if contracted public service delivery is to be a success:

> Legislators can do many things to help improve contract management. For one thing, Congress could add and should address the disconnection between the law of government contracting and administrative law. Traditionally, these two bodies of law have been separated, at least in part, by government contracting law's primary focus on prevention of corruption and administrative law's emphasis on administrative procedure. It would be particularly helpful if contracting laws could be better integrated with existing administrative law.
>
> (Cooper 2003: 163)

In a recent paper, two American scholars have documented how monitoring the contractual behaviour of the government's own employees is nearly as high as when tasks are contracted out to for-profit organizations, but monitoring seems to lessen when tasks are contracted out to non-profit organizations. There is no apparent reason for why this is so. It seems that when non-profits take over tasks, monitoring is simply reduced (Marvel and Harvard 2005).

Providers have become used to developing their own quality assurance systems. One example is the local government in Graested-Gilleleje in Denmark where it was a part of the contract that providers should come up with a quality system (see the case study in the Appendix of this book). Applying this system to a new service area will make it easier for providers to win new contracts. It can also enhance their legitimacy in the eyes of the wider public.

The market structure is also of importance to how regulation of contracted public service delivery works. If there are more providers in the marketplace, then regulation of contracted public service delivery should work better because the system will be the same for everyone. If there is only a handful of providers working together in a network arrangement, then regulatory conditions may be more complex. Therefore, Romzek and Johnston's (2005) recommendation for the design of contract regulation and accountability is that contract managers and contract designers must take the specific context into account.

The market for PPP projects is being regulated to allow for some competition. Private partners to PPP contracts have to compete for their contracts; they cannot assume they will just get the contract by having good connections in government. A number of companies have shown interest in the PPP projects. The government's regulatory role in this respect is to make sure that enough private companies stay interested in PPPs over the course of decades. If private companies suddenly directed their investments to other non-state industries, then a regulatory task for the government would be to win back that attention from the private companies.

156

Of course, the most visible evidence is often found in court and administrative tribunal rulings on violations of contracts, non-compliance behaviour and failure to deliver the promised results. The European Court has reached verdicts in many cases; this whole area is the subject of contract law, a huge subject in law studies and law research.

DISCUSSION: REGULATING CONTRACTED PUBLIC SERVICE DELIVERY

Regulating providers and holding them accountable for how they deliver the services is a complex matter. The 'chain of regulation' includes the hierarchical relationship between a ministry or the local government, and the purchasing division of that government. Looking at the relationship from a principal–agent theory point of view, the challenge for principals is to know what the agents at the various levels do and to find out what kind of knowledge the agents possess. Looking at the relationship from a broader governance perspective that takes the regulative, normative and cognitive side of institutions into account, the challenge is to form and influence the institutional arrangements so that providers will comply with the wishes that a ministry, a local government and their purchaser divisions establish.

There are signs, however, that the accountability framework in general has improved, and that Hodge's (2000: 241) hope for applying a cautious 'learn as we progress' approach may therefore be the most sensible option in thinking about organizational arrangements.

What are the options facing contract managers, policy-makers and administrative officers designing institutions for contracted public service delivery? There seem to be at least four options available based on the regulatory forms above.

- ■ Improve command-and-control regulation by writing stronger contracts. There is now a huge amount of theoretical knowledge on how providers may try to hide information and action from government purchasers (the principal–agent problem). One way out of this problem is for purchasers to be able to write more sophisticated contracts. Empirical experience should give information on the various strategies and tactics that providers are likely to follow. Given this knowledge, purchasers may be able to write and enforce contracts in more detailed ways. Building a good enforcement institution is also part of the game. This could be done by strengthening independent regulatory authorities, or by promising rewards for performance. A number of options are open to purchasers as contract-writers. A variation of this is to focus even more on performance targets and to build a performance-based management model around the contract. This is done in various ways and it is a safe means for governments to combine many aspects of the New Public Management model.

157

- Let providers regulate themselves through management-based regulation. Purchasers can work with providers to establish appropriate guidelines for how regulation should take place. Purchasers can encourage providers to have schemes of reporting and self-assessment and means for making the primary performance data available. That way, purchasers will save time, money and effort, and a fair deal of the actual regulatory behaviour will be in the hands of the providers. The purchasers or external regulators will only have to improve the self-regulation schemes and make control visits every once in a while. The dilemma is how much government providers should trust providers. It is likely that the bigger for-profit companies will be better equipped to have their own systems.
- Use the market as the prime regulation mechanism (maintain strong competition). This regulation strategy can be followed by the purchaser organization or by external regulators such as government ministries. Providers can be pitched against each other. This would entail ongoing observation of the organizational ecology of the providers. Encouragement of competition and monitoring of anti-competitive behaviour is often the key task of national competition agencies.
- Or use some combination of these options. The most evident form of combination model is the regulated competition model which uses both hierarchy and market-type mechanisms in its regulatory profile. The regulated competition model allows for some competition, but within the orbit of the regulatory state.

One of the most challenging aspects is defining the right conditions for accountability and regulation to flourish. A crucial feature – setting the right performance targets – is also the most difficult one:

> The key to successfully contracting out government business is the ability to say clearly, concretely, and completely what it is that the government wants to produce; that is, to define the value that the public is trying to capture through any given operation. This is, as it has always been, where the trouble lies. It is difficult for a collective to reach agreement on the precise attributes of public value that it wants to see produced in a given part of the public sector. Defining social utility functions in ways that they can be written into contracts is tough conceptually, analytically, and technically – and politically.
>
> (Moore 2002: 318)

What does setting up a regulatory framework for accountable contracting imply? And who should the architects of such a system be?

First, the regulation and accountability framework must be carefully designed around the contracting theme. Adding bits and pieces from various regulatory frameworks and applying them to the task of contracting is often futile. Both purchasers and providers will get confused, politicians won't know which set of rules is the most important one when faced with problems exposed in the media, and citizens will not receive the optimal

158

service they expect. Fligstein (1996, 2001) has argued quite convincingly that markets must be made and created in many areas of public service delivery, and that there is a huge institutional design task for legislators and administrators. Fligstein has also warned that in established markets, the incumbents (the dominant providers) will be against the challengers (the potential providers that try to enter a market). The government's role here is not to align with the incumbents (as they tend to), but to support the challengers. A particular problem arises in public service delivery because many of the incumbent providers will often be public sector organizations who have enjoyed monopoly status for years. Supporting private sector challenges against established public sector providers is often a tricky task for politicians who count on the votes from public sector workers.

Second, the regulation and accountability framework must be compatible with the overriding institutional framework in each country or region. It is of little use to set up a regulatory and accountability system that does not correspond with the existing institutional framework already in place. The institutional framework is gradually changing with NPM reforms, but sceptics have warned about believing too much in global convergence and instead recognizing divergence locally and nationally. There will be no one regulatory framework that can satisfy all governments and businesses around the world.

Third, the regulatory and accountability frameworks still need to be internationally coordinated. The approach to public–private partnerships in the European Union is a good example. Contractual regulation and accountability may not converge, but there must be at least some interchange among systems so that purchasers and providers can look across borders for new deals.

Fourth, it is evident that the actors involved in establishing and developing a robust regulation and accountability system must be drawn from various sources. Politicians and their civil servants will be best placed to deal with parliamentary accountability. Ministries of justice and ministries of industry must focus on the legal aspects of the accountability system. Finally, the managers of the purchasers and the providers themselves must be active in establishing and maintaining regulatory systems for managerial accountability. Managers can play an active role in constantly formulating and reformulating the institutional framework that surrounds managerial accountability in order to make the systems more efficient and useful in everyday practice.

Ideally, the various accountability forms should fit together, and regulation would therefore be on target for each accountability form. The combination models described above should guide that practice. What seems to be needed most is a solid contract management institutional context which asks: what are the rules and norms that contracts are embedded in, and are they shared by all the key players in the contracting process?

Does this amount to 'a regulatory state' that goes with the contract state? In certain ways it does, as the rules and regulations – and combinations thereof – are clearly important in making contracting for public service delivery work in practice. In other ways, contracting does not necessarily contribute to a regulatory state in the sense that more and more regulations are added. If designed smartly, contracting for public service delivery need not overemphasize the regulatory aspect, and, depending on how independent regulatory authorities are institutionalized and how effective they are, they might support contracting for public service delivery without overburdening contracting with rules.

CONCLUSIONS

Providers delivering public services through contractual arrangements must be accountable for their performance, and the purchasers must also be accountable to their principals higher up in the hierarchy for a contractual accountability system to function. The different forms of accountability have been defined as parliamentary accountability (hierarchical and political), legal accountability, and managerial accountability. How accountability is secured is through regulation. Regulation usually equals sustained and focused control, sometimes by a public agency, sometimes by inspector-free mediums such as a peer review process. There are at least four forms of regulation that have been described in this chapter: regulation through hierarchy, regulation through the use of market mechanisms, regulation through peer reviews, and regulation through randomness. The specific challenges of contractual accountability and regulation have been described. The importance of the institutional contract environment – the administrative and political traditions, the rules and norms of society – that contracts are embedded in is crucial in understanding how contractual accountability works and how it might be designed. Caring for the context, and establishing a clear and transparent relationship between targets and realistic outcomes, and between the key players of purchasers, providers and regulators are among the essential features in order to enhance contract accountability effectiveness.

DISCUSSION QUESTIONS

1   Why is there still a need for regulation when markets are supposedly liberalized?
2   What are the key components behind the notion of 'regulatory reform' and 'smart regulation', and how are they applied in a given policy area in your country?
3   How do you perceive the mix or the combination between regulation strategies (command-and-control, market-based, management-based regulation) in your own policy area?
4   Why and how do independent regulatory bodies differ from country to country?
5   What is the relationship between national independent regulatory bodies and international independent regulatory bodies?

160

REFERENCES

Ayres, I. and J. Braithwaite (1992) *Responsive Regulation. Transcending the Deregulation Debate*. Oxford: Oxford University Press.

Baldwin, R. and M. Cave (1999) *Understanding Regulation*. Oxford: Oxford University Press.

Baldwin, R., C. Scott and C. Hood (1998) Introduction, in Baldwin *et al.* (eds) *A Reader on Regulation*. Oxford: Oxford University Press.

Bardach, E. and C. Lesser (1996) Accountability in human service collaboratives – for what and to whom?, *Journal of Public Administration Research and Theory* 6(2): 197–224.

Braithwaite, J. (2001) *Global Business Regulation*. Oxford: Oxford University Press.

Broadbent, J., J. Gil and R. McLaughlin (2003) The development of contracting in the context of infrastructure, investment in the UK: The case of the private finance initiative in the NHS, *International Public Management Journal* 6(1): 173–197.

Coglianese, C. and D. Lazer (2002) Management-based regulatory strategies, in J.D. Donahue and J.S. Nye (eds) *Market-based Governance. Supply Side, Demand Side, Upside and Downside*. Washington, DC: Brookings.

Cooper, P. (2003) *Governing By Contract: Challenges and Opportunities for Public Managers*. Washington, DC: GQ Press.

Donahue, J. (2002) Market-based governance and the architecture of accountability, in J.D. Donahue and J.S. Nye (eds) *Market-based Governance. Supply Side, Demand Side, Upside and Downside*. Washington, DC: Brookings.

Drewry, G., C. Greve and T. Tanquerel (eds) (2005) *Contracts, Performance Measurement and Accountability in the Public Sector*. Amsterdam: IOS Press.

Fligstein, N. (1996) Markets as politics. A political-cultural approach to market institutions, *American Sociological Review* 61(4): 656–673.

Fligstein, N. (2001) *The Architecture of Markets*. Princeton, NJ: Princeton University Press.

Flinders, M.V. (2001) *The Politics of Accountability in the Modern State*. Aldershot: Ashgate.

Greve, C. (2002) *Privatisering, regulering og demokrati*. Aarhus: Aarhus Universitets Forlag.

Greve, C. and K.V. Anderson (2001) Management of telecommunication service provision: an analysis of the Tele Danmark Company 1990–1998, *Public Management Review* 3(1): 35–52.

Hodge, G. (2000) Privatization. *An International Review of Performance*. Boulder, CO: Westview Press.

161

Hood, C. (1998) *The Art of the State. Culture, Rhetoric and Public Management*. Oxford: Clarendon Press.

Jordana, J. and D. Levi-Faur (eds) *The Politics of Regulation. Institutions and Regulatory Reforms for the Age of Governance*. Cheltenham: Edward Elgar.

Kettl, D.F. (1993) *Sharing Power, Public Governance and Private Markets*. Washington, DC: Brookings.

Levi-Faur, D. (2006) The diffusion of regulation and diffusion of capitalism, in M. Conkey and P. Dutil (eds) *Dreaming of the Regulatory Village; Speaking of the Regulatory State*. Toronto: The Institute of Public Administration of Canada.

Levi-Faur, D. and J. Jordana (2004) The politics of regulation in an age of governance, in Jordan and Levi-Faur (eds) *The Politics of Regulation*. Cheltenham: Edward Elgar.

Majone, G. (1994) The rise of the regulatory state in Europe, *West European Politics* 17(3): 77–101.

Majone, G. (1996) *Regulation Europe*. London: Routledge.

Marvel, M.K. and H.P. Harvard (2005) Outsourcing oversight. A comparison between monitoring for in-house and for contracted services, Paper for the Public Management Research Association Conference in Berkeley, CA, October.

Milward, H.B. and K. Provan (2000) Governing the hollow state, *Journal of Public Administration Research and Theory* 10(2): 359–380.

Moore, M. (2002) Privatizing public management, in J.D. Donahue and J.S. Nye (eds) *Market-based Governance. Supply Side, Demand Side, Upside and Downside*. Washington, DC: Brookings.

OECD (2000) *Regulatory Reform in Denmark*. Paris: OECD.

Peters, B.G. (2005) Squaring several circles: coordination, performance and accountability, in G.C. Drewry, C. Greve and T. Tanqurerel (eds) *Contracts, Performance Measurement and Accountability in the Public Sector*. Amsterdam: IOS Press.

Power, M. (1994) *The Audit Explosion*. London: DEMOS.

Romzek, B. and J. Johnston (2005) State social services contracting: exploring the determinants of effective contract accountability, *Public Administration Review* 65(4): 436–449.

Scott, C. (2006) Regulatory fragmentation, in M. Conkey and P. Dutil (eds) *Dreaming of the Regulatory Village; Speaking of the Regulatory State*. Toronto: The Institute of Public Administration of Canada.

Swedish Public Management Office (2005) *Six Deregulations*. Stockholm: Swedish Public Management Office, Report 8.

Thatcher, M. (2005) The third force? Independent regulatory agencies and elected politicians in Europe, *Governance* 18(3): 347–373.

Vogel, S. (1996) *Freer Markets, More Rules. Regulatory Reform in Advanced Economies*. Ithaca, NY: Cornell University Press.

FURTHER READING

Matthew Flinders' book *The Politics of Accountability in the Modern State* (Aldershot: Ashgate, 2001) is an excellent discussion of various forms of accountability. Baldwin and Cave's *Understanding Regulation* (1999) is a good and widely respected introduction to the regulation debate. John Braithwaite's impressive *Global Business Regulation* (Oxford: Oxford University Press, 2001) puts regulation in a global context. Giandemenico Majone's (1996) *Regulating Europe* gives a good introduction to the European debate on the regulatory state. David Levi Faur and Jainct Jordana's edited volume *The Politics of Regulation* (Cheltenham: Edward Elgar, 2004) provides an in-depth analysis of the recent discussions on regulatory capitalism. Hood's *The Art of the State* (Oxford: Clarendon Press, 1998) is well worth reading for its many smart ideas on how to control and regulate in the public sector and beyond. Hood and colleagues write extensively on *Regulation Inside Government* (Oxford: Oxford University Press, 2000) and *Controlling Modern Government* (Cheltenham: Edward Elgar, 2004).

Chapter 9

Conclusions

Contracting for public services

LEARNING OBJECTIVES

By the end of this chapter you should:

- be able to assess the contract management model in light of the lessons learned from the earlier chapters of the book;
- view and gain insight into a mature contract management model that uses the insights from the various chapters to point to new combinations and relations in contracting;
- get a brief review of some of the future trends associated with contracting for public service delivery, including the type of state that administers contractual relations; and
- be invited to think about the future challenges facing contract managers in the age of globalization and increased pressure from citizens as customers, and to consider the strategies that are possible for changed contract management.

KEY POINTS OF THIS CHAPTER

- There is a basis for a more mature model of contract management given the theoretical advances that have been made, and the practical experience governments have all over the world.
- The mature contract model points to an interconnected model where policy, strategic purchasing, contract, service provision, partnerships, customers,

regulatory mechanisms and the institutional context are seen in combination.

■ A number of contract models for the future are plausible, and if some of the key trends are amplified, scenarios of contracting in the future are likely to be focused on 'the integrated contracting state', 'the globalized provider and subscriber state', 'the globally regulated market state', or 'the holistic governance state (with a lesser role for contracts)'.

■ New challenges arise for governments and contract managers in the expanded contract state and the strategic options will be different according to the actor's position in the system.

KEY TERMS

■ **Mature contract management model** – a model of contracting which incorporates the theoretical advances that have been made in the literature and the best practice experience of (mainly) OECD governments during recent decades.

■ **Integrated contract management model** – a public management model that is built around contractual relationships and where there are adequate resources and capacities for contracting to be conducted to its full potential.

■ **Globalized provider and subscriber state** – a public management model where the bulk of the power lies with the providers in an increasingly globalized marketplace where services are delivered by multinational providers, and where governments are reduced to 'subscribers to services' indicating a 'subscriber state' in Alasdair Roberts' (2004) phrase.

■ **The globally regulated contracting state** – a contract management model where the importance of the nation state (or local governments) is reduced in the light of regional or globally enacted trade regimes and/or international benchmarking institutions, and where most policy development and sanctioning takes place above the nation state in various globalized settings.

This chapter draws together the key lessons and issues for the public service manager in the management of contracts and the providers of contracted services, what has been learned in this text and key issues for the future. The key issues for the future include the need for more international and global regulation of providers, more international and global knowledge-sharing of contract management, and the development of new information technology tools to keep contractors accountable and help public managers manage contracts.

A MATURE CONTRACT MANAGEMENT MODEL

Contracting for public services has undergone a change in recent years. Gone are the days when contracting was only about putting the cleaning operations of the local school out to public tender and hoping that someone would be qualified as a provider, and eventually writing a badly organized contract that would cause trouble for local politicians because it was not clear enough, and cause agony for the providers because they thought it was just another business deal they were used to from the private sector. Today there is 'a new agenda' in contracting for public services. The new agenda is partly caused by more thinking and development within the contract management knowledge itself, and partly by developments in the marketplace where increasing globalization and specialization has led to new challenges for public services delivered through contractual arrangements. This leads us to consider a mature contract management model. The model is mature because:

- There have been several theoretical advances in contract management theory during the last decades with some, if not as much as could be wished for, academic attention given to the topic of contract management, and several empirical investigations from which to draw theoretical lessons.
- Countries around the world, especially OECD countries, have experimented with contracting out in public service delivery. Many governments have made contract management a key part of their overall public management reform agenda and daily public management practice.
- Contract management has become institutionalized from Wellington to Oslo, from Melbourne to New York City. Simply put, there is a wealth of best practice experience out there from which to draw lessons.

Many international organizations have already learned their lessons. The OECD, for example, has reached the conclusion that contract management and market-type mechanisms (here referred to as 'outsourcing') are integral to modernizing government:

> Outsourcing has grown significantly during the last 15 years. It has been shown to be applicable to a wide range of government services. Apart from traditional concerns relating to the disturbance of vested interests, or change in the familiar profile of government, the constraints relate to the degree to which the delivery of service can be monitored at arm's length, the need to maintain the government's capacity now and for the future, and the protection of other core governance principles. The benefits of outsourcing in terms of increased efficiency can be significant, and the services that have been outsourced rarely revert back to government provision. Outsourcing can be expected to increase substantially in the coming years.
>
> (OECD 2005: 139)

The mature contract management agenda is dominated by the following factors:

- coherent policy that includes partnerships (finding a balance between competition and collaboration);
- strategic purchasing;
- communication policy on contracting;
- upgraded contractual competence with managers;
- relational contracts with a neoclassical twist;
- networked providers and purchaser–provider partnership relations;
- globalized markets with incumbents and challengers;
- active consumers;
- varieties of institutional contract contexts.

Coherent policy that includes partnerships

There is a basis for developing a coherent policy on contracting for public service delivery in most OECD countries. After more than two decades of experimentation with contracting, and after a recent decade of trying out reforms with PPPs, governments should have been able to collect sufficient material to build a well-informed, evidence-based and

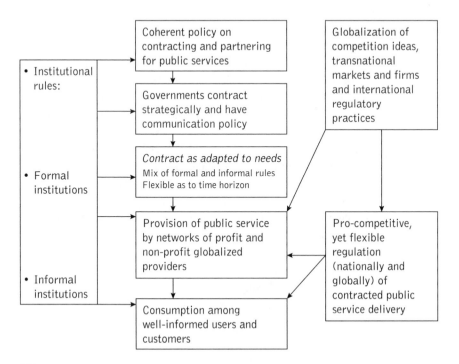

Figure 9.1 *A mature contract management model.*

theoretically underpinned contracting policy. Not all governments have done that – but the possibility is certainly there. One of the basic ingredients in such a policy is to be specific about what the theoretical and practical rationale of the policy is (Romzek and Johnston 2002). The rationale is the guiding light for both purchaser organizations and provider organizations, and the customers that are supposed to derive benefits from the contracting process. As we have seen during the course of this book, the rationale has changed over time in some cases. Economic efficiency gains and savings used to be at the top of the list for most governments. This has gradually been supplemented by reasons of synergy and innovation. While these concepts may be illusive, they nevertheless signal that governments want something more out of a cooperative arrangement than just saving money in a given budget year. Thus there has been a gradual shift towards a more open agenda for what governments want to achieve with contracting, and what providers can deliver.

The move towards innovation as a key argument is supported by the recent interest in PPPs. PPPs may be regarded as extensions of the contracting argument, not as a complete alternative to it. Often PPPs will involve contracts for public service delivery, but those contractual relationships are built on cooperation, (sometimes) trust, risk-sharing and a long-term commitment. This is unlike some of the previous period's short-term contracts where governments were tracing the quick savings bonus. PPPs have become a useful addition to the contract agenda in many countries, and in particular countries such as the UK, Australia, Canada and the Netherlands. In other places, PPPs are slowly picking up, but the institutional structures of states such as Denmark, Sweden, Norway, and some of the more state-oriented countries, for example, France, the invitations to private partners to participate in public action in infrastructure projects and in service delivery mechanisms have been more reluctant.

When contracting has been supplemented by PPPs, the natural thing to ask would be if 'a coherent policy' means that the two policy areas have to be integrated into one policy. There are good arguments for that. The already existing recommendations for contracting can include the more complex issues of risk-sharing, joint service production and private finance involvement that the PPP literature and practice has highlighted. What we will get then is a more developed contracting policy and theory, where 'traditional contracting' and 'PPPs' are a subset of the same phenomenon.

Another possibility is that the policies co-exist. The best example of how that can be done comes from the UK where there is both a Best Value policy for contracting and a PFI policy for economic partnerships. The most recent policy document on PPPs in the UK is 'PFI – strengthening the long-term partnerships' (HM Treasury 2006). It is the same in other countries. Parnerships Victoria is the name of the policy in the state of Victoria in Australia where they also have a policy for contracting out of government services (Department of Treasury and Finance, Victoria 2000).

Strategic purchasing

Governments must see contracting in a strategic perspective. 'Strategic contracting' is Steven Kelman's (2002) term for the trend. Contracting can no longer be put aside in the organization. Instead it must gain a place in the overall strategy of the organization. That goes both for the purchaser who has to specialize in contract management as well as for providers that will often specialize in a particular service or industry. A 'holistic' or 'whole-of-government' approach to contracting could be other contenders for terms. The key message from both theory and evidence-based information which governments can collect is that contracting needs to be an integral part of every government's activity, and that sufficient resources and political attention should support this. There is a focus on 'adequate resources' (Romzek and Johnston 2002), the need for training of contract managers (Cooper 2003; Kettl 1993; Van Slyke 2003), the need for building robust contract management capacity at various levels of government (Brown and Potoski 2003), thinking through in addition to the strategic recognition, and the integration of performance-based management sought by Kelman (2002). The OECD (2005) acknowledges that contracting and PPPs do not come easy, and that managerial effort and resources need to be allocated to the practice of contracting.

BOX 9.1 SOCIAL AND ENVIRONMENTAL ISSUES IN CONTRACTING

A recent trend in contracting is to interpose demands for responsibly social or environmentally friendly behaviour in contracts. Social clauses are promoted by governments. Environmental issues are also being addressed, including working environments. American scholar Archon Fung (2002) has showed the increasing attention that social and ethical issues are having in marketplaces. He first envisions what a social market would like:

> Imagine a world in which the environmental, labour, and other social aspects of products and processes of firms were fully transparent for everyone to see and judge. Such transparency would be a step toward building a well-ordered social market in which consumers and investors could act confidently on their ethical preferences. Those with preferences about how firms treat their workers or the environment could incorporate these values by accurately selecting appropriate securities and products.
>
> (Fung 2002: 147)

> Making social markets and helping consumers face providers is still not easy:
>
> > From the perspective of organizing economic markets and social regulation, the project of creating social markets now lies on a cusp. We can look back to a perhaps imagined time when social values did not enter into investment, consumption, and corporate management decisions. Given the degree to which individual moral and social preferences have already penetrated marketplaces, it seems impossible to recapture that separation between economic and social motives. Nevertheless, the chaos in emergent social markets – the difficulty consumers have in distinguishing firms that act on their values from those that just talk, the converse inability of forms to make credible social commitments, and the clash of conflicting or uninformed social preferences – makes many long for just such a divorce.
> >
> > (Fung 2002: 169)

In some respects there is a *rationalistic* current related to these calls to improve contracting. If only the area of contracting were given more financial resources, allocated more manpower and upgraded the performance management aspects, then contracting would be a viable and often recommendable practice of every type of government in the OECD questions. These types of advice appear to share a planning optimism that is not necessarily reflected in other types of research which look at the reasons why contracting sometimes fails. Indeed, some of the authors mentioned above have pointed to some of the potential problems with contracting: that the market for public services do not function like a well-oiled, efficient market with sufficient provider competition (Kettl 1993; Romzek and Johnston 2002), that horizontal relationships between partners to a contract often collide with vertical principal–agent relations posed by the constitutional framework of government (Cooper 2003), that the capacity to evaluate and find out what has been bought is sometimes hampered by unclear performance targets, and so on. In other words, despite the rationalistic cries for more resources and better training programmes, the strategic purchasing function is not always likely to work smoothly.

Communication about contracting

Communicating about contracting has long been a neglected area of study, and we found very few references to the communication aspect in the literature cited in this book. Savas (2000: 175) lists 'initiate a public relations campaign' as one of the elements on his list of steps in the contracting process. Nevertheless it would probably help governments if they think about a communication strategy before they go ahead with certain contracting out processes, especially when relations break down between purchasers and providers (or partners to a contract), and the communications skills are needed. A recent Danish publication focused on 'Contracting out in the crossfire', and analysed a number of cases where there had been 'media storms' about a particular contracting project (Council for Contracting Out 2005). Contract managers and the leaders to whom they are accountable frequently find themselves in the midst of controversies when some contracting scheme does not turn out as planned. There are also after-the-crisis discussions, as, for example, the contracting issue relating to the Challenger disaster in the USA. Here discussions arose as to whether NASA had not been a responsible buyer of equipment, or whether the contractors were under pressure not to do enough quality checks to ensure the product met the performance criteria.

The communication strategy for a contracting process would ideally be directed at the key stakeholders in the contracting process. It would have specific types of information for each group of stakeholders. Citizens worrying about change in service standards need assurance, and potential providers need to receive information about the market conditions and future competition prospects. The communication strategy would also be flexible in terms of manpower devoted to it. When the tender process is announced, there are likely to be many questions from media and stakeholders. When a problem with service delivery occurs in the middle of the contract period, that calls for another kind of communication. Both purchasers and providers must have professional staff who can handle communication. There is also a communication aspect to letting stakeholders know about the results that have been accomplished. Local government executives would be well advised to inform both the citizens and the central government ministers if a local government has succeeded in delivering the promised results through contracting. The missing focus on communication might be due to the more technical and rationalistic approach to contracting that is often taken by contract managers and academics.

Upgraded contractual management capacity

All of the above means that contract managers must be better educated and trained in the various factors that make up a contractual arrangement. Contract management cannot be left to former employees from the providers, or be treated as a side issue that collaboration with a consulting company will solve. Governments have got to train and prioritize managers working with contracts and contractual issues. Kettl (1993) pointed to the need for more focused training in the 1990s. Kelman (2002) renewed the call and asked for more strategic competence on behalf of the public managers, including managers at the top who work with contractual issues. Contract management is in need of competencies in institutional design, communication (including political communication), awarding contracts, implementing (through networks and partnerships), quality checking and dialogue, controlling, evaluation and regulation (see also Van Slyke 2003). Cooper (2003) has called for contract management to be taken up more systematically in training programmes for public managers, such as Master of Public Administration or Master of Public Management courses.

Relational contracts with a neoclassical twist

Contracts must fulfil many wishes at the same time. Contracts should be formally written agreements that allow for clear performance targets, and that will be subject to scrutiny, accountability and regulation. At the same time contracts are expected to be flexible, to allow for interpretation and consultation among the partners to the contract, and to be suitable for new learning processes once the results from the contracts become known. One way to describe the current pressure for flexible yet reliable contracts could be 'relational contracts with a neoclassical twist'. Contracts must be tools that can foster cooperation and partnerships. Yet if anything goes wrong, or someone has to be held to account, the contract must be formal and clear enough to allow some form of sanction. The relational aspects are well covered in the literature. 'Incomplete contracts' signal that contracts cannot specify every contingency beforehand, and that some interpretation and fulfilment along the way has to be allowed. The 'neoclassical twist' is also well addressed in the literature: the contracts must function as a document that will enable third parties to check performance figures and to impose sanctions on the partner that has broken some clause in the contract. As both purchasers and providers (or partners in PPPs) want to have both flexibility and the possibility for accountability and regulation, the ideal-type contract for the delivery of public services must be able to handle both aspects! Of course, that is not always possible, and governments around the world try to select one of these aspects in their presentation of contractual agreements. Recently, the partnership contract has been dominant in the discourse on contracting, and therefore the relational aspect and the promotion of cooperation as the main rationale have been in the foreground at the expense of the image of the 'traditional contract'.

Networked relationships

Contractual relations are no longer always just a matter between a single purchaser and a single provider. There may be several purchasers that form a 'purchasing alliance' and will make deals collectively. The same happens with the provider side. Providers may form consortia to deal with contracts, and several providers may operate neck-to-neck in providing a service, or they may be in different districts but still be in competition (as is the case in Phoenix, Arizona). Governments are trying to form relationships in networks with the providers (Milward and Provan 2000). The providers are looking for new ways to organize among themselves (Sanger 2003). Managing networks is an alternative challenge to managing a single provider (Considine and Lewis 2003; Romzek and Johnston 2005).

Consortia are an even more interesting feature in PPPs. Many PPP contracts are entered between one or more government principals and a host of sub-providers. Usually, the partnership contract will be negotiated by one organization, but the organizations doing the real work and delivering the promised service or infrastructure are a host of providers or partners. One problem arises if all partners feel that there is a special PPP spirit, or if they treat it like just another contract. In addition, the legal and financial complexities of many modern economic partnerships (of the PFI type) make the networked relationships a reality in modern public governance.

Globalized markets

Public services are not just delivered locally by locally known firms, or nationally by nationally known firms. In addition, public service delivery is becoming globalized (Dunleavy 1997). Global firms aim to sell their products and services to a wide range of countries across the globe. A good example is the Group Securicor company that has expanded its reach through mergers and aquisitions. The company operates prisons and delivers security services, but has also been engaged in health management. These companies seek to sell standardized products to a certain extent. Global standardization of services means that governments can no longer choose their own specifications of products freely. Governments become 'subscribers' to services instead of individual purchasers as Roberts (2004) has called it. Roberts also identified transborder service networks, where companies form alliances. This is related to the networked society mentioned in the previous section. However, as Roberts notes, the networks may not be a multiple cooperative channel of communication and dialogue envisaged by some public management scholars, but may instead be more closed networks of elite players that work together and leave other organizations out of the game.

There is no sign that the forces of globalization are slowing down. Companies all over the world are seeking new profit opportunities. If public service markets develop, there is no reason why global companies should stay away from them. Because of the focus on benchmarking and the whole evaluation trend in the public sector, public service organization will be meeting the same kinds of standards increasingly. This is exactly the stronghold of the global companies that have the capacity to meet the nationally or internationally set standards. We are therefore likely to see 'bigger and better markets'. Evidence from Sweden suggests that the smaller players on the market are likely to be squeezed out after a while (this is what happened with contracting out in Stockholm in the 1990s) (Almqvist and Högberg 2005). Despite the government's efforts to allow public employees to open up their own company, the trend is going in the opposite direction: firms will get bigger as markets are getting bigger.

Smart and responsive regulation

Regulation is going to be smarter, more responsive and increasingly global in outlook. Regulation has improved tremendously over recent years, and the science of regulatory

173

studies has also grown (Levi-Faur and Jordana 2004). There are several implications of the trend towards 'the regulatory state':

- *Regulation theory has become more sophisticated*. Regulation is not only about command-and-control regulation, but also relies on management-based regulation and market-based regulation.
- *Regulatory practice has improved through continued focus*. OECD now talks about smarter regulation and regulatory reform. There is a constant focus on how to improve the quality of regulation.
- *Regulation is becoming more focused*. Independent regulatory authorities (IRAs) have been established in large numbers across the OECD countries. They are especially designed to be concerned with regulation. Other regulatory authorities have strengthened their mission and their engagement in regulatory practice. This applies to national Audit Offices and other, more traditional regulatory authorities. The British National Audit Office, for example, is a highly respected institution when it comes to the regulation of PPPs.
- *Regulation is becoming more global*. Gone are the days when regulation was just a national matter. Regulation takes place in international organizations. The European Union has been characterized by its emphasis on regulation (Majone 1994). Regulation is also the issue for many international organizations (the International Telecommunications Union (ITU) is a prominent example of this). Regulation is a matter for global organizations such as the World Trade Organization (WTO). Cooperation between the different levels of regulatory authority is required in the future public sector. This is bound to affect the nature of contracting for public services. Regulation of contracted public service delivery is likely to involve more than just the individual local government as a regulator.

More focused and confident customers

Over a long period of time (at least two decades of NPM reforms) citizens have become used to being referred to as customers. Governments also sometimes speak of their citizens as customers. Customer orientation has reached the public sector, although nobody is sure what the exact implications are for identification as customers (Fountain 2001). Consuming public services may never be the same as going to the local supermarket: A research team from Britain conducted empirical research into the theme of citizens-as-customers, and they discovered that people were able to make the distinction clearly. 'It's not like shopping' was one of the expressions that summarized the findings. People thought differently about being served by a public service organization and being served in a restaurant or nearby supermarket. However, the rhetoric of the NPM reforms has continued, and there is likely to be more 'user demand' in the future as well.

Varieties of institutional contractual contexts

Contracts have to be sensitive to the features mentioned above. One factor is that the contractual arrangements must consider the specific institutional features of each polity. Although the trend towards a more globalized marketplace is present, various countries and parts of the world operate from their distinctive historical-institutional background. The importance of contractual institutions has been identified in this book. Entering into contracts without knowing the country or the region's history, legal requirements and norms associated with contractual arrangements can be problematic for the parties concerned. Therefore, there is a need to be more sensitive to the specific institutional frameworks in each country or region of the world in which contracts are embedded. Understanding the peculiarities will help form a better contractual relationship. The way to enter into a contractual arrangement in the United States is different from entering into a contractual arrangement in Iceland or Australia. However, more global agreements or international agreements on trade are likely to affect the contracting regime. The procurement rules of the European Union have a profound effect on the way contracting occurs in the all-member states. Germany, Ireland or the Netherlands cannot pursue contracting policies independently without adapting and enforcing EU procurement rules.

A GLOBAL PERSPECTIVE

A global perspective has been mentioned in most of the topics explored so far. A widely argued claim is that this is an age of globalization understood as 'a process (or set of processes) which embodies a transformation in the spatial organization of social relations and transactions – assessed in terms of their extensity, velocity and impact – generating transcontinental or interregional flows of networks of activity, interaction and the exercise of power' (Held *et al.* 1999: 16). What are the current discussions and challenges ahead regarding globalization?

Public management reform, of which contracting is an essential feature, involves two sets of questions for globalization. First, there is the globalization of public management reforms themselves. Second, there is the globalization of markets that provide public services on a contractual basis. In public management reform there is a growing need for international comparison. The work of Pollitt and Bouckaert (2004) has been one significant milestone for assessing public management reform across a number of OECD countries, and there has been important work on comparing the Nordic countries (Lægreid and Pedersen 1999). Kettl (2000) has already noted the 'global public management revolution', wondering why so many countries have turned to the same themes at the same time. It seems that public management reform needs to go further down this road of examining the international perspective. Just as the previous public administration research focused on Civil Service systems in comparative perspective there is a need to know how different implementations of public management reform have been

175

carried out. Some authors have noted how comparative or international public management is almost turning into a sub-discipline itself under the broader public management framework (Kelman *et al.* 2003: 14). In addition, public management reform is not just a question of how one country's response to an international trend differs from another country's response, but also about how the internationalization of public management discourse allows different actors to contribute to the discussion and shape the way people think about international public management (Sahlin-Andersson 2001). The second part of the globalization of public management reform is about markets. In many countries, privatization and contracting out has been on the agenda. New public services markets are emerging and these markets are increasingly international in scope. Sanger (2003) has reported on welfare markets in the USA. Dunleavy (1997) has previously seen a trend towards globalization of public service markets where private providers specialize in services and try to get governments as customers all over the world. Roberts (2004) sees global service provider networks as offering market-based services. He sees a trend towards governments taking out subscriptions of service delivery instead of contracting them out themselves. Governments thereby lose some of the capacity they were supposed to have by specifying contracts and being principals towards lower level agents. In Roberts' scenario, the agents have taken over the principals!

International public management reform is increasingly occupied with 'results' understood as the outputs and outcomes which governments produce. The main questions that have to be addressed in international public management reform theory and practice are essentially: 'What works, what doesn't, and in what context these successes and failures have occurred and why' (Kelman *et al.* 2003: 15).

Partnering or public–private partnerships are a global phenomenon empirically, at least in the discourse of public management reform, and the initial task was to compare the recent international experiences from countries around the world and draw some theoretical lessons from them (Hodge and Greve 2005; Osborne 2000). If partnering is 'the latest chapter in the privatisation story' as Hodge and Greve (2005: 3) has remarked, then partnering should be debated in the context of previous experiences in that field as well. An interesting observation about partnering is that the concept and the practice follow in the same footsteps as the public management reform/NPM debate. The most aggressive action takes place in the UK and Australia (New Zealand did not jump on the PPP bandwagon). The experience often cited is from early experiments done by the Major government and later the Blair government in the UK (just as the Thatcher experience was reported on privatization). Conceptually, Britain has been promoting the PPP concept widely (see e.g. IPPR 2001), although the term public–private partnerships has been used more loosely to cover all kinds of public–private cooperation in the US and elsewhere (Kettl 1993; Wettenhall 2003) and more 'economic' partnerships, as we have seen in this book. As the concept of partnering is used in so many settings, there is a need to agree on at least a minimum of conceptual clarification. At the moment, partnering seems to be used both in a 'loose' sense – social partnerships – covering also some sporadic interaction between public and private actors, and in a more 'narrow' sense – economic partnerships – describing deals when public organizations use private finance and operations expertise to build new infrastructure.

The challenge for further research is to ask: 'What is the nature of PFI/PPP and who is regulating its application? How are definitions of PFI/PPP in terms of value for money and risk transfer derived and operationalized? What is the merit and worth of PFI/PPP?' (Broadbent and Laughlin 2003). To that we might add: 'What can be learned about PPP from international experience?' (Hodge and Greve 2005; Osborne 2000).

Regulatory reform has been international in scope for a considerable time, and especially since Majone (1994) tried to learn from the American experience with regulation and to transfer that discussion into a European context. In a recent comparative study, the editors have remarked how 'Regulation as an art and craft of governance, as an institutional reality, as a field of study, and as public discourse is more salient and celebrated nowadays than ever before' (Levi-Faur and Jordana 2004: 1). To understand regulatory reform in an international perspective means asking at least three kinds of questions. The first and most obvious question is perhaps to examine the 'changing relations between competition and regulation and their implications for the role of politics in general and the state in particular in the governance of the capitalist economy' (Levi-Faur and Jordana 2004: 2). Markets across the world have been deregulated and re-regulated for a considerable time and we need to explore further how the relationship is unfolding in different countries and unions. The second set of questions relates to the different levels of regulatory bodies. What are the relationships between global regulators, European regulators, national regulators, industry regulators and competition authorities? How do governments and companies or decentralized organizations around the world interact with the regulators? Why and how do international organizations, such as the OECD, try to influence the regulatory process? The third set of questions relates to the regulatory system itself. Are we witnessing a more international regulatory system in the making or will there still be 'competing regulatory systems'? This is about the international cooperation on regulation. It is also about the way international agreements in trade generally, but also in specific sectors, is reached.

THE CONTRACT STATE OF THE FUTURE?

What will the future contract state look like? In Chapter 1, we discussed various terms that had been used in the research literature on contracting to characterize the contract state. The concepts included 'the hollow state' (Milward and Provan), 'the enabling state' (Deakin and Walsh) and the 'strategic contracting state' (inspired by Kelman 2002). We also noted how the evolution of contracting had transformed the view of the contract state. In the 1980s and early 1990s, the contracting state was seen as a threat (hollowing out), or an opportunity (enabling) while the later aspects focused on developmental perspectives ('strategic').

The aim of this section is to discuss if there are other visions that will signify what kind of contract state we are likely to see in the future. There are four possibilities we will focus on after the discussion in this book that reflect both the theoretical development and the empirical experience with contracting during the past decades.

The integrated contract management state

The integrated contract management state characterizes a situation where contracts are wired into the organization of public service organizations. Contracting occurs at all levels, and contracting with private providers (for-profit and non-profit) are institutionalized and accepted as the norm. As Jan-Erik Lane has written:

> The contracts in the new contracting state using a giant nexus of contracts from the top to the bottom of the state hierarchy, including governments at various levels, whether there is a unitary or federal state format, will be different from the contracts used earlier. . . . In the new contracting state, there would thus still be short-term principal–agent relationships, but there will also be spot market contacts, the use of both reflecting the drive towards tendering/bidding.
>
> (Lane 2000: 195)

We could add that an integrated contract management state will also involve partnership contracts. The PPPs appear here to be a special form of long-term contract that emphasizes risk and sharing of resources and gains. PPPs make sure that private finance will be an integrated part of financing public service provision. As the contracts become more institutionalized, governments and providers will stop to think of contracts as something special. Contracts are therefore likely to be something that is taken for granted. If you want a public service delivered, contracting is an appropriate way to do it.

The globalized provider and subscriber state

The globalized provider and subscriber state characterizes a situation where the markets have become internationalized and even globalized. Global service providers have systemic service and standardized service concepts. The companies will expand in an increasing number of countries. Just as we have had 'coffee house chains', and 'burger chains', we will have service provider chains where public services are part of a global concept, recognizable anywhere in the world.

The globally regulated contract state

The globally regulated contract state is characterized by an increasing focus on common rules for contracting. International agreements will specify what a good contract is, and what responsibilities the parties to the contract have. The procurement rules of the European Union are an example of an international rule set that governments and providers in the European Union have to accept as a necessary part of their purchaser–provider relationships. The implications of this trend are that the international rules – the institutional frameworks at the international level – will achieve a high level of importance, and the individual contract will not be as important. Most clauses in contracts are covered in the internationalized legislation. The interpretation of the rules will be left to the courts, and to competition and regulatory authorities. The political and managerial conditions for strategic action will be strongly limited in this scenario. The trend is towards institutionalization of the contracting process that will leave little room for independent action with individual purchasers and providers.

The partnership state (with a lesser role for contracts)

The partnership state (with a lesser role for contracts) is inspired by the wider governance literature, and the literature that has declared NPM as dead (Dunleavy *et al.* 2006). This literature generally argues that governance of public service organizations is part of a wider governance approach where also the third sector and citizens are drawn more into the governance process. These relationships are said not to be guided by principal–agent type contracts, but by more fluid models of interactions. The 'network' is the preferred metaphor for this kind of society and relationship between public and private actors. Governments and observers are talking about a 'whole-of-government' approach where the ties that bind organizations loosely together are celebrated, but in ways that do not entail formal contract relationships. The possible room for contractual relationships in this scenario is through partnerships. But partnerships are meant to be 'social' partnerships and not the neo-contractual PFI-type economic partnerships that have been associated with PPPs for infrastructure projects that involve private finance, risk-sharing and complex legal and financial deals between governments and private partners in the construction industry. The partnership state signals a looser, more organic type of contractual relationship than the other scenarios.

A DEMOCRATIC PROBLEM?

Do contracts, contract management models and various versions of a contract state pose problems seen from a democratic perspective? Contractualism is sometimes charged with being undemocratic. Some of the usual concerns involve lack of accountability, the exclusiveness of the deals, lack of wider public participation, secrets involved in dealings with private sector providers, and the complexity which renders too much power to lawyers and economists. There is bound to be some truth in certain of these accusations. But it is also clear that contracts can make positive contributions to democracy:

■ *Better basis for accountability through contracts*: Through available performance data and the exposure these data receive in contracts, regulators and the public gain a significant insight into the practice of public service organizations.

■ *Contracts clarify responsibilities*: In traditional bureaucracy, the exact lines of command may become blurred over time as more layers are added to the bureaucracy. A contract can help specify the responsibilities of the partners to the contract, and enables a clearer distinction between purchasers and providers.

■ *Publicness*: Secret or sensitive information is a problem, especially in large infrastructure PPP contracts. A smart way for governments to overcome this is to publish the contents of contracts on the internet, but, due to legal implications, this may not always be possible.

■ *Public participation*: The formulation of contracts, especially concerning performance measures, can be made subject to public debate and deliberative democracy processes. The government can involve a wider part of the public in specifying what the performance measures should be in a contract, By having an active communications policy, the government can also do more to involve and communicate with citizens during the contract period.

■ *Communicate about complexity*: The complexity of the legal and financial contents of a contract – especially a PPP contract – may be formidable, but an active communication policy on behalf of the partners to the contract can eliminate much speculation and can help the various stakeholders to understand the contractual issues better. Independent reviews and checks on the partners' advisers and results can also be a way of tackling the complexity issue. The UK government orders independent reviews on a regular basis, and this could be institutionalized in government contracting as well.

CONTRACTING: FINAL REMARKS

Contracting is a fascinating issue. Contracting is engaged in connecting public and private organizations for public service delivery. Contracting involves both institutional and even constitutional questions related to the state, but also more focused questions on how to achieve best value for the public. Contracting involves a number of actors besides the main parties to the contract itself: the purchasers and the providers. These include the public that has to consume the services, the regulators who have to oversee the purchaser and the provider, the politicians who lay out and revise the contracting policy and the various international organizations that are framing the rules for contracting to take place. After more than two decades of widespread contracting, the fears and the hopes of those involved are more defined. Contracting is no longer ruled by actors that are either 'for' or 'against' the government or the market. Purchasers are beginning to be smart buyers. Providers' profiles expand as non-profit providers, other public providers and global actors supplement the traditional for-profit providers from the public sector.

The increasing use of partnerships has helped this understanding of more sophisticated contractual relationships, but also added new challenges. A much more reflective stage has been reached where there is room for informed choices and balanced judgements. The development is theoretical as our understanding of the theories behind contracting has improved in the new institutional economics, in institutional theory in sociology and political science, and in the public administration and public management research that deals with the challenges facing public managers. The development is also practical as governments and providers around the world have gained more experience and learned more during the past decades about what works in contracting for public services. Luckily, international organizations such as the OECD collect and systematize this wealth of empirical information and distil the best or smart practices for governments to follow in the future. Contracting is therefore likely to be central to public management systems in OECD countries in the years to come, and the tools and approaches that contract managers can use now are improved, and rest on a theoretically sound and evidence-based grounding. The future is likely to be dominated by digitalization, globalization and increasing network interdependency, but a key mechanism to facilitate many of these trends is going to be contractual.

DISCUSSION QUESTIONS

1   Consider the mature contract model outlined in the first part of this chapter. In your opinion, is it a realistic possibility or is it an idealized version of the contractual relationships that purchasers and providers experience?

2   To what extent do you see contracting as influenced by the forces of globalization? Or are contracting issues still primarily dealt with at the local level?

3   How do you view the different future contract states that the chapter depicts? Try to discuss the chances of one of the models becoming the contract state of the future.

REFERENCES

Almqvist, R. and O. Högberg (2005) Public–private partnerships in social services: the example of the city of Stockholm, in G. Hodge and C. Greve (eds) *The Challenge of Public–Private Partnerships. Learning from International Experience.* Cheltenham: Edward Elgar.

Broadbent, J. and Laughlin, R. (2003) Public–Private Partnerships. An Introduction, *Accounting, Auditing and Accountability Journal* 16(3): 332–341.

Brown, T. and M. Potoski (2003) Contract management capacity in municipal and county government, *Public Administration Review* 63(2): 153–164.

Considine, M. and J. Lewis (2003) Bureaucracy, network or enterprise? Comparing models of governance in Australia, Britain, the Netherlands, and New Zealand, *Public Administration Review* 63(2): 131–140.

Cooper, P. (2003) *Governing by Contract, Challenges and Opportunities for Public Managers*. Washington, DC: GQ Press.

Council for Contracting Out, Denmark (2005) *Udlicitering i krydsild*. Copenhagen: Schultz.

Department of Treasury and Finance, Victoria (2000) *Partnerships Victoria*. Melbourne: Treasury.

Dunleavy, P. (1997) The Globalization of Public Services Production. Can governments be 'best in the World'?, in A. Massey (ed.) *Globalization and Marketization of Public Services*. London: Macmillan.

Dunleavy, P., H. Margetts, S. Bastow and J. Tinkler (2006) New public management is dead. Long live digital-era governance, *Journal of Public Administration Research and Theory* 16(3): 467–494.

Fountain, J. (2001) *Building the Virtual State*. Washington, DC: Brookings.

Fung, A. (2002) Making social markets. Dispersed governance and corporate accountability, in J. Donahue and J.S. Nye (eds) *Market-based Governance*. Washington, DC: Brookings.

Held, D., A. McGraw, D. Goldblatt and J. Perraton (1999) *Global Transformations*. Cambridge: Polity Press.

HM Treasury (2006) *PFI-Strengthening Long Term Partnerships*. London: HMSO.

Hodge, G. and C. Greve (eds) (2005) *The Challenge of Public–Private Partnerships. Learning from International Experience*. Cheltenham: Edward Elgar.

IPPR (2001) *Building Better Partnerships*. London: Institute of Public Policy Research.

Kelman, S. (2002) Strategic contracting management, in J. Donahue and J. Nye Jr. (eds) *Market-based Governance*. Washington DC: Brookings.

Kelman, S., F. Thompson, L. R. Jones and K. Schedler (2003) Symposium: dialogue and definition on the field of public management, *International Public Management Review* 4(2), 1–19.

Kettl, D.F. (1993) *Sharing Power. Public Governance of Private Markets*. Washington, DC: Brookings.

Kettl, D.F. (2000) *The Global Public Management Revolution*. Washington, DC: Brookings.

Laegreid, P. and O.K. Pedersen (1999) *Fra opbygning tel ombygning af staten*. Copenhagen: DJØF forlag.

Lane, J.E. (2000) *New Public Management*. London: Routledge.

Levi-Faur, D. and J. Jordana (eds) (2004) *The Politics of Regulation*. Cheltenham: Edward Elgar.

Majone, G. (1994) The rise of the regulatory state in Europe, *West European Politics* 17(3): 77–101.

Milward, H.B. and K. Provan (2000) Governing the hollow state, *Journal of Public Administration Research and Theory* 10(2): 359–380.

OECD (2005) *Modernising Government*. Paris: OECD.

Osborne, S. (ed) (2000) *Public–Private Partnerships*. London: Routledge.

Pollitt, C. and G. Bouckaert (2004) *Public Management Reform: A Comparative Perspective*. Oxford: Oxford University Press.

Roberts, A. (2004) *Transborder Global Networks*. Arlington, VA: IBM Center for the Business of Government.

Romzek, B. and J. Johnston (2002) Effective contract management and implementation. A preliminary model, *Journal of Public Administration Research and Theory* 12: 423–453.

Sahlin-Andersson, K. (2001) National, international and transnational construction of new public management, in T. Christensen and P. Laegreid (eds) *New Public Management*. Aldershot: Ashgate.

Romzek, B. and J. Johnston (2005) State social services contracting: exploring the determinants of effective contract accountability, *Public Administration Review* 65(4): 436–449.

Sanger, M. (2003) *The Welfare Marketplace*. Washington, DC: Brookings.

Savas, E.S. (2000) *Privatization and Public–Private Partnerships*. New Jersey: Chatham Books.

Van Slyke, D. (2003) The mythology of privatization in contracting for social services, *Public Administration Review* 63(3): 296–315.

Wettenhall, R. (2003) The rhetoric and reality of public–private partnerships, *Public Organization Review: A Global Journal* 3: 77–107.

FURTHER READING

The future of the contract state is implicit in many of the writings that have been referred to in this book. The 'hollow state' argument is best explored through the various writings of H. Brinton Milward and various colleagues. Jan-Erik Lane's *New Public Management* (London: Routledge, 2000) is perhaps the most consequential book on what contract theory means for public service delivery and the way the public sector is organized. John Donahue and Joseph S. Nye's *Market-based Governance* (Washington, DC: Brookings, 2002) is the book that casts its net most widely and considers a host of new global issues. The discussion on networks and the management challenges that relate to networks has been covered most recently in E-H. Klijn and J. Koppenjan's *Managing Uncertainty in Networks* (London: Routledge, 2004). The partnership question is covered in S. Osborne's *Public–Private Partnerships* (London: Routledge, 2000) and G. Hodge and C. Greve's *The Challenge of Public–Private Partnerships. Learning from International Experience* (Cheltenham: Edward Elgar, 2005).

Appendices

Contracting out for railway services: the case of market entry by Arriva in Denmark

Carsten Greve

During the last days of December 2001, the Danish Minister for Transport made a decision to award a contract for railway services to the Danish subsidiary of the British-owned company Arriva. The railway routes were in parts of Jutland, the peninsular of Denmark. The Danish railway system had been mostly run by the public enterprise Danish State Railways (*Danske Stats Baner*) (DSB). The exceptions were small local railways that were run by private providers on contract with local governments. The most used railway tracks had been state-run for over a century.

The government had changed in November 2001. A Liberal-Conservative government had taken over from a Social Democrat government. The previous Social Democrat Minister for Transport had been sceptical of privatization and contracting out. The incoming Minister for Transport from the Conservative Party was generally in favour of privatization and contracting out. The stakes were that if private providers were not allowed to run railway services this time around, few doubted that private providers would ever gain entry into the market, and that DSB would be the sole player on the market for years to come. The decision was therefore anticipated with excitement.

The decision to award the contract to Arriva came as a surprise to many, not least the public enterprise DSB. DSB had undergone a long-term efficiency strategy since the early 1990s where it had made huge efficiency gains and cut down costs. DSB had prepared carefully for making an efficient bid to win the contract. DSB submitted the cheapest bid, and had the track record for running railways. DSB was therefore very surprised when it turned out that the contract was awarded to Arriva. Arriva was pleasantly surprised of course. The company has already been responsible for the operation of buses in the Greater Copenhagen area since the 1990s.

DSB submitted an enquiry to the Minister for transport. DSB first refused to accept that the public enterprise had lost the contract. The Managing Director of DSB said that DSB knew the route inside out and knew how much it would cost to run the service efficiently and well. The chairman of the Board and the Director arranged a meeting with the Minister, but little was resolved at the meeting. The Minister for Transport remained steadfast in his decision. The reason for turning down DSB's offer was that it was judged to be unrealistically cheap. In short, the Minister did not believe that DSB's calculation of costs was possible to implement. Arriva, on the other hand, was pleased to be the provider of train services in addition to the bus services it was already responsible for. Media reports announcing throughout January 2001 that Arriva's poor running of selected services in Britain had led to fines did not seem to affect Arriva's standing in Denmark. Arriva was now going to be a bigger company with a much larger portfolio in Denmark, and would use that to make further expansion plans.

ARRIVA TAKES OVER

According to the plan, Arriva would take over the service of running the trains from DSB in January 2003. The takeover occurred on 5 January 2003. There was a celebratory mood to the day. Arriva raised the flags. DSB people were disappointed. A new era was about to begin. Soon after Arriva took over responsibility, problems began to appear. The trains were not running on time. Many trains were cancelled. The passengers began to show disappointment too. Many passengers disapproved openly of the new company. In addition, the snow in January and February did not make the situation any better. Passengers were freezing on the platforms, waiting for trains that never came or arrived late. The media picked up the story quickly. It could report the views of passengers who voiced their disapproval in public. Arriva came under intense pressure in the media.

Arriva began a crisis management strategy during the winter. Buses covered routes where trains were not operating. At the same time, Arriva tried to cope with the media strategy. Arriva claimed that not enough train operators had been transferred from DSB to Arriva. Arriva was short on trained people to operate the trains. Arriva tried to put the blame on DSB and the Ministry for Transport. To the media it appeared that Arriva was playing a blame game when it should have been concentrating on getting the services running.

Members of Parliament asked questions of the Minister. Politically, something had to be done. In May 2003 it was decided that DSB should operate some of the services again for a limited time period. From the autumn of 2003 Arriva began running the services again.

MISSING INFORMATION IN THE CONTRACT

The lack of train operators was one problem to cope with. Another problem – but this time seen from the perspective of the Ministry for Transport – was that price for peak hour traffic was not calculated properly. There was a need to make changes to put in extra trains at certain times during the day. For Arriva to make changes to the train schedule the company had to pay extra because of peak hour traffic. An amendment to the original contract was formulated and signed by both parties, but this time it cost the Ministry for Transport dearly.

Regarding the train operators, the problem turned out to originate with the Ministry for Transport and DSB. It was revealed that training and education of new train operators were the sole responsibility of DSB. As DSB and the unions were sceptical towards the new competitor, no special effort had been made to educate enough train operators in time for Arriva's enty into the market. Arriva had assumed that enough train operators were available, and that it would be possible to train and educate new train operators. Arriva found – not altogether wrongly – that their operations had been obstructed in some ways.

The contract itself, however, asked Arriva to 'be responsible for preparing fully by taking all necessary activities so that the operator is ready in all areas when the services should start running'. To be able to bid for the contract, Arriva had to put up 10 per cent of the economic value of the contract. The contract ended up being worth DKK 160 million, and DSB had originally bid half that amount. The purchaser has put a service and reliability factor into the contract. If service and reliability is between 95 and 97 per cent, there is no effect to the payment. If service and reliability is below 95 per cent, the payment is reduced by 2.5 per cent.

The original Arriva contract was a 386-page document. The main part of the contract was 16 pages long. The contract period that Arriva signed up for was 5 January to 14 December 2007. A possibility for renegotiation during the period was left open.

The public and the passengers' expectations had also changed dramatically. Train services were not always reliable and efficient when DSB was in charge of the operations, but people had higher expectations about the services from the new provider. People were perhaps also more watchful about mistakes because of previous media stories relating to privatization and contracting out. The attitude changed over time as people got used to the train services from the new operator, Arriva.

In 2006, the trains were running reasonably efficiently. Arriva met all its key targets. Arriva did manage to cash a bonus for fulfilling the contractual objectives. DSB was still the main competitor, but DSB had also formed a strategy to bid in other countries for train routes, notably in Britain and Sweden. DSB was not successful, but it had tried to follow the same strategy as Arriva and go abroad for gaining entry into new markets.

STRATEGIC CONTRACTING IN A POLITICAL CONTEXT

Railway privatization and contracting out remain a controversial area for many people and stakeholders. DSB had been running the majority of the Danish train services for over a century. People were used to DSB. When privatization and liberalization of markets became a trend from the 1980s onwards, the railway service in Denmark was not the first type of service to be marketized. In Britain, as we all know, this was different, with railway privatization an issue already from the early 1990s.

DSB had prepared for the new situation nevertheless. DSB had streamlined its organization during the 1990s. It had sold some parts of the public enterprise to other companies, and was in the process of privatizing buses and sea lanes. In the railway services, DSB had enjoyed a *de facto* monopoly though, and clearly regarded itself as the future market leader as well. When contracting out railway services in Jutland became an issue, DSB began preparing for that in earnest, but DSB was also sure it would win eventually. Therefore, the shift in government attitude, and the award of the contract to the competitor 'from outside' Arriva, was something of a surprise.

Politically, however, contracting out to a private provider was perhaps not such a big surprise. Various governments had officially endorsed contracting out in the transport sector. The incoming Conservative Transport Minister was pro-contracting out. If he had decided against involving private sector companies, the outlook for contracting out in years to come would have looked bleak.

In management terms, the government as a purchaser made the two blunders mentioned above. The government did not foresee that DSB would be reluctant to train and educate train operators. And the government did not foresee peak hour ratios, and the tactics of Arriva to exploit that weakness and to demand specialized pay to change the schedule and put in more trains.

The provider did not accept the criticism at the time, but had a hard time defending itself in the first six months of service operation. The managing director later blamed the Ministry of Transport for promising better quality at a lower cost to the public, while at the same time preferring to pay a lower price for the train service. Despite a lack of enough train operators, Arriva chose to go ahead with the task anyway, knowing that it would be difficult to live up to the public's expectations. The managing director later blamed the Transport Union for being 'a department in DSB', and blamed the employees for lacking the capacity to transform to a new, businesslike culture. Still, the managing director said, the contracting out of train services is part of the process, and there is a natural learning process when new initiatives are being implemented.

Did the purchaser gain anything from the deal? Arriva put in new trains to operate the services. The change of trains may not have occurred as quickly if a contracting out process had not taken place. Arriva has plans to introduce new services to customers, such as television screens in trains. The Danish National Audit Office noted that the economic gains expected from contracting out had not been realized.

The contracting out experience in the railway sector has introduced competition for real for the state-owned company DSB. DSB knows now that it cannot take any route for granted in the future. DSB has to compete for every contract. Arriva cannot afford to rest on its laurels. Arriva knows that it also has to make a competitive bid next time around in order to stay in business. This should in theory benefit the customers. Other factors, including a run-down track system, have prevented train passengers from enjoying the full fruits of competition.

CONCLUDING REMARKS

Contracting out railway services represents a challenge to a country's public service delivery. The challenge is first to governments as purchasers to get the contract right. The Danish Ministry for Transport had some problems in this respect. Another challenge is to providers to get the service delivery right. Arriva in Denmark had underestimated the difficulty in getting able train operators to keep the trains running. In addition, Arriva had underestimated the huge public and media interest that followed from the contracting process. The challenge was also to the public, the passengers and the politicians from the opposition parties to allow for some time before the new provider had become confident with all aspects of the new job. In the end, most of the challenges were met in contractual terms. The government had to amend the contract to get Arriva to put more trains on at peak hours. The government also had to take the training and education of train operators out of the hands of DSB to enable neutral education opportunities. Arriva had to acknowledge that it should have guarded itself against any obstruction from a public enterprise that had managed the route for many years, and be better prepared to deal with situations where a sufficient number of train operators may not be available.

Was contracting out of railway services a costly experiment that has cost the taxpayer, or was the process a necessary lesson to be learned in order to improve the way contracting out procedures are handled?

In the short term, there is little doubt that transaction costs have occurred to get the contracting process running. Costs were associated in speeding up the education and training of train operators, of getting buses to run services when train services were not operating, and costs associated with informing and sometimes compensating unsatisfied customers. In the long run, however, outcome may improve. Passengers have become used to the 'new' operator. Arriva has learned the system and gained more experience in how to run train services in Denmark. The government has shown that it has a credible contracting out strategy – that it is possible to challenge the traditional monopoly delivery organization in DSB. Competition has therefore been introduced in the railways sector, and companies must now prepare to compete in order to win contracts. Efficiency strategies are therefore a necessary element in all transport companies' profile.

DISCUSSION QUESTIONS

1   Should the government as purchaser have chosen another strategy to make sure more contingencies were covered in the contract?
2   Did the government take enough notice of railway privatization and contracting out in other countries, such as the UK?

3   Was the political context too obvious for the contracting process to be judged fair in management terms?

4   How do you view the accountability structure for Arriva? Has the company earned its bonuses, or have the targets been set too low by the purchaser of the services?

5   Can the government go back and choose DSB as the next provider of services for the route, and what will be the consequences for the longer term perspective for contracting out in this sector?

REFERENCES

Infomedia: Newspaper articles on Arriva 2003.

Interview with Johnny Hansen, managing director, in *Spektrum*, May 2003.

National Audit Office, Denmark (2002) *Beretning om Trafikministeriets valg af operatør på jernbanestrækninger i Midt- og Vestjylland*. Copenhagen: National Audit Office.

National Audit Office, Denmark (2004) *Beretning om Trafikministeriets håndtering af kontrakten med Arriva*. Copenhagen: National Audit Office.

Strategic contracting in local government: the case of Graested-Gilleleje in Denmark

The local government in Graested-Gilleleje (GG) in Denmark embarked on a strategy for contracting for public services in the early 1990s. The impetus was both to deliver better and less costly services, and also to look for new and alternative ways of delivering public services. One of the key means GG used was to invite (in 1992) and involve private providers to deliver public services. The local government enjoyed a liberal-conservative majority in the city council. The political backing for the project was secured. The mayor was one of a limited number of local governments in Denmark at the time that found it interesting to try out alternative service delivery mechanisms. The city council had employed an active chief administrative officer (CAO). He had a political science degree from a university in Denmark, and he was keen on inducing change into the organization of public service delivery.

At the beginning of the project, the local government tried to establish a public–private partnership with a private company – Scancare. The private company was a subsidiary of two larger, Danish-based multinational companies – Falck and ISS. The multinational companies wanted to achieve new markets in the public sector, and went along with the idea. A good dialogue was established between the private company and the local government about possible private service delivery in the future. Soon, however, the company and the local government found out that the contracting out situation would demand that the private sector organization be independent of local government. The close public–private partnership that had been developed was an impediment to the contracting out process ahead. After that the private company withdrew its initial interest in the original project.

CONTRACTING OUT FOR PUBLIC SERVICES IN LOCAL GOVERNMENT

The local government went ahead with the project of contracting out welfare services. The first service was elderly care. The local government wanted to contract out elderly care in part to private companies. The city council had initiated an investigation into the pros and cons of contracting out in 1994 which was done in connection with the private sector company involved. The report was made public in 1995 – after the private sector company had withdrawn from its close cooperation with the local government. The report was entitled 'The future elderly service delivery – a proposal for private sector involvement'.

The proposal raised a storm of protests. There was an outcry among public employees already working with the elderly. There were also protests among citizens in the local government. The unions also mobilized against the effort.

The local government decided to take up the challenge and to proceed with the contracting out policy. The local government leadership could rest assured that they were on the right track and would not face much opposition. First, the mayor held a secure majority in the city council. There was little chance that the mayor would be ousted in the next local election. Second, the management of the local government was eager to proceed with new public management reforms. The local government was already picking up an image of being an innovative local government that was prepared to take risks and try something new in public service delivery. Therefore, the protests were foreseeable, but would not stand in the way of the experiment about to take place. In national politics, there had been pressure since the 1980s to adopt market-type mechanisms in the delivery of public services.

FIRST ROUND OF CONTRACTING FOR PUBLIC SERVICE

The first contracting out process was carried out in 1996. The result was that the local government contracted out part of the provision of elderly services to a Swedish-based private company called Curatus. Elderly services involve running homes for the elderly and helping elderly people in their homes. A remaining part of the service delivery was kept in-house as a check on the private provider. The aim, however, was clear: to allow the private sector companies to take over as much as possible gradually to enable the local government to concentrate on being a smart buyer.

The local government worked hard at implementing the project. There were several factors influencing the implementation. First, widespread public attention was given to the project: the employees, citizens and the media watched the project's implementation closely. National politicians were also showing interest in whether or not the local government achieved progress with contracting out. Second, the local government had to cope with discussions on the rules and regulation surrounding contracting out. What was allowed and what was not allowed was up for discussion constantly. The local government was pushing new boundaries in contracting out services so closely connected with the welfare state.

In the end, the first round of contracting out went well. Services were delivered. Targets were met. Despite intensive media coverage, the project was not hampered by any scandals or failures in service delivery that are sometimes experienced in these kinds of high-profile exercises.

SECOND ROUND OF CONTRACTING FOR PUBLIC SERVICES

The relative success of the first period made the local government hungry for more. The local government initiated a new contracting out tender in order to contract out the whole of the elderly service delivery to private sector providers. The purposes of contracting out were described as quality development of services, consumer choice between two providers, quality competition between providers, human resources systems and social clauses in top-class, economic advantages, to prevent a monopoly situation, and to specify a contracting structure that maximizes possibilities for designing the optimal organizational solution.

A long and detailed document on the conditions for tendering was issued which would form the basis for the contract. The new model of contracting out a whole policy area to private providers was described. The call for tenders was issued in 1999. In 2000, three private providers were chosen. They were a Swedish-based company (Partena) and two Danish-based companies (SeniorCare and Senior-Service, Denmark). Senior-Service was formerly known as Curatus, but is now under new management. The private providers delivered services at four elderly centres within the local government district. Partena Care had responsibility for two elderly centres. In addition to those, elderly citizens were able to choose services from a number of smaller providers for selected, specialized services. There were approximately 740 users to whom the private providers delivered services.

The local government was reorganized to be better equipped to handle contractual relations with three private providers. The purchaser function was organized centrally. It was called 'Elderly service, visitation and purchasing'. The purchaser function was accountable to the Select Committee for Elderly Services within the city council. Users in their own homes were able to choose from a menu of services: personal care, care-related tasks, cleaning and practical help, and add-on services for which they paid. The main organization principle was to put the citizen (or the customer) at the centre. The core values pursued were self-determination, individualism and safeness.

The contract was divided into different sub-agreements. One agreement concerned 'help in the elderly's own home'. A second agreement concerned the daily operations of the elderly centres (which again were divided into subgroups such as personal care, cleaning, training and so on). A third agreement concerned laundry. A fourth agreement concerned food. A fifth agreement concerned development, which had the objectives of furthering effectivness and user satisfaction. This part of the contract emphasized that personnel had to be motivated and aware of what quality is. Thereby, there were big ambitions tied to developing human resources throughout the contracting period. The contract also had a clause on corporate social responsibility (CSR). The clause calls for private providers – without reimbursement – to take on a social responsibility, for example, by giving the unemployed a chance to do job-training.

Coordination between the purchaser and the provider was also written into the contract. As a minimum, the purchaser undertakes that an annual meeting will be held in order to discuss general questions and developments. More meetings in the period leading up to the start of the contracting period are expected. The local government implemented a new information technology system at the time which was developed in cooperation with another private sector IT company. In the contract, the purchaser demands that the private service providers will integrate the purchaser's IT systems in the registration of the services delivered to citizens. This also encompassed use of handheld PalmPilots in registration and which were novel and innovative at the time. The local government made the IT systems available to the providers without charge.

Control and accountability systems were put in place from the beginning of the contract period. In the contract, it is emphasized that the local government as a purchaser expects problems to be solved through dialogue and by preventing problems from happening in the first place. Control meetings are scheduled on a fortnightly basis between the purchaser and the provider. A purchaser representative will be present physically at the elderly centre for at least three hours a week. There has to be an office available to the purchaser representative, and a mailbox. The purpose of the control is to set up a dialogue forum between (1) the users, (2) the relatives, and the (3) staff of the provider.

A 'traffic-light' control system was also established in the contracts. If a complaint is filed, the purchaser expects the provider to correct the matter within seven days ('green light'). If the purchaser notes that misconduct has taken place, the purchaser issues a warning that has to be dealt with within two days ('yellow procedure'). If gross misconduct is found, the provider must reply in writing within 12 hours ('red procedure'). Quality of services is described in three ways: (1) the user/customer's own experience of quality; (2) the checkable quality related to performance indicators, and (3) the described quality. Performance indicators are used in four ways: (1) amount of personnel per user per day/week; (2) time of delivery of service in relation to agreed time; (3) amount of delivered services in relation to required services, and (4) number of yellow/red warnings and procedures. The registration was carried out regularly and summoned by the end of each month. Besides this quality control, providers are encouraged to apply their own quality control system to the GG local government. The programme is regarded by the local government in isolation and is not integrated into the local government's own quality assurance programme.

If the contract is not held, the purchaser will seek negotiations between the purchaser and the provider. A neutral third-party arbitrator is appointed in common cause between the purchaser and the provider to settle differences. The purchaser and provider will split the cost of hiring the arbitrator. If differences cannot be settled, the matter will go to court. In the last part of the contract, GG notes that any change in level of service will be communicated six months in advance.

The contract was renewed in 2004. The local government decided to carry on with the contracting out project. Private providers are still responsible for delivering public services today. The city council still has the same majority. Both the mayor and the CAO still have their jobs. Citizen satisfaction has been stable throughout the period. The media has stopped reporting intensively. The GG model has been copied by other local governments in Denmark. GG has visitors from many parts of the globe in order to study its model. In 2007, as part of a new structural reform in Denmark, GG local government has joined forces with the neighbouring local government. The use of new public management models and contracting out in particular is set to continue.

CONCLUDING REMARKS

The case of GG highlights several issues in the contracting for public services model introduced in the first part of this book. The political conditions surrounding the project were stable. The mayor enjoyed a comfortable majority throughout the period. There was enough time and space to describe the targets and formulate the policy goals. There was no hurry in drawing up contracts in the first place. The local government made an effort to collect material to understand the process and implications of contracting in the best possible way. GG sought to establish a close connection with the private sector early on. A public–private partnership was underway and was almost established formally, but the degree competition made the furthering of the original public–private partnership between the local government and just one selected firm impossible. GG went ahead gradually. Only part of the elderly services was contracted out in the first period. The local government tackled the media and the public from the beginning. Although there were protests, the local government tried to get its way. It did not allow the protest to overwhelm the whole project. The project still went ahead. Protesters at the time – both employees and citizens – might say that they were being sidelined. The first period was used to collect evidence and gather experience about contracting. When the time was ready (i.e. when a new contract period was approaching), the local government took the next step, and wanted to contract out all of the elderly services to private companies. The local government managed to get enough companies interested in the bid. Three private providers were awarded the contracts in 2000. By that time, the local government had reorganized its own operations to be better prepared to deal organizationally and managerially with the contractual relationship with the providers (where one was known from the previous period, and the other two were new).

197

Throughout the period, both the mayor and the CAO had known where they wanted to go. The goal was to get better services for citizens, but also to try to involve private providers in the delivery of public services. This strategy has succeeded. Throughout the period, there has also been a constant focus on communication. The focus has been on communication both with the media, and with the key stakeholders more specifically. Private providers have been interested in winning contracts in this local government. The private providers have agreed to the terms set by the purchaser.

At the same time, the contracting for public service in GG has been unusual in some aspects. It was one of the pioneer local governments in Denmark to conduct experiments with contracting out and other alternative service delivery mechanisms. The institutional rules and norms were not entirely in place when GG began. This both gave the local government an advantage because it could pursue new strategies, but it could also be a disadvantage because all media eyes were on the activities of the local government. The local government had a consistent political and managerial leadership throughout the period which allowed for stable progression in the strategy.

DISCUSSION QUESTIONS

1. How is Graested-Gilleleje's contracting experience an example of strategic contracting?
2. In what ways did the institutional context that Graested-Gilleleje was in shape the strategy?
3. Who is dominating the relationship? The purchasers or the providers – or do they appear to have constructed a real dialogue?
4. How do you rate the accountability structure for Graested-Gilleleje's contractual relationships?
5. Was the gradual strategy necessary – or should GG have gone for the quick change in the beginning?

REFERENCES

Andersen, N.Å. (1995) *Udlicitering*. Copenhagen: Nyt fra samfundsvidenskaberne.

Fuglsang, M. and Midjord, C. (1995) Udlicitering af ældreområdet. Græsted-Gilleleje som eksempel, in C. Greve (ed.) *Privatisering, selskabsdannelser og udlicitering*. Aarhus: Systime, pp. 136–157.

198

Graested-Gilleleje homepage: www.ggk.dk (from 1 January 2007 the local government has merged with another local government in a new Gribskov local government; see www.gribskov.dk.

Graested-Gilleleje (2000) Tendering material for the contracts for elderly care.

Hegnsvad, M. (2001) Udlicitering kræver styring og ledelse, in S. Hildebrandt and K.K. Klausen (eds) *Offentlig ledelse på dagsordenen*. Copenhagen: Børsen Publishing, pp. 85–104.

Index